Labor Movements

Labor Movements
Global Perspectives

Stephanie Luce

polity

First published in 2014 by Polity Press

Polity Press
65 Bridge Street
Cambridge CB2 1UR, UK

Polity Press
350 Main Street
Malden, MA 02148, USA

ISBN-13: 978-0-7456-7059-1
ISBN-13: 978-0-7456-7060-7(pb)

A catalogue record for this book is available from the British Library.

Typeset in 11 on 13 pt Sabon by
Servis Filmsetting Ltd, Stockport, Cheshire
Printed and bound in Great Britain by Clays Ltd, St Ives plc

For further information on Polity, visit our website: www.politybooks.com

Contents

Acknowledgments

The material in this book was gathered over many years, and I am grateful to colleagues and scholars who helped me understand the labor movement in a more global context, including Sara Abraham, Emiko Aono, Ralph Armbruster-Sandoval, Carolina Bank Muñoz, Anannya Bhattacharjee, Edna Bonacich, Anita Chan, Dan Clawson, Eli Friedman, Ellen David Friedman, Sarita Gupta, Jeroen Merk, Pun Ngai, Matt Noyes, Ashim Roy, Gay Seidman, Yamasaki Seiichi, Akira Suzuki, Hirohiku Takasu, and Ben Watanabe. A special thanks to Naila Kabeer, who invited me to visit India and Bangladesh with her to interview activists, workers, and scholars, which helped me understand labor standards from another perspective. Thanks to Shannon Lederer and Ashwini Sukthankar for sharing time to discuss their work. I have also learned a great deal from working with the Asia Floor Wage Campaign, National Guestworkers Alliance, the Retail Action Project, and Labor Notes.

The book is immeasurably improved by insightful feedback from Paula Chakravartty, Ellen David Friedman, Heidi Gottfried, Amy Hanauer, Penny Lewis, and Ruth Milkman. I have benefitted enormously from working over many years with my students, colleagues, and staff at the University of Massachusetts-Amherst Labor Center, and the Murphy Institute, at the School for Professional Studies, City University of New York. Ilana Berger, Johanna Brenner, Eli Deuker, Kim Gilmore, Jen Kern, Catherine Sameh and Erin Small all provided support of various kinds to

Acknowledgments

help me through the writing process. I am also grateful for the support of my family and the Brenner family.

I am thankful for Emma Longstaff at Polity Press for her vision that such a book should be part of the social movement series, and for inviting me to contribute. Thanks also to Jonathan Skerrett, Elen Griffiths, and Clare Ansell who patiently guided me through this process, and Ian Tuttle for copyediting.

I owe deep gratitude to my partner Mark Brenner, who read the manuscript multiple times and helped me formulate my ideas, making the book much better as a result. It was he who convinced me to write this book, as his own persistent optimism in the labor movement pushes me to keep working.

This book was inspired by the hundreds of activists, organizers, students, union members, and leaders I have met in dozens of countries. Some have risked their livelihoods, and even their lives, in the fight for a more just world. It is to them that I dedicate this book.

1

Introduction

Vignette #1:

When the BJ&B hat factory opened in a free trade zone in the Dominican Republic in 1987, it brought the promise of jobs and a better life for local residents. Over 2,000 workers, primarily women, were hired. But soon, the women realized the jobs came at a cost. Managers were verbally abusive, sometimes threatening physical violence, forcing most workers to work overtime shifts, and firing or refusing to pay workers for small infractions. By the late 1990s, a small group of workers began to organize a union. But when they declared their union in 2001, 20 union supporters were fired. The workers enlisted supporters in the Dominican Republic and abroad, and over the next two years, they waged a campaign against BJ&B. The company asserted that unionization would result in factory closure (Gonzalez 2003; Ross 2004).

The U.S.-based United Students Against Sweatshops launched a campaign against Nike and Reebok, two of the largest purchasers of BJ&B products, urging the companies to pressure the factory owners to recognize the union. After much effort, in 2003, BJ&B agreed to let workers decide whether to form a union, remain neutral during the process, as well as negotiate a contract if that was the workers' decision. They also agreed to rehire the fired workers. Workers won raises, scholarships, and better working conditions. The victory was hailed as groundbreaking, since unions have had little success organizing workers in the free trade zones of the Dominican Republic or elsewhere (Ross 2004).

But soon after the victory, the large brands began reducing their orders and moving work to cheaper factories in other countries. In February 2007, the brands abruptly ended all orders and BJ&B shut its doors without warning, leaving the workers without jobs and with little recourse (Greenhouse 2010; Dreier 2011). Like so many cases where garment workers have organized, the victory at BJ&B was short-lived. In the end, the factory owner's dire predictions that work will dry up were not just idle threats (Armbruster-Sandoval 2005).

Vignette #2:

In August 2008, 134 workers at the Stella D'oro bakery in the Bronx, New York went on strike, two weeks after their union contract expired. The company was demanding significant wage and benefit cuts. Stella D'oro was founded in 1932 by a New York family, who grew it to a successful business with 575 employees. In 1992 the family sold the company to Nabisco, which sold it to Kraft, which then sold it to Brynwood Partners, a private equity firm, in 2006. Brynwood obtained over $425,000 in tax abatements from the city to upgrade machinery at the plant, but by 2008, it argued that wages must be cut to retain profits (Jaccarino 2009; Lee 2009).

The workers, members of the Bakery, Confectionery, Tobacco Workers and Grain Millers Local 50, went on strike for the next 10 months. The union filed charges with the National Labor Relations Board (NLRB), one of which claimed that Brynwood had refused to provide the union with a copy of its 2007 financial statement, thereby failing to bargain in good faith. In June 2009 an NLRB judge ruled in favor of the union, and ordered the company to reinstate the workers.

The next week Stella D'oro invited the workers back but within a few weeks announced that it would close the factory and move production elsewhere. Brynwood sold the company to the Lance

Corporation, which moved the production to a non-union bakery in Ohio.

Despite a strike, significant community support, favorable court ruling, and media coverage in major newspapers, the union was unable to keep the plant open or maintain the jobs of its members. While the company ended up moving production inside the U.S., the dynamics are indicative of the reduced power that unions have in an era of global capitalism. Whether companies threaten to move overseas or to the neighboring city, they can still use their mobility to break a union. When employers are free to move investments and production with little penalty, what can unions do?

*　*　*

Just a few decades ago, mainstream economists predicted that increased international trade and the spread of free markets around the globe would lead to new jobs for many and an increased standard of living for all. Noted economist Paul Krugman argued for increased free trade, dismissing those who raised concerns as "silly," protectionist, or simply wrong (Greider 2013). But while globalization has led to a massive increase in wealth, and an average increase in gross domestic product per capita, a closer look reveals a troubling picture for many of the world's workers.

In the world's biggest economy – the United States – unemployment, including long-term unemployment, is at levels not seen since the Great Depression of the 1930s. Worse, millions of workers are underemployed in various ways – working part-time when they want to be full-time, or stuck in seasonal and temporary work. A 2012 report found that over half of new college graduates were either unemployed or working in jobs that did not require a college degree (Associated Press 2012).

The picture is similar across much of the world. Since the great recession of 2008, youth unemployment has skyrocketed. Almost 13 percent of young people around the world – 73.8 million people under the age of 25 – are officially unemployed, and the numbers are much worse when we include those who are underemployed or not in the formal economy. For example, 12.7

percent of European youth are not in the labor market or in school as of 2012 (ILO 2013).

It isn't just young people that are suffering. The International Labor Organization (ILO) found that 197 million people worldwide were without jobs in 2012 – almost 6 percent of the formal labor market. But 39 million people have dropped out of the labor market due to the recession, meaning that unemployment is actually much higher – and the ILO predicts things will only get worse in the coming years. In 2012 part-time employment increased in two-thirds of wealthy countries (ILO 2013).

More disconcerting is the growth of workers in the informal economy and in "precarious employment" or contingent work – people in temporary or seasonal work, or other forms of work with no job security and lack of social protection.[1] Neoclassical economics predicted that as capitalism spread, and economies experienced economic growth, formal employment would rise. Yet in many countries this has not been the case, as the past few decades of economic growth have come hand in hand with an increase in informal employment.

High unemployment and underemployment, and increasing precarity comes alongside stagnant, or even falling, average wages. What is most remarkable is that in many countries, wages have stagnated while labor productivity has increased. For example, between 1999 and 2011, labor productivity grew over twice as fast as wages in wealthy countries (ILO 2013). Figure 1.1 shows that whereas wages and labor productivity moved together in the United States for several decades after World War II, the two began to diverge in the 1970s, resulting in a serious gap. And where the postwar period saw workers maintaining their share of the expanding economic pie, over the past four decades employers have captured the gains from increased productivity.

Even before the global financial meltdown, some analysts noted the alarming trend of stagnant wages. Morgan Stanley economist Stephen Roach wrote in 2007:

The pendulum of economic power is at unsustainable extremes in the developed world. For a broad collection of major industrial economies

4

– the United States, the euro zone, Japan, Canada and the U.K. – the share of economic rewards going to labor stands at a historical low of less than 54% of national income – down from 56% in 2001. Meanwhile, the share going to corporate profits stands at a record high of nearly 16% – a striking increase from the 10% reading five years ago. (Roach 2007)

After the 2008 crisis, things looked even worse. The global labor income share continued to fall in the OECD (Organization for Economic Development and Cooperation) countries as well as most developing countries, as the share of national income going to corporate profits rose – particularly in the financial sector (ILO 2013).

There are some exceptions. China has experienced real wage growth in the last decade, even when controlling for cost of living increases. Real wages went up for salaried workers in India for most years since 2005. The growth in wages and employment in

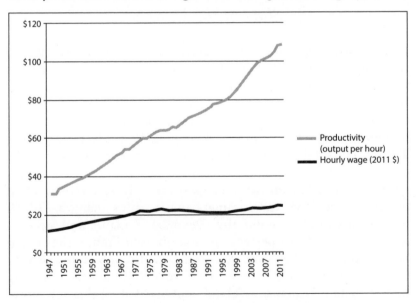

Source: The State of Working America, 12th edn., Figure 4U.

Figure 1.1 U.S. Wages and Productivity, 1947–2011

China and India means that absolute poverty has fallen in those countries, and on average, worldwide. But despite these gains, over one-quarter of the world's workers are living in poverty. In 2012, 397 million workers in developing countries were living in extreme poverty, despite holding a job, and another 472 million were above extreme poverty but did not have enough income to regularly meet their basic needs (ILO 2013).[2] Furthermore, despite wage growth in China and India, inequality is rising rapidly as the share of national income going to workers is not rising nearly as fast as the share going to corporate profits (ILO 2013). In most countries the wealthy have done well in good times and bad, while workers fall further and further behind. Historically, labor unions have been the primary institution to counter inequality and fight for worker rights, but today they do not appear able to address the crisis. Where are the unions?

State of the Unions

Unions would seem the natural vehicle to raise wages and improve working conditions, but in most countries, unions have grown weaker over the past few decades. In a 2006 report, the U.S. Bureau of Labor Statistics (BLS) compared union membership and density (the share of wage and salaried workers that belong to unions) data for countries belonging to the OECD (Visser 2006).[3] The total number of union members grew in many of the countries in the 1970s and 1980s, but since 1990, those numbers decreased in 18 countries and grew in only six. International union density rates vary dramatically, with as many as 70–80 percent of workers unionized in Denmark, Finland, and Sweden, while as few as 8–15 percent are unionized in France, the United States, Korea, and Poland. According to the BLS study, density rates fell in 20 countries from 1970 to 2003, increasing in only four (Belgium, Denmark, Finland, and Sweden). Table 1.1 shows data for countries from 1999 to the most recent year available, along with the percent difference and the total number of union members. In all but two of 33 countries, union density fell over this period, and fell by almost 4 percentage points for all OECD countries.

There are no comparable statistics for non-OECD countries (sometimes called the "global south"). The New Unionism Network compiled data from the International Trade Union Confederation (ITUC) and U.S. State Department to track union membership since 2000 for 94 countries. This data shows that union membership has increased in 50 of the countries, while declining in only 32. Six countries were relatively stable, and six do not allow unions. This suggests that the phenomenon of declining union power is not as universal as some might believe. Some of the countries that show large percentage growth are those that do not allow independent trade unions, such as China, Syria, and Vietnam. But a number of other countries show substantial increases in union membership. The countries with large growth as well as relatively large union membership include Argentina, Belgium, Brazil, Canada, Egypt, Luxembourg, Nigeria, Singapore, Taiwan, and Turkey. It is clear that union growth was not confined to one particular region.

Still, growth in members did not translate to increases in union density in all cases, suggesting that unions are not keeping pace with a growing workforce. In addition to membership decline in some global south countries and most in the global north, union power measured in other ways suggests unions have become much weaker. Historical alliances between political parties and trade unions are fraying or have been severed entirely in a host of countries, including Spain, England, Argentina, South Africa, and Sweden. In the past decade, labor-backed parties have come into power in many countries and instituted reforms that undercut union power or benefits.

Some measures suggest there is also a drop in public support for unions. In the U.S., Gallup polls show public support for unions is at near historic lows in the post-World War II era, with just 52 percent of those polled saying they approve of unions (Jones 2012). Some Canadian polls suggest that the public trusts management more than labor unions (Hébert 2012).

Many argue that unions have outlived their usefulness, if they

Table 1.1 Union Density Rates and Total Union Members, OECD Countries

Country	1999	Current	Most recent year available	Percent difference, 1999–most recent year	Total union members, most recent year
Australia	24.9	17.9	2012	−7.0	1,840,400
Austria	37.4	27.8	2011	−9.7	990,000
Belgium	50.9	50.4	2011	−0.5	1,946,673
Canada	28.1	26.8	2011	−1.3	4,625,777
Chile	13.5	15.3	2012	1.8	821,041
Czech Republic	30.0	17.3	2009	−12.6	709,475
Denmark	74.9	68.5	2010	−6.4	1,662,000
Estonia	16.3	8.1	2010	−8.2	42,000
Finland	76.3	69.0	2011	−7.2	1,473,500
France	8.1	7.8	2010	−0.2	1,850,000
Germany	25.3	18.0	2011	−7.3	6,300,000
Greece	26.8	25.4	2011	−1.4	672,880
Hungary	24.5	16.8	2008	−7.7	566,709
Iceland	87.4	79.3	2008	−8.1	124,000
Ireland	38.7	31.2	2012	−7.5	476,000
Italy	35.4	35.6	2011	0.2	6,053,856

Japan	22.2	18.0	2012	−4.2	9,892,000
Korea	11.7	9.9	2011	−1.8	1,720,000
Luxembourg	43.3	37.3	2008	−5.9	122,640
Mexico	15.8	13.6	2012	−2.1	4,355,294
Netherlands	24.7	18.2	2011	−6.5	1,350,432
New Zealand	21.7	20.5	2012	−1.2	379,185
Norway	54.8	54.7	2012	−0.1	1,312,618
Poland	20.5	14.6	2010	−5.9	1,738,107
Portugal	22.5	19.3	2010	−3.1	738,720
Slovak Republic	34.2	16.7	2011	−17.5	330,000
Slovenia	41.9	24.4	2011	−17.5	190,000
Spain	16.0	15.6	2010	−0.5	2,371,600
Sweden	80.6	67.5	2012	−13.1	2,815,200
Switzerland	20.9	17.1	2010	−3.8	703,300
Turkey	10.6	5.4	2011	−5.2	802,470
United Kingdom	30.1	25.8	2012	−4.3	6,455,000
United States	13.4	11.1	2012	−2.3	14,366,000
OECD countries	20.8	17.0	2012	−3.8	79,796,877

Source: OECD Stat Extracts. Data for union density and union members are for the most recent year available.

were ever useful. In the global economy, the argument goes, companies engage in cut-throat competition with others from around the world. They do not have the luxury to pay higher wages than competitors in low-wage countries like China, and they cannot compete if they have to provide generous benefits. The global economy is fast-paced and fickle, and employers need to be flexible when faced with the demands of the market. Against this new reality, unions artificially inflate the price of labor and erect rigid work rules that stifle employers' ability to hire and fire when needed.

Furthermore, in emerging economies, much of the workforce operates in the informal sector, where individuals are afforded few, if any, legal protections and often lack a formal employer. The trade union model, resting on collective bargaining agreements and industry standards, does not apply to workers who are technically self-employed, often working from home.

But the fall in wages, and marked rise in inequality within and between countries, could also suggest that unions are more necessary than ever. It may be that the dynamics of a globalized economy introduce new challenges and obstacles for unions, but that does not make them irrelevant.

Indeed, survey data suggests that many workers still want to join a union. The Worker Representation Survey, conducted by Harvard economist Richard Freeman, shows the proportion of workers in the United States who want a union increased from the mid-1980s to 1995, and again by 2005, when a majority of workers indicated that they would join a union if they could, and over three-quarters of workers said they would like some form of representation in the workplace (Freeman 2007). While there is less research on this question in other countries, existing studies suggest the results are similar. Charlwood (2003) found that about 40 percent of non-union British workers overall, and 50 percent of manual workers, would likely join a union if given the option. Bryson (1999) found similar results for Canadian workers. Givan and Hipp (2012) analyzed survey data from 24 countries and found that, on average, workers have a positive perception of unions' ability to improve working conditions.

Unions may be one of the only institutions capable of correcting the great imbalances in today's global economy. Even some conservative analysts see that the growing inequality between wealthy and poor creates an unstable situation, a risk for massive unrest, and weak aggregate demand (Roach 2007; Blodget 2012). In 2002, the World Bank released a report reviewing over 1,000 studies on collective bargaining and economic outcomes, and concluded that while union density seems to have no correlation with most economic indicators, it does have a negative relationship to wage inequality and dispersion. In other words, countries with higher union density have lower wage inequality. They also found that while greater collective bargaining coverage alone can correlate with higher unemployment, countries with *highly coordinated* collective bargaining (such as the Scandinavian countries) are more likely to have lower unemployment and less persistent periods of unemployment, as well as stronger productivity growth (Aidt and Tzannatos 2002).[4]

This decline in wages, employment conditions, and union power are not just the outcome of a global economic crisis. Rather, they represent a longer-term trend connected with the rise of neoliberalism: a set of policies that promote free trade, deregulation, privatization, downsized government, liberalized financial markets, and fiscal austerity. These policies are driven by an economic and political philosophy that is based on a belief that "free markets" are efficient and desirable, and that governments should prioritize policies that promote expansion of markets and individual property rights, and de-emphasize government programs and democratic collective institutions, such as unions. Neoliberals argue that when investors and employers are free to pursue maximum profit, the world as a whole will benefit. They see unions as a major barrier to profit maximization.

While globalization itself it not new, neoliberalism (what some call corporate globalization) gained prominence in the last several decades. In the mid-twentieth century, the labor movement grew strong in many countries because governments regulated everything from trade to labor standards, creating restrictions on what employers and investors could do. With the ascendance of neoliberalism, governments have transformed their regulatory functions, dismantling many rules and practices that leant power to workers and unions while reregulating in a way to give more freedom to employers. Globalization itself is not a problem for unions, but neoliberalism is.

In this book, I argue that unions are still necessary in the global economy. Despite major challenges for union effectiveness and even survival, the labor movement must find a way to adapt in order to provide a voice for billions of working people who otherwise have little power and few resources. By most metrics of individual well-being and qualitative measures of a healthy economy and environment, the neoliberal policies adopted throughout much of the world have failed. The labor movement represents one of the best options for generating the dialogue needed, and the organizing required, to create a more sustainable model. While not the only solution to global inequality, unions are one of the largest and most well resourced options that workers have to represent their interests. In addition, unions have access to certain kinds of power that other social movements or organizations do not – notably, power to withhold labor and stop or slow production.

To make the case for unions' key role in turning our imbalanced economy upright, I close this chapter with a more detailed review of the phenomenon known as "globalization," including its impact on workers and labor organizations. In chapter 2, I provide arguments for why, despite challenges, there is still a need for unions and labor movements today. Chapters 3 and 4 discuss the external challenges that unions face, from labor law to capital mobility, trade agreements, international institutions, political ideology, and dramatic changes in global labor markets. These factors set the legal and policy parameters in which unions must function, at the same time that unions attempt to build enough strength to reshape the political and economic landscape through protest or legislation.

It is important to recognize that not all challenges unions face are external. Unions have also made errors of their own, failing to adapt to a changing economy and labor force. In some countries unions have been prone to corruption of various forms, and in many places, have relied on limiting the labor supply and excluding workers from the workforce in order to gain power. Even under the harsh political and economic climate of today's global economy, union leaders could make better decisions concerning their internal functioning, and how to use their resources and set priorities. These are the subject of chapter 5.

Chapter 6 provides a discussion of potential sources of power that unions might use to rebuild. Most analysts agree that the global economy favors corporations over workers, and it will take tremendous effort and organizing to change that balance. I start with a closer look at how neoliberalism has given more power to employers in relation to workers. I then review a few theories of power, and discuss traditional strategies that unions have used to win: workplace organizing, strikes – including general strikes – and political action.

In chapter 7, I analyze the ways in which unions have had to look for additional sources of power as their traditional methods have become weaker under neoliberalism. I explore the various ways in which unions and workers today are attempting to revitalize and renew, including adopting new organizing models, forming labor–community coalitions, and building non-union worker organizations.

Finally, I conclude with a look at some of the experiments that have been underway in the past few decades, where unions are attempting to challenge the constraints they face and remain relevant in the global economy. These examples vary in scale and scope, and few can claim major success. Still, they are instructive as potential components of a revitalized labor movement. This book is not a comparative study of labor movements, nor does it intend to cover all parts of the world. Rather, I focus on the U.S. labor movement through a global lens, in relation to movements in other regions.

How Did We Get Here?

The roots of our current situation revolve around different theoretical models coming out of the collapse of the global economy of the 1930s. These models have been labeled as socialism, communism, social democracy, and free markets, but in fact the majority of countries have adopted various forms of capitalism that have had different roles for workers and labor organizations.

Most of the global north countries (the U.S., Canada, Europe, Australia, New Zealand, and Japan) adopted variations of "managed capitalism" (Stiglitz 2006). This camp argued that, despite the Depression, capitalism could still provide benefits to the population, but a strong role for government was necessary to regulate markets, and to develop programs to provide social goods and redistribute wealth. Today, the British economist John Maynard Keynes gets the most credit for the theoretical perspective that arose from the period, though Keynes' thought was similar to and built off of other scholars. The United States' version of this was known as the "New Deal" – much less ambitious than what was adopted in much of Europe – but still operating on the theory that government intervention was required to maintain a healthy capitalist economy.

For the most part, unions played a large role in managed capitalist economies – in some cases, they were brought in to ward off movement toward a more radical economic model. Capital was weak in Europe and Japan postwar, so labor had greater relative strength in those countries and could assert a voice in national economic rebuilding. Most industrialized countries had established labor or socialist parties that supported the establishment and political participation of mass industrial unions during this period.

In the U.S., unions experienced a major upsurge and gained legal recognition in the 1930s, but this growth was rooted in a historically compromised context, including decades of severe repression, no established labor parties, and almost no institutional foundations. In general, unions in the global north were strong enough to win some major demands, but not strong enough to challenge the fundamental logic of capitalist production and global managerial control.

The second model coming out of the 1930s was the command economies, or central planning. The Soviet Union and China declared themselves workers' states run by workers, for workers. But in reality, trade unions were connected to the ruling party, and independent trade unions were not allowed. Without autonomy, unions were one-directional institutions helping implement production goals set by government planning agencies rather than giving workers voice on the job. Unions generally served the interests of managers rather than workers – and in places like China and Vietnam operated more like an insurance program, or at best, a social services agency.

Many of the remaining countries, called the "Third World" by some, were still under colonial rule – approximately 30 percent of the global population lived under colonial rule in 1945 (Brutents 2010). Sometimes referring to themselves as the Non-Aligned Movement, many of these countries fought for national liberation and political independence, and also attempted to create their own models of economic development, not necessarily tied to or governed by the Western model or the USSR (Prashad 2007).

Two of the dominant economic models that developed in these countries were Import Substitution Industrialization (ISI), and export-led growth. The ISI model developed in Latin America, where Argentinean economist Raul Prebisch proposed a path for economic development using high tariffs and "infant industry protections" in order to move up the development ladder from raw material extraction, to greater value-added production. In the process, countries would reduce their dependence on imports from wealthier nations.[5] Many Latin American countries, and some in Asia, adopted variations of ISI. The state assisted by subsidizing the purchase of imported machinery and establishing high tariffs on the import of finished products like automobiles (Gereffi and Evans 1981). For the most part, labor unions in Argentina, Brazil, Mexico and elsewhere were partners in the ISI development regime, via populist labor parties that governed for many decades (Murillo 2000).

The second major model, export-led growth, aimed to develop industry aimed at international markets. Theories about the role of export promotion in economic growth go back to the nineteenth century, but the theory was put to the test in a handful of Asian countries in the postwar period. South Korea, Taiwan, Hong Kong, and Singapore in particular adopted export-led strategies in the early 1960s, pursuing growth by liberalizing the economy, increasing exports, and, in theory, reducing the role of government. Neoliberal economists held up these countries as models, suggesting that neoliberal reforms led these countries to experience significant sustained economic growth for several decades (Lin 2012). Yet in reality, the countries only adopted a modified form of neoliberalism. For example, although the countries did increase exports, the states played a strong role in industrial planning and provided protections for infant industries, via import barriers and direct subsidies for certain domestic firms, depending on performance and production goals. The state also controlled labor: workers did not have many basic rights, and the state used direct repression against workers organizing, although union rights were sometimes expanded in response to protest, such as in South Korea in the late 1980s (Rodrik 2002; Hart-Landsberg 2009).

The 1973 Crisis and the Rise of Neoliberalism

While the post-World War II era witnessed different models and paths toward economic development, and different roles for unions, by the 1970s, political and economic trends began to create more uniform conditions for unions and workers across countries. In particular, in the late 1960s, economic growth began to slow in many regions, and in 1973, a severe global recession hit. This created an opening for the critics of Keynesianism. With economic instability and stagnation affecting much of the world, theorists, politicians, and activists stepped up efforts to implement new models. Some critics came from the Left, arguing that it was necessary to move from managed capitalism, or social democracy, to socialism or communism. There was a growth in Left organizations around the world in the 1960s and 1970s. The Left took power or came close to it in many countries, including Portugal, Bangladesh, Jamaica, and parts of Italy and Spain.

But other critiques came from the Right – particularly a group of economists and political philosophers advocating for the expansion of "free market capitalism." Geographer David Harvey (2005) asserts that this period created the conditions for the birth of neoliberalism. Keynesianism was failing to generate enough capital investment, which had slowed by the late 1960s, leading to lower growth and job creation. The debate became, how to reinvigorate investment? Neoliberal thinkers asserted that the free market was the solution. The key was to make the economy friendly to investors and finance. This required changing regulations to make it easier to invest or run a business; it also required reducing any "rigidities" that impede investment, from higher taxes to labor protections, including unions. Neoliberalism became an ideology and a practice. While neoliberal reforms in practice did not always coincide with its theory, they generally represented a move to reregulate labor and capital markets in favor of property owners and investors, and away from social protections and worker rights.

From the 1970s to the 2000s, neoliberalism spread throughout the globe – first as an ideology, then as a political program. Neoliberal policies were first tested in Chile in 1973, after the U.S. government helped overthrow the democratically elected president Salvador Allende and put in place a military dictatorship that enacted major neoliberal reform. A coup in Argentina in 1976 brought in military dictatorship that also began to plant the seeds for neoliberal reform (Teubal 2004). Under President Carter, the U.S. Congress began deregulating the banking and transportation sectors. In 1978, Chinese leader Deng Xiaoping announced that the country would experiment with markets, including establishing market pricing and allowing foreign trade and investment. In 1979, the U.K. elected Margaret Thatcher as prime minister, and the following year, the United States elected Ronald Reagan as president, and the shift to neoliberalism seemed assured (Harvey 2005). Massive capital restructuring in the 1980s, followed by the fall of the Soviet Union in 1989, sealed its fate. Although neoliberalism eventually came to dominate, it took different paths in different parts of the world.

The Liberal Market Economies Countries that followed a path of "managed capitalism" can be divided into liberal market economies (LMEs) and coordinated market economies (CMEs) (Hall and Soskice 2001). The LMEs (U.S., U.K., Canada, Australia, New Zealand, and Ireland), or Anglo-American countries, are those where firms rely primarily on market arrangements and hierarchies to function. These countries emerged from the war with weak social programs and institutions. While the trade unions in these countries won certain rights and had even enjoyed periods of relative strength, they never obtained a formal role in running the economy or in setting industrial policy. Some did not even have strong labor parties, or saw increasing distance between unions and labor parties starting in the 1980s.

While there was conflict over economic models in the 1970s, in the 1980s it was the neoliberals who won out as leaders and began implementing their reforms in earnest. The global economy began to open up and capital began to restructure. With increased international trade and investment, corporations and investors found it easier to move to regions or countries with fewer restrictions. Corporations looking to restore profit rates of earlier decades sought ways to cut costs, and one major way to do so was through cutting labor costs – moving production to countries with lower wages, freezing wages at home, eliminating unions, and increasing the pace and intensity of work.

It was not only CEOs, but also elected officials who backed this approach. While neoliberalism started as a political ideology, as it took root, it created a vise in which all politicians were forced to operate. The first neoliberals were Republicans and Conservatives, but eventually, the Democratic Party in the United States (the closest thing to a Labor Party in the United States), the Labour Party in the United Kingdom, and the Australian Labor Party all adopted parts of a neoliberal platform.

A key plank in the neoliberal program was an attack on unions.

In the United Kingdom, Thatcher went after the miners and railway unions; in the United States, Reagan broke the Air Traffic Controllers' union in the famous PATCO strike. Labor law in the United States had never been strong relative to other parts of the world, and was weakened considerably with the Taft-Hartley Act in 1947, which restricted many union rights. Efforts to strengthen labor law, including eliminating the right of employers to hire replacement workers during a strike, were unsuccessful – including in the late 1970s when the Democratic Party controlled the Presidency, House and Senate. But over time, the National Labor Relations Board – the main agency in the U.S. responsible for implementing labor laws related to unions – became even more conservative, issuing rulings that further restricted union rights, and further undermined freedom of association in practice (Estlund 2002; Gould 2007). Unions were on the defensive throughout the 1980s, and continued to be so into the 1990s under Bill Clinton in the U.S. and Tony Blair in the U.K.

Workers' rights were further undermined by the proliferation of free trade agreements, which first led to more capital flight in the manufacturing sector where unionization was historically concentrated. The rise of free trade agreements strengthened employers' bargaining power. For example, labor scholar Kate Bronfenbrenner found that following the implementation of the North American Free Trade Agreement in 1994, employers used the threat of plant closure more frequently during organizing drives (Bronfenbrenner 2000). Approximately 68 percent of employers in mobile industries (such as garment or electronics manufacturing) used such threats in the 1990s, compared to 36 percent of employers in non-mobile industries (such as hotels and restaurants). The threats were effective in reducing unionization and even had an impact on bargaining first contracts. A 2009 study found that these trends had persisted, and in fact had intensified (Bronfenbrenner 2009).

Coordinated Market Economies Other global north countries, primarily in Western Europe, have been classified as CMEs (Hall and Soskice 2001). Here, labor unions were more successful at

19

integrating their role in government post-World War II – through stronger social policies and workers' rights, and a formal role for unions in establishing wages and working conditions via tripartite governance. As a result, restructuring in the 1980s was not as harsh for workers and unions as it was in the LMEs (Phelan 2006). In countries such as Germany, Sweden, and the Netherlands, unions were able to assert their role in some of the restructuring, thereby mitigating the negative impact. In Sweden, union density even rose for a bit in the 1980s and 1990s (Phelan 2006). For a few decades, it appeared that some of the European unions would be spared the attacks seen in the Anglo-American world.

But even in the CMEs, neoliberal globalization eventually had an impact, particularly in the arena of labor market flexibility. Transnational corporations attempted to cut costs and look for greater returns, in part due to heightened global competition. States and regions got pulled into bidding for capital, trying to become hospitable to business – including foreign capital looking for investment opportunities, or domestic capital threatening to leave. In this context, policymakers moved to create the European Union. Several European nations were operating in coordination via the European Economic Community formed in 1957, but a larger and more formal alliance, named the European Union (EU), was established under the Maastricht Treaty in 1993. The EU established an economic and political entity, with a single market and standard set of rules and regulations, governed by the European Commission (EC) and other supranational institutions. They created a monetary union, called the Eurozone, in 1999, establishing the currency of the euro. There are now 28 countries that belong to the EU, though not all are part of the Eurozone, and not all share the same benefits.

The principle behind the EU was to harmonize upwards: to take the considerable variation in wealth, living standards, policies, and programs across the member states and adopt EU-wide standards that would attempt to lift up those at the bottom. However, built into the EU were competing goals. Alongside the goal of higher standards was the mandate of the "convergence criteria" of the

Maastricht Treaty, including that member states keep inflation at no more than 1.5 percentage points above the average of the three lowest inflation member states; that member states not allow deficits to exceed 3 percent of gross domestic product (GDP) each year; and that gross government debt not exceed 60 percent of the prior year's GDP. These financial criteria – promoted primarily by German Chancellor Helmut Kohl – created constraints on domestic economic policymaking, which grew increasingly restrictive. Overall, the convergence criteria of the EU embody a neoliberal philosophy that prioritizes low inflation and low government spending in the name of attracting investment.

This tension could be seen in the EU labor market policy as well. As early as 1993, the European Commission issued the "White Paper on Growth, Competitiveness and Employment," which called on European countries to examine the rigidities in their labor market policies in order to expand employment creation (Sbragia 2004). The White Paper stated that flexibility should not come at the expense of those already employed, but the 1997 Luxembourg Summit laid out clear and detailed recommendations, such as "more adaptable types of contracts," and revised benefit and training policies that would give the unemployed "incentive to look for work." These recommendations were framed as creating more opportunities for women to enter the labor force, and finding work for the unemployed. The formal goal of EU policy became to balance labor market flexibility with job security, or "flexicurity." But the other policy interests laid out by the EU institutions, such as price stability and low inflation, were at odds with the goals of security, and instead pushed governments simply toward flexibility.

Conservative, moderate and even some left governments implemented neoliberal reforms in a number of CME countries, particularly in the 2000s. For example, the Socialist Party in Spain began the process of labor market deregulation as early as the 1980s, and this was expanded by José María Aznar, when the conservative People's Party was elected in 1996 (Burgess 2004; Perez 2004). By 2000, Aznar was in alliance with Tony Blair in the United Kingdom, pushing the EU in the direction of neoliberal change. Soon, Silvio Berlusconi was elected in Italy and joined the alliance, creating a powerful coalition that pushed a host of policies, including labor market flexibility, within the EU (Sbragia 2004).

International competitive pressures, as well as EU policy goals relating to finance, have pushed most EU member countries further in the direction of flexibility in recent years. A 2012 study evaluates the labor market policies of 18 EU countries from 1985 to 2008 and finds that most countries have not met the dual goal of "flexicurity" (van Vliet and Nijboer 2012). Overall, flexibility has increased, primarily for those who are already "outsiders" – such as women, or migrant workers, who did not have access to full-time jobs before (Vosko 2000). Such policies created greater inequality between "insiders" and "outsiders," as well as a larger pool of temporary workers in many EU countries. The stratified impact of these measures may also be the result of unions' unwillingness to make existing contracts more "flexible," while being willing to accept increased flexibility for temporary workers who are not their members (Davidsson and Emmenegger 2012). In any case, the result is increasing labor market flexibility without corresponding increases in security for workers in the EU.

The Global South   Global south countries were among the first to be subjected to neoliberalism, starting with Chile and Argentina in the 1970s, and spreading rapidly throughout Latin America, Africa, and Asia in the 1980s and 1990s. Like Chile, some countries were forced to adopt neoliberal reforms after military coups – often with the backing of the United States or European governments, and sometimes involving assassinations, in their efforts to overthrow leaders seen as communist or sympathetic to communism. In addition to Chile and Argentina, between 1950 and 1973 left-leaning leaders were ousted in Bolivia, Brazil, Cambodia, Congo, the Dominican Republic, Ecuador, Guatemala, Indonesia, Iran, and Zaire (Keating 2012; Prashad 2007). This set the stage to bring in new leaders identified with the United States, and willing to go along with U.S.-backed neoliberal reforms starting in the 1970s and early

1980s. Soon, the neoliberal path was no longer a choice as all alternatives were gradually closed off.

Some global south countries found themselves pushed into neoliberalism through the policies of international financial institutions and the Structural Adjustment Policies of the International Monetary Fund (IMF) and World Bank. Countries that pursued ISI policies were vulnerable because they had borrowed large amounts of international money to implement ISI. When interest rates spiked in the early 1980s, some tried to, but could not, secure private refinancing and were forced to turn to the IMF and World Bank for assistance. These institutions imposed conditions on the loans. Placing conditions on loans is standard and unremarkable in most cases – such as when a bank requires a certain annual income before approving a mortgage. But with structural adjustment the conditions were extreme, requiring countries to adopt a wide range of reforms designed to liberalize the economy and open it up to the world market. Sometimes the demands were even contradictory to the Constitution or basic laws of the country. For example, the Mexican government agreed to hold down wages in the context of structural adjustment despite a Constitutional right to a living wage (Alarcón-González and McKinley 1999; Anker 2011).

Some African countries were under the leadership of corrupt dictators, supported by their former colonizers or the United States in the 1960s and 1970s. During this period they accumulated substantial debt as they pursued large, sometimes foolhardy, development projects, so when these debts became insurmountable in the 1980s, these countries also began to adopt structural adjustment programs and economic restructuring at the hands of the IMF and World Bank. Over two decades later, most analysts – including the IMF and World Bank – acknowledge that structural adjustment failed, overall, to create healthy economic development. Joseph Stiglitz, who was chief economist at the World Bank in the late 1990s, describes the many ways in which structural adjustment made conditions worse in countries – and made it almost impossible for the new slew of leaders to pursue healthy growth. In fact, even some of the advances countries had made – in health care or public education – were reversed under structural adjustment (Stiglitz 2006).

Still other countries pursued neoliberal policies under the leadership of domestic politicians trained in economics or political science in the United States (such as Carlos Salinas in Mexico and Francisco Flores Pérez in El Salvador). In South Africa, the African National Congress (ANC) adopted neoliberalism on its own after the fall of apartheid in the 1990s (Schneider 2003). But by that period, after the collapse of the Soviet Union and what appeared to be the triumph of free market capitalism, it seemed impossible to pursue any other path to economic development. If the ANC pursued any policies other than neoliberalism, international investors threatened to take money out of the country, destabilizing the economy. Later, leaders such as Luiz Inácio Lula da Silva of the Brazilian Workers' Party, would face the same constraints. Neoliberalism became the "common sense" among politicians and policymakers across the globe.

Neoliberals claimed that liberalization was the key to explaining the dynamic growth of Asian countries including South Korea, Taiwan, Hong Kong, and Singapore. But in fact, these countries did not adopt a full neoliberal program until after the Asian Financial crisis in 1997, particularly in relation to labor markets. For example, in 1997 South Korea passed a series of reforms as part of the IMF rescue package which included reducing labor market standards in order to attract foreign investment – eliminating lifetime employment, easing the ability to hire and fire, and weakening union rights, such as allowing firms to hire replacement workers during strikes. Unions protested the proposals, and so the government included a few reforms favoring unions, such as expanding the right to unionize in the public sector, and creating a Tripartite Commission that gave labor a voice in policy setting. But while workers and unions were gaining some rights on paper, and, in some ways, increased voice, the country was pursuing a path that decreased job security for workers, and dramatically increased irregular or "nonstandard" work (Kim 2004).

Neoliberalism came to India slowly, in the form of privatization and deregulation in the 1990s. In 1991 India adopted the

New Economic Policy – a slew of policies that would make them eligible for aid from the IMF and World Bank. The country moved from a state-led, ISI economy to a market-led liberalized one. They accepted a multi-billion dollar bailout from the IMF that required India to agree to a host of conditions, a number of which had major implications for labor (Ahn 2010). This included downsizing the public sector, leading to massive lay-offs and a reduction in the proportion of workers employed in the formal sector. It included reforms that gave greater rights to private sector firms and investors relative to unions and workers. This opened up a period of broad attacks against unions. Unions were quickly on the defensive, working against reforms that would enhance labor flexibility (Sundar 2000).

The Transition Economies Countries that have moved from a centrally planned to a market economy are called "transition economies." The political collapse of the Soviet Union in 1989 provided neoliberal reformers more evidence that capitalism had triumphed, and planned economies were a failure. But at the time, there were still various models of capitalism that countries could choose, ranging from Nordic social democracy to United States' "free markets." For the most part, the formerly centrally planned countries plunged into a "shock therapy" – a set of policies recommended by economists such as Jeffrey Sachs, and the IMF and World Bank to get these economies quickly operating on market principles. A big part of this was selling off state-owned enterprises and public assets to private bidders. It also involved other standard elements of the neoliberal model: opening up the economy for investment and trade, instituting macroeconomic policies to prioritize low inflation, and creating private financial institutions.

It also meant establishing labor markets and wage labor. Suddenly, the trade unions were autonomous from the state, and had to move swiftly to adjust to a whole new environment and set of rules. Instead of the government setting wage rates, employers now did. Public industries were privatized, and employers now had the ability to hire and fire at will.

China adopted markets in a much more measured fashion, starting with experiments in Guangdong province, in southern China, in the late 1970s. The Chinese government set stronger regulations about how much foreign investment could come into the country, and under what conditions joint ventures could operate. The government had previously allocated jobs via government institutions and government-controlled trade unions; government policies set a wage structure and provided basic income and social security. To move to a market economy, the country needed to create a labor market where workers sold their labor power to employers, and job allocation and wage determination were no longer controlled by the state. The first step was to end the concept of the "iron rice bowl" in 1978, where workers would be assigned to a work unit in state-owned enterprises (SOEs), which provided workers with lifelong employment. China began privatizing SOEs in the 1980s and 1990s, pushing millions of workers out of work. In 1989, 70 percent of urban dwellers worked for the state; this dropped to less than 30 percent by 2010 (Zenglein 2008; Warner 2010). The state also subsidized new development in the private sector – including massive investment in infrastructure in Southern China and export zones, and employing government recruiters to bring workers from rural areas to work in the new factories (Ross 2006).

The 2008 Crisis and Beyond

Despite taking a variety of paths, and considering that there are still great differences in legal and political structures, demographics, and levels of development, by the mid-2000s most countries had adopted at least some neoliberal reforms. Then the next global economic crisis hit in 2008. Five years after the crisis began, certain indicators, such as profits, CEO salaries and stock market levels appear to have recovered. Yet the situation for workers is bleak, and there is little sign of recovery to date.

The expansion of neoliberalism has meant that workers in many parts of the world face similar conditions, despite the variations between countries. There are differences related to the strength and creation of unions and their legacies, but everywhere there are parallel trends in corporate restructuring, toward lower labor standards and informal employment, and in relation to governments.

The trends in corporate restructuring result from the changes in regulations that allow corporations to consolidate power. There has been massive conglomeration, through mergers and acquisitions, leading to a small number of large transnational firms in many industries. For example, due to mergers and acquisitions in the international hotel industry, the top 12 companies controlled 75 percent of the total hotel rooms worldwide by 2001 (Woodside and Martin 2008). In the United States, the 10 largest grocery firms went from a 27 percent market share in 1994 to 50 percent in 2000 (Drake 2001). Supermarket consolidation is even more extreme elsewhere: in Sweden, three chains control 95 percent of the market; in Argentina, Belgium, Denmark, France, Great Britain, the Netherlands, and Spain, a handful of grocery firms control 45–60 percent (Vivas 2009).

Corporations have also entered complex relations with other firms, including "supply chains" that convert raw goods to finished consumer products, sometimes involving multiple companies and countries. Through economic restructuring, increased subcontracting, and the interpenetration of finance into much of the economy, the boundaries of each individual firm have become more blurred. Workers and unions have more challenges in working directly with employers. Employers still have authority over workers, but that employer also is in a complex relation with their suppliers or purchasers. This is not necessarily new: subcontracting systems existed in previous eras. But the nature of the globalized economy has led to much larger scale firms, broader networks, less transparency, further complicated by dense regulations, trade agreements, and accounting practices. This is ironic, as the tenets of free markets call for less regulation, but many scholars note that we should not mistake neoliberalism for deregulation, as in reality, many of the neoliberal reforms resulted in increased regulation, just for different ends.[6] In this sense, corporations restructured in ways that obscure relationships and make it much more difficult for workers to organize in their workplace and

27

bargain for better wages or working conditions. The restructuring has made it easier for corporations to shift legal responsibility for their actions to others further down the supply chain.

Corporate restructuring has developed alongside changes in the labor market. Neoliberal policy frequently diverges from the theory, but its adherents assert that labor flexibility is a necessary, though not sufficient, condition for economic growth. Initially, some employers restructured using "just-in-time" production and inventory systems. This allowed them to reduce the amount of capital tied up in inventory, and to make it available for other purposes. "Just-in-time" staffing can do the same thing. Employers want to hire and fire parallel to fluctuations in contract orders or sales volume.

But what happens to unions and workers? In the past, many unions succeeded by controlling or limiting the supply of labor. For example, they were able to win contracts that mandated employers only hire union workers, or that workers join the union when hired. They established training and apprenticeship programs that workers had to complete in order to work in the trade.

Some unions shifted from this model to a more inclusionary model, where unions represented skilled and unskilled workers. Some even moved to a political model where unions and parties represented the broader working class – but even this was premised on the idea of closed borders – limited immigration flows and restrictions on capital outflow and jobs leaving the country. What is the role for unions in a global economy that has labor flexibility as a fundamental assumption?

The labor movement has seen contradictory trends in the modern world. On the one hand, international institutions and some countries have pushed for greater labor rights and "free unions" – such as in Poland and the former Soviet Union. The United States and ILO pushed Middle Eastern and Latin American countries to improve labor standards and legal frameworks before adopting free trade agreements. And by many indicators, such as number of ILO conventions adopted, or the legalization of certain trade union rights, conditions have improved on a global level over the past two decades (ILO 2008). On the other hand, much of this same push has come with, or alongside, requirements for greater labor market flexibility, such as increasing employer rights to engage in subcontracting, reducing worker rights to job security, and undermining trade union rights in practice (Burgess 2010; Cammett and Posusney 2010; Cook 2010).[7] The spread of neoliberal globalization has given more power to capital vis-à-vis workers and citizens, making it easier for investors to use the "threat effect" to change laws. Employers can threaten to take their jobs and/or investments to another country, or even a neighboring city, if they are not given tax cuts, looser regulations, or relaxed enforcement of certain laws.

This leads to a third similarity that many workers face, in different parts of the world: changes in the role of the state. More power for employers relative to workers, and unions, has also weakened the power of political parties, and in turn, weakened or severed some historic union–party alliances. This does not mean that the state is no longer relevant, or impotent in the face of global capital. In many ways, certain states are as powerful as ever. But neoliberal policy requires a state that is active in enforcing favorable conditions for capital – reregulating labor markets and property rights in ways that end up exacerbating inequality, unemployment and underemployment, contingent work and working poverty.

Conclusion

Despite the expansion of markets to most of the globe, and the corresponding increase in total wealth, most workers around the world face bleak conditions. Neoliberalism has led to increasing job insecurity, flat or declining wages, and a large spike in inequality. Employers have gained rights relative to workers, and governments have failed to champion worker interests. But neoliberalism came to prominence in part due to the failures of the prior system. The era of managed capitalism had its own weaknesses, leading to economic crisis in the 1970s.

Just as the economic recessions of the 1930s and 1970s opened up debate about the kind of economic system we want to live in, so has the 2008 global crisis. There is a growing consensus that neoliberal globalization has created serious problems. The ILO, in its Declaration on Social Justice for a Fair Globalization, notes that while globalization has had some positive effects, it also "has caused many countries and sectors to face major challenges of income inequality, continuing high levels of unemployment and poverty, vulnerability of economies to external shocks, and the growth of both unprotected work and the informal economy, which impact on the employment relationship and the protections it can offer" (ILO 2008).

One of the reasons neoliberalism has been bad for workers is that the model stresses the role of competition as a force for growth. As Panitch and Gindin (2012) argue, competition can harm individual businesses but overall makes the capitalist class stronger, as a class. On the other hand, competition in the labor market has the opposite result. Competition between workers means that individuals lose, but the class as a whole is also made weaker. Whether the competition is between black workers and white workers, men and women, permanent and temporary workers, or workers in the United States and workers in China, workers as a whole are worse off when they compete with one another in unfettered free markets.

On the other hand, while neoliberalism has led to severe problems for workers, it also creates new opportunities for unions. As sociologist Peter Evans notes, the emergence of large global corporations and supply chains creates common targets for workers around the world, and may provide new incentives and leverage (Evans 2010). While political systems vary greatly, workers find their elected representatives reregulating economies in ways that give corporations and investors more rights, also creating a potential common thread for labor organizers attempting to counter that trend and expand rights for workers.

As we once again debate the kind of world we want to live in, it is imperative that workers have a voice in the discussions and space to help build a new model. Unions have historically been one of the best ways for workers to enter these debates. But unions, like the workers they represent, are facing hard times. If unions are to survive, it is crucial that they understand these same contradictions of the global economy. But even more important than the survival of unions are the conditions of the global working class, and indeed, the health of the global economy and environment. If there is to be any hope for a more balanced and sustainable world, the labor movement must find ways to address these contradictions together, across borders. This includes the need to deal with "flexibility" as well as the overall shortage of living wage jobs, and the need for a foundation to global citizenship.

Part I

Background

2

A Role for Unions?

While labor unions have existed since the birth of industrialization, the trade union movement experienced most of its growth in the U.S. and Europe in the post-World War II era, from the 1940s to the 1970s. There were many unique things about that period, including that the world was relatively less globalized than it had been before or since. Partly as a product of two world wars, many countries tightened borders to global capital flows and immigration. But through diplomatic agreements such as the General Agreement on Tariffs and Trade (GATT), influenced by economic and foreign policy interests, international tariffs began to decline, leading to increased international trade. That, combined with advances in technology and communication, as well as containerization in the shipping industry, laid the groundwork for a resurgence of the global economy in the last 30 years.

As mentioned earlier, globalization is not new – the 1800s were perhaps more global than much of the 1900s. Doug Henwood (2003) cites a 2002 speech by Anne Krueger, head of IMF, to illustrate this point:

> The phrase "emerging market" only came into common use in the 1980s, but capital flows into developing countries of course have a much longer history. Stock markets were operating in Turkey by 1866, India by 1875, and Brazil by 1877. Widespread sovereign borrowing – in the sense that we think of it now – got under way in the late eighteenth century, when the spread of constitutional forms of

government led to more stable nation-states that recognized continuing liabilities to lenders . . .

But while the 1800s may have been more globalized, trade unions have had their greatest growth and power in the mid-1900s: a period when global trade and investment was much more regulated. In fact, economies overall were regulated with a greater balance of power between corporations and workers at that time. Can unions be effective in a more integrated world, where regulations are designed in a way that gives corporations more power over workers?

Some critics assert that unions are outdated, as they are best suited to represent blue-collar, manufacturing workers. In wealthy countries, manufacturing has declined significantly in terms of the share of jobs, and retail, food service, education, and health care are now the dominant employers. Unions, they say, are not appropriate for service sector workers, workers with higher levels of education and training, or workers who may consider themselves to be "professionals" rather than part of the working class.

Other critics assert that unions are not effective ways to organize the modern worker, who is more likely to be a migrant, moving within a country or across borders. The informal sector is a large and, in many places, growing segment of workers (Chen and Vanek 2013). Can unions be relevant for this workforce?

In this chapter I argue that despite changes in the global and domestic economy, unions still have a vital role to play. While they may need to change the way they operate, unions are one of the only organizations with the capacity and interest in representing workers in the global economy. First, I begin with some basic facts about unions and union members, which will dispel a few myths about who unions do or can represent. Then, I show how unions have played a positive role in most countries by decreasing inequality and stabilizing the economy. However, the ability of unions to play this role is constrained by the political and economic context. Even if unions were somehow able to achieve their higher density rates of the past, it is not clear that they could have as large a positive impact on wages and working conditions on the micro- and macroeconomy due to major structural neoliberal changes, such as deregulation of industries and the increased role of finance. But to reverse those structural changes, workers need more power. Unions are still necessary for addressing the large imbalance of power between workers and corporations. In fact, unions may be one of the few counterforces to drastic inequality.

Beyond the potential for unions to impact wages and the economy, unions have intrinsic value. Unions are one way to expand and deepen democracy in its fullest sense. They may also provide a path to global citizenship in a new world order dominated by corporations and international financial institutions. Finally, unions are a natural vehicle for raising key ideological questions about the kind of world in which we want to live. As we debate the future – whether we return to the days of managed capitalism, or move to something new – unions have a valuable role in shaping the conversation and moving toward a worker-friendly outcome.

Who Belongs to Unions?

A common perception is that labor unions are primarily for white men, who work in blue-collar jobs – manufacturing, truckdriving, construction, or on the docks. It is true that these types of workers have historically been in unions. But the demographics of union membership varies by country, and has changed over time in many places.

In the U.S., the majority of union members are now in the public sector. The two occupations with the greatest number of union members are "education, training and library services" and "office and administrative support occupations" (Bureau of Labor Statistics 2013). There are more men in unions than women, but the gap has been closing over time.[1] Black workers are now more likely to be union members than white, Asian, or Latino workers. In fact, black men and black women are more likely to be in a union than white men (Bureau of Labor Statistics 2013).[2]

Surveys of EU countries show that on average, more men are

members of unions than women, but that in recent decades, male membership has declined significantly, and women's membership has increased slightly, closing the gap. Overall, women's share of trade union confederations varies significantly across the EU, with a low of 18 percent of members of the Italian Union of Labor to a high of 68 percent of members in the Finnish Confederation of Professionals. Of 27 union confederations surveyed, women made up 40 percent or more of the members in 16 (Dumont and Harcourt 2003). These high numbers are in part a reflection of the types of occupations and industries that are unionized in EU countries.

Unions still represent blue-collar workers, but around the world they also represent professional and service workers as well, including teachers, health care, public sector, finance, and retail workers. For example, the bank workers union in Brazil is among the country's most active – in 2011, the union struck and shut down over 8,000 banks in 26 states (La Botz 2011). German retail workers struck against Walmart long before Walmart workers struck in the U.S., back in the 2000s (Associated Press 2002a). Likewise, one of the most militant and active unions in South Korea is the teachers union. A 2007 report of call centers found that 50 percent of global call center workers are covered by a collective agreement; representation is particularly high in Brazil, France, the Netherlands, and Sweden (Holman et al. 2007).

While unions are more diverse in composition and in the occupations they represent than common perception might suggest, they are still far from representative of the global working class – particularly in relation to young workers. International labor organizations have noted the crisis facing young workers in general in terms of unemployment and underemployment, and the corresponding impact on trade union membership. Still, globally, unions are far more diverse – and far larger – than any other form of worker representation. The New Unionism Network estimates that over 460 million people belong to unions worldwide.[3] Even with a drop in density in many countries, labor unions still play a significant role in raising wages and improving working conditions for millions of workers. But beyond the micro benefits unions bring to individual workers, they can benefit macroeconomies as well.

Unions Reduce Inequality and Stabilize the Economy

Unions can provide many benefits to their members: higher wages, better job security, and stronger benefits. But they can also have a positive impact on the macroeconomy, benefitting all workers, even those not in unions. Two ways they have historically done this is by reducing inequality and stabilizing the economy.

Inequality is rapidly increasing on a global level – both within and between countries. Of course, inequality can be measured in different ways and the period of time you select to measure can influence the degree to which these changes are evident. However, there is consensus that the divide between the very wealthy (measured by income or wealth) and the rest of the population has grown over the last 30 years in many countries.

Two of the pre-eminent scholars on inequality are economists Thomas Piketty and Emmanuel Saez. They have measured income inequality across the world, going back in time. In a series of studies, they find an increasing gap between top earners and middle and lower income earners, particularly in the U.S., but also in English-speaking countries, as well as in India and China. In some cases, wages at the bottom and middle rose over time, but the inequality is explained by very large surges in the top wage earners' incomes (Piketty and Saez 2006). Piketty and Saez do not find the same trends in continental Europe or Japan, but other data suggest inequality is growing there too, if not at the extreme levels as in other countries – particularly because tax policies and government programs help soften the worst effects of inequality (International Labour Organization 2013).

But it isn't just academics who note these trends. The IMF has noted the same phenomenon in a series of papers, showing that while average per capita incomes have risen for much of the world, the gap between rich and poor has grown significantly, with big gaps in places like the U.S. and China (Kumhof et al. 2012). The IMF study concluded that increased trade narrows the gap between rich and poor, but this is trumped by the impact of financial globalization and new technology (Juamotte et al. 2007).

Labor movement theorists have argued that unions are one of the best ways to reverse the inequality growth. A host of studies have found that unions reduce inequality within a workplace, such as reducing the race and gender wage gap. An ILO study reports a strong correlation between wage inequality and the degree to which wages are set through collective bargaining. Countries with high levels of bargaining coverage have less inequality, while countries with low coverage – such as Poland, Hungary, the U.S., and South Korea – have higher inequality (Hayter and Weinberg 2011).

Economist David Card found that the drop in U.S. union density from 1973 to 1993 explained 15–20 percent of the increase in wage inequality among male workers. Card did not find similar outcomes for women workers, but concluded that increasing unionization in the public sector during this period slowed the growth in wage inequality (Card 2001). Bruce Western and Jake Rosenthal find similar results. They write: "Accounting for unions' effect on union and nonunion wages suggests that the decline of organized labor explains a fifth to a third of the growth in inequality – an effect comparable to the growing stratification of wages by education" (Western and Rosenfeld 2011). Unions also appear to reduce wage inequality within a firm – reducing the wage gap between highest- and lowest-paid workers, and also between workers of different races and genders (Yates 2003).

However, not all studies find similar results, and there is much debate about the reasons behind increasing inequality. Some scholars assert that technology is one of the main determinants, rather than union density. Others argue that the conditions of the country matter, and that it is not possible to make a blanket generalization about the relationship between unions, collective bargaining, and wage inequality. For example, Casale and Posel (2011) found that in South Africa in 2000–6, unionization decreased the wage gap among union members, but increased the wage gap between union and non-union workers. They also found that the gender wage gap was larger in the union sector.

Others argue that while unions once played a strong role in creating a more equal society through redistribution, the changing economy has lessened their impact. For example, Baccaro (2008) examined 51 countries and found that union influence on equality has diminished in most countries since the 1970s. Only in Central and Eastern Europe did trade unions still play such a role by the 2000s. Baccaro argues that in part due to globalization, unions no longer had the latitude or power to negotiate wages, therefore reducing their ability to contribute to wage compression between low-skill/low-wage jobs and higher-wage jobs.

Related to the relationship between unions and inequality is the ability of unions to stabilize the economy. Standard neoclassical economic theory predicts that unions destabilize the economy by raising wages and creating unemployment. Labor is a commodity in this model, and raising the price of labor (wages), will result in a decrease in demand for that good. It also argues that unions cause other "rigidities" in the labor market – with a union contract, employers are not as free to hire and fire workers at will or implement certain production changes without restriction. Employers need to be flexible to the ever-changing consumer demand and product market, and cannot be constrained in their decisions. Therefore unions, according to this theory, slow growth and are undesirable. Furthermore, investors may see countries with strong unions and labor laws as less attractive. Removing regulations and eliminating unions is seen as a way to improve the "business climate" and attract capital.

Yet there is a growing body of research that challenges some of the assumptions and findings of these theories. Labor movement theorists have long argued that unions have a unique role to play in stabilizing the economy. John R. Commons and John Maynard Keynes both argued that markets, left to their own devices, would lead to crises and dysfunctionality. Unions could mediate the excesses of the market, by restraining the worst tendencies of firm competition, and redistributing wealth into the hands of workers, who were also consumers and drivers of economic activity.

A 2002 World Bank report summarized a wide range of studies and concluded that countries with greater union density had less severe business cycles, greater GDP growth, and faster recovery out of recessions. However, they also found that the effects changed over time, with a stronger impact of unionization on macroeconomic variables in the 1970s and 1980s, and less impact in the 1990s (Aidt and Tzannatos 2002).

For a while, there was debate about the relationship between inequality and growth, but increasingly, economists see that high inequality can hurt growth, particularly balanced growth. In 2011, IMF researchers released a study that showed high inequality stands out as a strong impediment to sustained growth spells (Berg and Ostry 2011). While it is possible to observe economic growth in countries with high inequality, they found that "high 'growth spells' were much more likely to end in countries with less equal income distributions," and that "the effect is large." They found that a "10-percentile decrease in inequality . . . increases the expected length of a growth spell by 50 percent." Therefore, to the extent that unions reduce inequality, they can also indirectly influence sustained economic growth. But for unions to reduce inequality, they must address the imbalance of power between employers and workers.

Unions and the Balance of Power between Corporations and Workers

The studies here suggest that unions' capacity to reduce inequality and stabilize the economy has lessened to some extent in recent decades, coinciding with the rise of neoliberalism. This suggests that even if unions were able to achieve their prior density levels, they may not have as much power to influence the macroeconomy. This is in part due to the massive changes brought about by neoliberalism. Managed capitalism, or Keynesianism, reduced the power of corporations to "exit." Unions were also able to extract wage gains from large profitable, oligopolistic firms, and there were laws and regulations in place that made firms more likely to have to bargain with unions and agree to collective bargaining contracts.

Today, there are still large oligopolies, but these companies now have more power relative to unions, due to massive industry deregulation (of industries like trucking, telecom, and utilities), deregulation of the financial sector, privatization, and trade and investment laws. As the role of finance increased dramatically, many new opportunities for investment emerged. Now, if employees in a fast food restaurant were successful in organizing the company, converting low-wage part-time jobs into full-time living wage jobs with benefits, the investors could pull out and put their money elsewhere. Thus, the power of "exit" has grown for corporations relative to workers and unions. The structural conditions that made it possible for unions to redistribute profits, reduce inequality, and stimulate balanced growth no longer exist.

David Harvey, a geographer who studies political economy, argues that the widening gap between rich and poor is not just coincidence or the innocent by-product of advanced technology. Rather, it is the outcome of a deliberate program of neoliberal change. Harvey (2005) states that neoliberalism can be understood as an attempt to restore average profitability to the capitalist economies after the 1970s recession/slow-down – in this, neoliberalism has failed. But, it can also be understood as a political project on the behalf of the top earners to restore and increase their share of income. In this, the neoliberal project appears to be a great success.

There is much evidence to show that neoliberalism was as much about the balance of power between corporations and workers as it was about economic theory. As mentioned earlier, both Margaret Thatcher and Ronald Reagan went on the offensive against labor unions in their countries. Federal Reserve Chairman Paul Volcker, initially appointed to his position by the Democrat Jimmy Carter, shared Reagan's view that unions had to be controlled. When Reagan broke the air traffic controllers' strike in 1981, Volcker remarked, "The significance (of PATCO) was that someone finally took on an aggressive, well-organized union and said no" (Neikirk 1987). The neoliberal attack on unions could be seen as early as the 1973 coup in Chile. According to one scholar,

> The wave of repression associated with the military takeover was directed particularly against the trade union movement. One of the military's earliest decree laws . . . outlawed the CUT [Workers' United Center of Chile]. A subsequent Decree Law . . . deprived unions of the right to hold meetings . . . It also required vacancies to be filled by seniority or government appointment rather than by union elections. (Remmer 1980: 282)

The initial attacks against unions as part of the neoliberal agenda were often direct and ideological. Elsewhere, the changes were indirect, and came as a result of conflicting policy demands or contradictory goals. The EU in particular created itself with two souls: one based on social integration and the other based on austerity. Given the built-in mandates covering debt and budgets, countries are constrained in their ability to engage in deficit-spending during economic recession, and they are pushed toward cutting social programs, and/or public sector wages and employment.

Similarly, free trade agreements and the IMF/World Bank Structural Adjustment programs did not necessarily undermine trade unions outright, but instituted policies that had the same effect. For example, opening up markets to foreign imports has had a negative impact on domestic firms in many countries, leading to lay-offs or closures – often in unionized firms. Neoliberal reforms often brought in export processing zones (EPZs) that were exempt from domestic labor and employment laws. Therefore, even if new jobs are created in EPZs, they are far less likely to be unionized than the jobs that were cut with domestic employers. Structural adjustment encouraged privatization as well, and again, public services that were more likely to be unionized were then converted to private sector non-union jobs.

The spread of neoliberalism did not unfold the same way in every country, and did not even result in across-the-board cuts to labor rights and union strength. For example, Murillo and Schrank (2005) argue that many Latin American unions were able to intervene in the reform process, with the help of domestic political parties and international labor allies, to resist some of the most harmful reforms. In fact, they note that there were 18 labor reforms implemented in Latin American countries between 1985 and 1998, and that 13 of those strengthened collective bargaining rights. This indicates that while the balance of power between corporations and unions has shifted in favor of corporations during the spread of neoliberalism, there has been space for some resistance, and in fact some unions have managed to expand labor rights. This suggests that unions can still play a role in mitigating neoliberal reforms and the balance of power between corporations and workers.

Beyond the impact unions may have on wages, inequality, and the macroeconomy, they also have intrinsic value, helping to expand democracy and rebuilding the global economy in a more just way.

Democracy

Labor unions can contribute to expanding democracy under a liberal definition or a more radical definition. Advocates of Western-style "liberal democracies" have asserted that trade unions should be allowed as voluntary associations that provide worker voice and balance market failure. Organizations ranging from the ILO to the U.S. State Department assert that freedom of association is essential for democracy. In fact, several leaders of Western nations argued that the former Soviet Union and modern China are not democratic because their citizens have no right to form independent trade unions. Ronald Reagan famously spoke in favor of trade union rights, when he said this of the Solidarność trade union in Poland, in 1980:

> They remind us that where free unions and collective bargaining are forbidden, freedom is lost. They remind us that freedom is never more than one generation away from extinction. You and I must protect and preserve freedom here or it will not be passed on to our children and it would disappear everywhere in the world. Today the workers in

Poland are showing a new generation how high is the price of freedom but also how much it is worth that price. (Reagan 1980)

The conservative U.S.-based non-profit Freedom House uses freedom of association as a key indicator in its index of "Freedom in the World." A U.S. State Department official explained in 2002, "Trade unions are often the only institutions that give a voice to workers, whose circumstances are often neglected by those in power. More important still, sometimes they are the only mass-based organizations that stand against authoritarian regimes" (Craner 2002). Unions can provide workers freedom of expression in the workplace, because they can provide some protections for workers who may have no rights otherwise.

For example, U.S. employment law is founded in the principle of "employment-at-will." This assumes that both employer and employee have the freedom to voluntarily enter, or leave, the employment relationship. In theory, this sounds positive, but in practice, because employers tend to have far greater resources than the average employee, and therefore more bargaining power, employees are vulnerable. They can be fired for a wide range of reasons, and even no reason at all. It was only in the 1960s that the federal government passed laws providing some protection for workers against employment-at-will, by making it illegal for employers to fire workers based on certain protected categories (race, color, creed, sex, nationality, religion). Subsequent laws protect workers for being fired due to age or disability status. However, an employer can still fire you if he simply does not like you – as long as he can prove that it was not due to discrimination. The only other form of protection that workers have is a contract, including a union contract. Without employment protection, workers are not free to express their opinion, and they have no due process for arbitrary discipline or firing. Unions provide some degree of democratic rights through collective bargaining agreements or other forms of agreements that offer protection.

Research also shows that unions are effective in enforcing existing laws and enhancing good government. For example, David Weil (1991) found unionized workplaces are more likely to have health and safety inspections, and that the monitoring and enforcement of standards is more thorough, and Stephanie Luce (2004) found that union involvement improved the implementation of living wage ordinances in the U.S. In these cases, unions serve as a mechanism of accountability for employers and governments, and can even increase the capacity of governments to do their job. In a cross-national study of 54 countries, Lee found that when union mobilization is connected to civic mobilization, unions balance not only class power, but also power within state institutions, making government more transparent and responsive (Lee 2007).

In addition to their role in liberal democracies, political theorists have advocated that unions could have a role in a more radical version of democracy, taking worker voice beyond the voting booth and into the workplace. Despite the protections that a union contract can provide, there is no guarantee that union members have a voice in how a firm is run. In fact, in countries like the U.S., many unions abandoned fighting for a role in production, hiring or investment decisions, accepting certain economic benefits (higher wages and benefits), and leaving major decisions to managerial prerogative.

This is not the case in all countries. In some European countries, unions participate in a system of co-determination. This system began in Germany after World War II, in the coal and steel industries and spread to other sectors. The laws governing co-determination require that worker representatives be given formal seats on the supervisory body of the enterprise. Workers have one-third of seats for smaller enterprises and one-half of seats for firms with 2,000 or more employees (although management has the tie-breaking vote). Worker representatives have a full vote on these boards, which govern basic managerial decisions, including those regarding production, hiring and layoffs, and productivity.

In addition, German workers in any workplace with five or more employees have the right to a works council – a body independent of management or the trade union. Workers elect representatives to the council, which has the right to make decisions on some matters and give input on others. Their rights are greatest on "social matters" (such as changing work days or establishing a cafeteria in the workplace), less on human resources (hiring and firing), and least on economic planning (such as where the company plans to invest).

According to Michel (2007), 18 of 25 European countries have some form of employee representation on enterprise boards. There is great diversity in how these function in practice, which made it difficult for the European Union to reach a consensus on establishing co-determination throughout the EU. Instead, the countries agreed to a "European Works Council" model. Established in 1994, this applies to any company in the EU with over 1,000 employees. The works council is advisory, however, and only gives employees the rights to information and consultation. In 2004, the EU enacted regulations governing a company's right to establish itself as a European Company. The law requires the company to negotiate with employees over the issue of co-determination. If they cannot reach an agreement, the company must adopt a minimal program of providing information and consultation rights to employees.

Observers note that globalization has impacted the works councils and co-determination models in Europe. As companies have expanded operations overseas, and changes in regulations and trade law make it much easier to offshore jobs or move entire operations, the employer gains an advantage because management can now threaten to move if employees don't accept concessions (Looise and Drucker 2002; Michel 2007).

Globalization poses numerous challenges for unions, and may dilute their capacity to provide workers with greater democratic voice in the workplace. However, the challenges do not undermine the principle that workers need some mechanism for democratic voice. Unions may need to adapt, but they can protect worker rights under a more traditional liberal definition, and expand rights toward a more radical definition of democracy.

Global Citizenship?

Beyond providing a method for democratic voice in the workplace, unions might also be an avenue for establishing broader citizenship rights in the global economy. With the formation of the World Trade Organization (WTO), the world has a global institution with enforcement powers. This may be the first example of actual global governance, or the beginnings of an international "state."

The largest employers all operate in multiple countries, and most participate in global networks (including the WTO, but also the World Economic Forum and associations like the American Chamber of Commerce). Through formal and informal channels, employers are able to advance their interests in the global economy by lobbying governments around trade agreements, international law, diplomatic treaties, and domestic regulations and laws that affect them. Not all employers have the same interest, and in fact they may be opposed to one another as competitors in the same industry, or as different industries. For example, small businesses may have different interests than large businesses in relation to trade. A large firm has the resources to move production overseas and import products back at a cheaper price, whereas a small business is unlikely to be able to do the same thing. But despite different perspectives, there are venues for employers to lobby and enact regulations. The WTO administers over 60 agreements, covering trade in goods, services, investments, and other arenas. It governs over 97 percent of world trade and has the authority to make binding decisions. Furthermore, bilateral and multilateral trade agreements and investment treaties usually include mechanisms for enforcing rulings against countries.

For example, the North American Free Trade Agreement (NAFTA)'s Chapter 11 gives individual investors rights against potential expropriation – the potential loss of profit. Under NAFTA, individual investors can sue countries that pass laws or engage in practices that alter the potential profits an investor might have accrued. The first maor case filed under Chapter 11 came from the U.S.-based Ethyl Corporation. Ethyl supplied a chemical called MMT to Canada, used as a gasoline additive. The United States had banned MMT due to health risks, and Canada was about to do the same. Ethyl brought a case against Canada under NAFTA Chapter 11 for $200 million in lost profits. The

Canadian government decided to avoid the suit and reversed the ban, and paid Ethyl $13 million for damages incurred (Hallward-Driemeier 2003). The investor rights clauses may also be used to dismantle public services. UPS sued the Canadian government for $160 million, claiming that Canada Post enjoyed an unfair advantage over private companies due to public subsidies. UPS lost the case but only on a technicality. Meanwhile, Canada and the EU are negotiating a trade agreement that would allow EU companies access to municipal contracts in Canada. This would mean that Canadian cities and provinces could not give preference to local contractors or local hiring.

At the same time, the trade agreements and WTO have no similar provisions for worker rights. A few trade agreements include language regarding labor standards, such as the NAFTA labor side agreement, but the enforcement process is complex and weak, and to date workers have not won any case (Kay 2011). While the investor rights chapters often include clear, direct mechanisms that can result in binding arbitration, this is not the case for worker rights. The major institution governing workers is the ILO, but that has no power of enforcement, and little authority, particularly over large countries like the U.S.

Furthermore, the WTO, trade agreements, and changes in domestic regulation have made it easier for corporations and money to move across borders. This happens through changes that reduce restrictions on capital flows, reduce taxes on capital transactions, reduce tariffs and trade barriers, and increase opportunities for foreign investment. However, workers have not enjoyed this same trend in easing barriers to movement. While the number of people migrating across borders is at an all-time high (discussed further in chapter 4), many of these people are crossing borders without documentation or full rights. This includes people travelling on guest worker visas, which tend to provide workers with limited rights and second-class citizenship.

What we see is an emerging system of global governance that is being created and utilized by corporations, where workers have no citizenship. Investors have more rights in the international arena, and workers have few or none.

Unions, and international union federations, may provide a way for workers to lay the foundation for worker rights in a system of global governance. Unions are unmatched in size and resources among worker organizations and are the closest parallel to the industry associations and trade groups that corporations belong to. While not as extensive or powerful as employer groups, unions have relationships with elected leaders, political parties and civil society organizations. If workers are to have any chance in asserting their citizenship rights in this global arena, unions are the most likely choice.

Life beyond Capitalism

Finally, unions have a role to play in debating the path out of our current period of economic crisis. Will neoliberalism continue to be the dominant model? Should we – and can we – return to managed capitalism? Or are there new models that should be tried?

All economic and political systems have evolved over time, and it seems likely that neoliberal capitalism will as well. The global economic crisis called into serious question the viability of neoliberal capitalism, and there is an increasing consensus that neoliberalism has failed in many ways. In fact, after the 2008 global economic crisis, some of the main advocates of capitalism expressed skepticism about their model. Martin Wolf, chief economic commentator for the *Financial Times*, wrote this on March 8, 2009:

> On June 19 2007, I concluded an article on the "new capitalism" with the observation that it remained "untested." The test has come: it failed. The era of financial liberalisation has ended. Yet, unlike in the 1930s, no credible alternative to the market economy exists and the habits of international co-operation are deep.

Wolf adds, "Another ideological god has failed. The assumptions that ruled policy and politics over three decades suddenly look as outdated as revolutionary socialism."

Wolf is not the only one to raise questions about an alternative model. Historically, union leaders and labor movement theorists have played a role in generating healthy debate about the kind of economic and political system we should have. From the early days of industrialization, unions fought the spread of unfettered capitalism. Some fought the system of wage labor altogether, while others argued that if capitalism is to prevail, then workers should at least have the right to form unions and bargain for higher wages.

In the late 1800s and through the 1930s Depression, union leaders were divided about the role of the labor movement in capitalism. One school fought to integrate into capitalism, using unions as a way to be on a more level playing field with employers. Others pushed for the development of Labor parties of various forms, to regulate capitalism and give workers more power via the political arena. Still others saw unions' role as fostering class-consciousness among workers, building support to overthrow capitalism. This might happen through electoral means, such as through a socialist party, or it could happen through revolution. There was no consensus view among labor movements or scholars about the role of labor unions, and debate was heated and significant for many decades, including up through World War II.

In the post-World War II period, the debates took another form, as the world divided into political blocs. In the U.S., a strong anti-communist movement developed soon after the war ended. The Taft-Hartley Act was passed in 1947, which included a provision that required all union leaders to sign affidavits and take an oath declaring that they were not communists. Many unions purged their ranks of known or suspected communists and sympathizers. Although the Supreme Court ruled this provision of Taft-Hartley unconstitutional in 1955, the impact had already been felt, leaving the remaining union leadership much more ideologically conservative and homogeneous than they had ever been. Many unions, particularly in the U.S., stopped debating economic systems, and instead accepted "managed capitalism" and their role in it. On the international level, two global labor federations formed: the International Confederation of Free Trade Unions to represent unions in the "free world," and the World Trade Union League, representing unions in communist countries. U.S. unions were reluctant to participate in any international body (Evans 2010). We will discuss these more in chapter 8, but suffice it to say, a strong ideological divide kept unions from working together on a global scale.

When the 1970s crisis hit, U.S. union leaders were in no position to engage in ideological or theoretical debates about Keynesianism versus Communism, or managed capitalism versus neoliberalism. Their counterparts in other countries were more effective, not having undergone the degree of "red scare" seen in the U.S.

In the wake of the 2008 crisis, unions must keep alive the space for debating alternatives to unfettered capitalism. This does not necessarily require labor to come to a consensus on an alternative model, but it does suggest a need to keep the questions alive. If a worker-friendly system is to emerge, it will take tremendous political will and organizing. Unions are the most likely institutions to have the power and capacity to do that work – alone, or in alliance with political parties.

The theoretical seeds of an alternative system may well be in existence. A host of thinkers have put forward models and inspiration for a post-capitalist world, from the model of Participatory Economics (or Parecon) developed by Michael Albert and Robin Hahnel; versions of market socialism by John Roemer and David Schweikart; revived forms of socialism that are more democratic and perhaps more true to the initial visions of Marx, such as those by Michael Lebowitz. Many, such as Joseph Stiglitz, advocate a new form of "managed capitalism," or more regulated capitalism that might look like a "New New Deal." Others promote a form of "solidarity economy" that is based on cooperation as the fundamental basis, rather than competition. The "solidarity economy" model is broad, and includes such things as worker or consumer co-ops and bartering.

A few unions engage in debates about alternatives. The Congress of South African Trade Unions (COSATU) has had a long-term alliance with the South African Communist Party. While the two are separate organizations, COSATU leaders and thinkers have always engaged in debate about the nature of the South African economy. After the end of apartheid, the South African government adopted many elements of a neoliberal program in a package of policies called GEAR (Growth, Employment, and Redistribution), such as privatizing and restructuring state-owned enterprises, cuts in social spending, and tight monetary policy to control inflation. COSATU criticized GEAR and called on the government to adopt an alternative economic path that would lead the country toward socialism. Part of this called for short-term policies focused on job creation and increasing union power, but in the longer term they adopted a plan described in the following quote:

> A better coordinated international policy is required that contributes in the struggles to build a better world based on equitable redistribution of resources and closing the growing gap between the rich and poor within and between countries. . . . Deepening our work to establish socialist forums as a platform where debates on all major challenges facing the working class take place and at the same time playing a major role in delivering membership education and deepening the political consciousness of the working class on the ground. (COSATU 2003)

COSATU struggles to advance its agenda in the neoliberal economy, but continues to stick to its core vision of building the National Democratic Revolution. This includes keeping debate alive about the nature of capitalism and possible alternatives.

The United Steelworkers (USW) is also exploring alternatives to neoliberal capitalism in a small way. In 2009, the USW announced a partnership with the MONDRAGON Internacional, a worker cooperative in Spain run on the principle of one worker, one vote (I will discuss MONDRAGON in detail in chapter 7). The USW and MONDRAGON signed a framework agreement for establishing manufacturing cooperatives in the U.S. and Canada. USW president Leo Gerard remarked that employee stock ownership plans (ESOPs) were not good enough, as workers needed to have full ownership and control of their workplaces (Witherell 2009).

In Venezuela, many unions affiliated with the National Union of Workers have supported Hugo Chavez's Administration's set of policies aimed at building "21st Century Socialism," which includes nationalizing a number of key industries. However, not all unions support the recently deceased Chavez, and some argue that his reforms led to greater government control rather than increased worker voice. The debate is alive in Venezuela about what "21st Century Socialism" looks like in theory and practice, and what the role for worker voice and unions should be (Suggett 2010).

In Argentina, two opposition unions – not aligned with the ruling party–union coalitions – merged forces with a growing movement of unemployed workers in 1998, to form two new organizations, the Federación Tierra y Vivienda (FTV) and the CCC–Trabajadores Desocupados, which became part of the *piquetero* movement – protestors who relied on pickets in the form of blocking streets to make political demands. This movement has explored pathways out of the 2001 Argentinean crisis, including the "solidarity economy" of bartering, small worker collectives, and cooperatives of "the cobblers, bakery, tool shop, metal workshop, orchard, block-making workshop and clothes shop" (Chatterton 2004: 557).

In the last decade, some unionists have supported or participated in formations of anti-capitalist parties, such as the *Bloco de Esquerda*, or Left Bloc, in Portugal, and the New Anti-Capitalist Party in France. These parties bring together heterogeneous groups and voices to run for office, promote legislation, and build social movements. The Left Bloc moved from a group of outside protestors in the late 1990s to winning seats in Parliament. In 2009, they won approximately 10 percent of the votes in the Assembly and European Parliament. Their strategy is a combined one of fighting to maintain the welfare state and "managed capitalism," while attempting to keep alive debate about anti-capitalist models for the future. It has called for Portugal to renegotiate its debt, nationalize its banks, and increase taxes on the rich (Drucker 2013).

Finally, an increasing number of spaces have allowed labor movement activists to participate in dialogue about economic models, and whether unions should push for a return to managed capitalism or move beyond it. This includes the World Social

Forums and regional social forums; and via organizations such as the European Trade Union Institute, the Global Labour Institute, and the Friedrich-Ebert-Stiftung Foundation; and journals and blogs. Sociologist Peter Evans (2005) argues that labor movements are part building these spaces that enhance "counter-hegemonic globalization" keeping the global connections and networks, but building those from the bottom up, with a focus on sustainability, local communities, and human need rather than corporate profit.

Conclusion

Despite their weaknesses, labor unions still have an important role in our global economy. Unions have historically reduced inequality and stabilized the macroeconomy via collective bargaining agreements and redistributive social policy. Neoliberalism has drastically altered the balance of power between corporations and workers, but unions have managed in a few places to resist and intervene, organizing to win labor rights and victories for workers. If unions are again going to play a major role in stabilizing the economy, they must organize against the broader structural reforms of the last several decades and restore some balance in the global economy.

Beyond these concrete roles, unions contribute to expanding democracy, whether in a traditional liberal definition or a more radical view that expands political and social democracy into economic democracy, where workers have voice and power in the workplace and the actual labor process. As we create global institutions with real mandates and power, such as the WTO, the labor movement must push for equivalent institutions for worker rights. Unions could assert that workers have "citizenship" in this new global order, so that they have rights just as investors do.

Finally, we have seen that prior global crises opened space for deepening dialogue and debate about economic and political models. Unions were active participants in those debates in the past, particularly in the 1930s crisis. The 2008 crisis has raised serious questions about the viability of neoliberalism, and possibly even capitalism of all forms, even among some of its strongest supporters. Yet the labor movement has been slow to jump into this debate except in a few places. Unions must be at the forefront to insure that worker rights are central to any discussion of alternatives. Furthermore, a worker-friendly alternative of any kind will not be able to move from theory to practice without serious political organizing. Here, the labor movement is a vital player. Unions are more necessary than ever.

3

Why Unions Decline:
External Challenges on the
Macro Level

Labor unions have an important role to play in the twenty-first century. But rebuilding the labor movement will require solutions to a number of problems, including some historic challenges within the movement, as well as new ones created by the global economy. Unions operate in conditions that favor employers over workers, making it particularly difficult for workers to organize. This chapter discusses some of the "external challenges" that worker organizations and unions face (Kumar and Schenk 2006). These challenges can be grouped into trends in capitalist development and corporate restructuring, and those related to trade agreements, regulations, and laws. A second set of external challenges relating to changes in labor markets will be discussed in chapter 4.

Corporate Restructuring

Neoliberalism rose alongside a period of corporate restructuring, and indeed, some scholars argue that this was one of the main reasons for neoliberal policy: to assist struggling corporations in regaining profitability (Panitch and Gindin 2012). Restructuring included direct changes in labor practices – shifting the risks of employment from the firm to the worker, and breaking unions. Neoliberal policy also made it easier for corporations to expand global operations and supply chains, particularly as they restructured coming out of economic downturns. Finally, this was all happening as financial markets gain power and prominence, having major impacts on investment patterns, public budgets, and spending. All these trends have negative impacts on workers and unions, as they increase the power of employers relative to employees either directly, by shifting the costs and risks of employment onto workers, or indirectly, by increasing the power of firms to move production or investment.

Flexibility

I discussed the concept of flexibility as a foundation of neoliberal reform in earlier chapters. Here I provide some detail on its prevalence in a few countries. Flexibility encompasses a number of trends pushed by employers which shift the risk of employment from employers and governments onto workers: converting fulltime jobs to part-time, eliminating job security, increasing use of temporary, seasonal, and limited-term contract work, developing "just-in-time" scheduling, and increasing subcontracting. These trends can overlap with what we see in the informal sector, but in this section I focus on the ways in which employers are restructuring employment relationships.

According to Cook (2010), "Flexibility refers to the elimination or moderation of legal, political, and social restrictions on hiring and firing of workers, contracts, mobility, pay scales, and task assignments." Given increased competitiveness in the global marketplace, firms must look to cut costs. With a union contract, labor is a "fixed cost": employers are committed to hiring a given number of people for a given number of hours at a set wage through the life of a contract. Without unions – or contracts – employers can convert this fixed cost to a variable cost, adjusting the number of workers, hours worked, or even the wage paid, by the hour or day, according to consumer demand. By converting labor from a fixed to a variable cost, employers can demonstrate to shareholders that they are more easily able to adapt to the vagaries of the market. Firms can reduce labor costs when orders slow down and increase labor supply when demand increases. By weakening or eliminating contracts and commitments to provide benefits, firms increase managerial control and their own ability to plan.

Many countries have weakened labor laws to reduce the costs of hiring and firing. This includes reducing or eliminating mandatory severance pay and payment for unjust dismissals, introducing temporary contracts, and reducing unemployment insurance eligibility and payment. For example, England, France, Germany, and Spain all made reforms to allow temporary contracts in the 1980s (Kugler 2004).

Corporate restructuring and neoliberal globalization have led to a pattern of employment that is different from what already-wealthy countries experienced in their development. Industrialization in Europe and the United States led to a shift from agricultural work to informal and precarious work, to formal work. But in much of Asia and Latin America, economic development is not leading to formal work. Rather, most workers move from agriculture into service or industrial jobs that are temporary, part-time, contracted out, or precarious in other ways. Existing formal sector industrial work is often becoming more precarious, not less (Hewison and Kalleberg 2013).

For example, despite strong economic growth in the past decade, government data shows that employers in many countries increased their use of subcontracting in the 2000s. In part, this was because they lacked access to adequate capital to expand production, so by subcontracting, they could shift costs and risk onto the smaller subcontracted firms and workers. Data from India shows that the percentage of workers in informal work arrangements in the service and manufacturing sectors went up from 1999 to 2005 (Maiti 2013).

In the U.S., employers are shifting the risks of employment onto workers in several ways (Hacker 2006; Kalleberg 2009). They have shifted from offering defined benefit pension and health plans to defined contribution plans. They have increased outsourcing, particularly for certain services once done internally – such as janitorial, accounting, legal, and food service. They have also increased use of temporary workers. Recent work shows that employers have begun to adopt "just-in-time" scheduling practices, where they hire more workers than they need and have them available for "on-call" shifts. For example, in retail work, the worker must be available during a shift, but the employer will decide the night before, or morning of, whether the employee is needed, based on predicted customer flow. The employee may be called in to work and sent home early if there are not enough customers. The employer only pays for time worked, and so if the shift does not materialize, the worker is not paid (Lambert 2008; Luce and Fujita 2012).

Union-busting

Unions are an obstacle for employers who want to shift the risks of employment onto workers and implement non-standard work arrangements. Corporations began turning to union-busting consultants more and more, starting in the U.S. in the 1970s and 1980s. Also known as the "union avoidance industry," these consultants, lawyers, personnel psychologists, and strike-management firms offer strategies for employers to break an existing union and keep new ones out. Starting in the U.S. but now spreading overseas, the industry helps firms create anti-union literature and videos, construct anti-union committees in the workplace, hold one-on-one meetings with employees, develop anti-union training for new employees, and more – including activities that are illegal under labor law. It is a multi-billion dollar industry with thousands of firms, a number of which now operate internationally advising transnational corporations (Maher 2005; Logan 2006).

In a 2009 report, Kate Bronfenbrenner studied 1,004 U.S. organizing drives and found that employers fired pro-union workers in 34 percent of campaigns, threatened to cut wages and benefits in 47 percent, and threatened to close the plant in 57 percent – all violations of labor law. Here is just one example of anti-union activity. In 1998, employees at the Catholic Health Care West Hospital chain in California worked with the union SEIU (Service Employees International Union) to organize hospitals in Los Angeles and Sacramento. Catholic Health Care West hired the

Burke Group – the largest anti-union consultant in the U.S. (Logan 2006). Over the next two years, with the assistance of Burke, hospital managers engaged in a host of anti-union, and some illegal, behavior, from surveilling and disciplining union supporters to conducting one-on-one interrogations of workers to find out how they intended to vote in the union election. The hospital, which receives a large amount of public funding via Medicaid, paid $2.6 million to Burke for their services. In 2000, the union election was held and the union lost. The California State Assembly issued a report arguing that the union-avoidance tactics and anti-union management behaviors were key to the defeat (McIntosh 2000; Logan 2006).[1]

Global Operations and Supply Chains

A number of researchers have argued that globalization is not as extensive as some might think, in that the bulk of investment and trade still occurs within and between wealthy countries. Still, most data shows an increase in different measures of global expansion, from foreign direct investment to employment. For example, employees of U.S. multinationals increased from 24.8 million in 1989 to 34.5 million in 2011 – an increase of 39 percent, compared to an increase in total U.S. employment of 22 percent (Bureau of Economic Analysis 2013, Bureau of Labor Statistics 2013). At the same time, the percentage of employees in those multinationals that worked in the U.S. parent company fell from 79 percent to almost 68 percent. This means that U.S. multinationals were expanding rapidly, and hiring a greater share of workers via non-U.S. subsidiaries (Bureau of Economic Analysis 2013).

The number of global transnational enterprises and their affiliates has increased over several decades, from approximately 37,000 companies with 200,000 foreign affiliates in 1994, to 79,000 companies and 795,000 affiliates by 2011.[2] In 2011, those companies employed 69 million people.[3] UNCTAD's annual survey of the 100 largest transnational corporations shows that even post-crisis, these firms continue to expand and grow production and employment faster overseas than in their home countries

(UNCTAD 2012). Data from 2003 shows that for U.S.-based transnational corporations, 21 percent of their foreign affiliates were based in Europe – but 24 percent were in Africa and 18 percent in Asia and the Pacific (UNCTAD 2007).

Much of the expansion of global operations happens through mergers and acquisitions, which means that globalization does not necessarily mean new construction and new jobs, but instead the conversion of domestic ownership to full or partial foreign ownership. From the 1990s to mid-2000s, this form of investment accounted for more than half of total foreign direct investment (Chang 2008). This trend began to change after the economic crisis, but it is important to note that not all global expansion reflects job creation.

As corporations expanded global operations, they deepened and expanded global supply chains: the systems of producing, transporting, distributing, and selling goods and services via multiple firms. Gereffi and Korzeniewicz (1994) developed the global commodity chain (GCC) framework to analyze the different steps involved in production and distribution of products, and where power lies along this chain. For example, an automaker sells cars to individual consumers, but is a consumer as well, buying supplies from other firms, subcontracting work to other firms, and overseeing the assembly and movement of autos, usually across borders.

Global commodity chains are not just economic relationships. They are embedded in political structures, where the rules and regulations of a home country, as well as the rules and regulations that govern relations between countries, are crucial in determining the nature of the chain. Thus, chains may differ in their governance structures in terms of which firms "drive" the chain; but they can also vary based on the countries they are located in or travel through.

Workers must be able to relate to the supply chain as an economic entity that configures the way value is created and distributed. Workers in a particular factory may be constrained in achieving wage gains because their employer is constrained in retaining profit from the larger firm they produce for. At the same time, workers in one location are tied politically to workers throughout the supply chain. They have common interests in relation to the value produced throughout the chain, but also in relation to the rules and regulations that govern the chain. For example, if the United States increased tariffs on t-shirts coming from China, it could impact workers all along the supply chain who produce, distribute and sell those t-shirts.

In the 1990s, major retailers consolidated and gained power in the global market. For example, a 2008 report by Clean Clothes Campaign notes that there was not a single retailer on the list of the 100 largest global firms in 1993, but by 2003, there were 14 (Merk 2008). These companies, who buy and sell tens of thousands of products in multiple countries, have consolidated and grown to gain enough power to set the terms of trade with their suppliers. The industry has also seen the growth of large-scale buying agents who coordinate transactions between the large retailers (or brands, such as Nike), and manufacturers. Manufacturers have also begun to consolidate. There are large factories that primarily handle production for multinational brands (Applebaum and Lichtenstein 2006).[4]

Workers are not powerless in supply chains. For example, Selwyn (2007) shows how grape pickers in northeast Brazil have gained leverage vis-à-vis their employer due to changing work conditions. As retailers demand higher quality grapes, and continuous improvements in the production process, workers have increased their skill level and structural power, winning higher wages and better working conditions. But overall, workers are not on a level playing field with employers in supply chains.

Supply chains have been influenced by deregulation, or reregulation, of laws that allow for fair competition between firms. Most countries have some form of antitrust legislation that prevents individual firms from gaining too much power and becoming "price-setters" in a market. Firms can have monopoly (single seller) power if they control enough of a consumer market to set prices. However, they can also exercise unequal power in relations with suppliers. This is monopsony (single buyer) power: where a large firm is the main purchaser of inputs and is able to dictate the terms of contracts with suppliers, by setting prices and conditions.[5]

The United States passed the Sherman Antitrust Act in 1890. Barry Lynn (2006) argues that antitrust law was one of the most important policies shaping the U.S. economy in the twentieth century as thousands of antitrust cases were filed by the federal government, states, and firms, against firms that grew too large. But in the early 1980s, President Ronald Reagan set in place key changes to how monopoly regulations were interpreted. In particular, new guidelines "redefined the American marketplace as global in nature, and . . . severely restricted who could be regarded as a victim of monopoly" (Lynn 2006). Whereas prior regulations interpreted monopolies as excess power to harm other firms or suppliers, new regulations narrowed this so that monopolies were only understood as price-gouging of consumers.

This new interpretation laid the groundwork for Walmart to begin its massive growth. By keeping prices low for consumers, Walmart could not be found guilty of violating antitrust legislation. That it utilized monopoly or monopsony power to become a price-setter with suppliers, against other firms, and in labor markets, was no longer relevant. Hugill (2006) shows how this was one major difference for Woolworth's and Walmart. Both became global retailers, but in very different regulatory environments that determined how much power each would gain. Similarly, the U.S. government repeatedly charged the A&P grocery chain with violations of antitrust regulations, as it attempted to use its market power to coerce lower prices from suppliers (Lynn 2006).

The U.K. regulates monopolies via the Competition Act of 1998. An independent regulatory body, the Competition Commission, oversees mergers (particularly if a company will gain more than 25 percent market share), market competition, and competition in regulated sectors. Over the past few years, complainants called on the Competition Commission to investigate monopsony power among supermarkets. Interestingly, the complainants included Walmart CEO Lee Scott, who claimed that the British government should take action against the chain Tesco, claiming, "there is a point where government is compelled to intervene" when market share is close to 30 percent (Lynn 2006). In 2007 and 2008, the

Commission ruled that supermarkets were in fact abusing their power in supply chains. The Commission did not find negative results for consumers, but did find evidence that large grocery chains dominated the market, creating excessive barriers for new entrants. In addition, the Commission found that "the transfer of excessive risk and unexpected costs by grocery retailers to their suppliers through various supply chain practices if unchecked will have an adverse effect on investment and innovation in the supply chain, and ultimately on consumers" (Competition Commission 2008).

The Commission called for remedies including a tighter Supermarkets Code of Practice, and the creation of an ombudsman – the Groceries Code Adjudicator – to oversee implementation of the revised code. This ruling applies only to food items and not other products sold in grocery stores, such as apparel. However, it is a major decision by a government body regarding the power of major retailers in "buyer-driven" commodity chains. While it has been a lengthy process to get the Adjudicator role clarified and established, in December 2012 the Competition Commission announced that the Adjudicator will have the ability to investigate complaints from direct or indirect suppliers, whether in the country or not, arbitrate disputes, publicize findings, and, importantly, impose fines (Department for Business Innovation and Skills 2013).

Other regulations impact global supply chains and the power relations within them. For example, in France and Spain, large retailers have not been able to develop as much power as those in the U.K. and U.S. because in the former, the state has helped promote and maintain the power of large wholesale markets in certain industries. This means that the retailers don't deal directly with producers. Instead large retailers do most of their business with large domestic wholesalers, and the power relations are more equal (Palpacuer et al. 2004). France passed a law in 1953 to create a national network of fruit and vegetable wholesalers. The law protects 17 large produce markets. Other wholesalers are not allowed to sell produce within 20 kilometers. According to Gibbon (2003), French supermarkets purchase about 40 percent of their produce from these wholesale markets. In contrast, British super-markets buy all of their produce from producers, which allows for greater monopsony power among British grocery stores.

France and Germany have other regulations that impact the power of buyers in global commodity chains. For example, regulations prevent retailers from setting a price below cost. These countries also do not allow suppliers to offer different terms for different buyers, which, according to Palpacuer et al. (2004), was a key factor in Walmart's poor performance in Germany. In 2002, the German Supreme Court ruled that Walmart violated policies by selling items such as milk, butter and flour below wholesale cost, which was harmful to other retailers (Associated Press 2002b).

While the U.S. and U.K. have some similar regulations, monitoring and enforcement seems far less rigorous. For example, around the same time that Germany investigated Walmart for predatory pricing, the state of Wisconsin considered a similar complaint against the corporation. While the German case reached its highest court and ruled against Walmart, in Wisconsin, the investigation ended with a settlement at the level of the Wisconsin Department of Agriculture, Trade, and Consumer Protection. "Walmart admits no wrongdoing and will not pay a fine," said news sources on the settlement (*Hometown Advantage* 2001). Lawsuits around corporations' power are on-going, challenging the legal framework in which they operate, but global trends show corporate power growing in supply chains.

Financial Markets, Investment, and Public Budgets

Another external factor that has impacted workers and unions is the increasing size and power of the financial sector, or what some call "financialization" of the global economy. By almost any measure, the size of the financial sector has dramatically increased in domestic and international markets since the early 1980s, albeit with dips during recessions.[6] This can be seen in the share of profits by financial firms relative to national GDP, international financial market funds as a percentage of global exports, the daily volume of foreign exchange transactions, the share of national income going to financial institutions and holders of financial wealth, and more (Epstein 2005). Foreign financial flows have become more complex and volatile over time (UNCTAD 2012). These changes were facilitated by investor strategies and neoliberal reform, including deregulation (or reregulation).

One implication is that corporations have shifted from longer-term investment and growth strategies to short-term tactics designed to please or attract investors. Increasingly, managers make decisions that will raise stock prices rather than decisions that prioritize long-term growth and stability (Epstein 2005). "Short-termism" kept U.S. manufacturers from investing in research and development, new technologies, and retraining their workforce to compete in the global economy, because such strategies might require large initial investments that would not pay off for several years. Instead, they chose to cut expenditures in these areas in order to meet expected performance projections for the current quarter. A host of studies found greater short-termism among U.S. and U.K. managers in the 1990s and early 2000s, compared to German, Japanese, and Swedish managers (Laverty 1996; Grinyer et al. 1998; Segelod 2000). However, rather than changing practices in the former countries, it appears that short-termism is spreading. For workers, this means that more wealth is generated in financial services where there are fewer employees on average, and where labor unions were less present and less powerful.

Financialization also has implications for workers indirectly, via impacts on governments. As investors have more power to move their money, they can pressure local and state governments to lower corporate taxes or provide lucrative subsidies. This results in less income for governments and shrinking budgets. In turn, governments adopt austerity measures, cutting services, cutting or holding stagnant public sector wages and benefits, and even laying off public sector workers. This impact is summed up by this op-ed from the *Toronto Globe and Mail*: "Wherever you live in Canada, whatever party your provincial government happens to belong to, strife in the schools is about to become a way of life. The public-sector pie is shrinking, and everybody on the public payroll will have to take a hit" (Wente 2013).

The public sector pie is not shrinking simply due to a slow economy. In the U.S., while corporate profits grew significantly post-World War II to the present, particularly since the 1980s, total corporate taxes as a percentage of GDP fell from a high of about 6 percent in 1950 to just over 1 percent by 2010 (Marr and Highsmith 2012). Corporate tax rates are relatively high, but the effective tax rates are much lower, as the codes have numerous loopholes. Some studies found that closing corporate tax loopholes could cover all or much of state budget shortfalls in certain recessions (Braunstein 2003).

The average corporate tax rates in the EU have declined as well. For example, from 1995 to 2012, the average top rate on corporate income fell from 35.3 percent to 23.5 percent (European Commission 2012). This contributes to budget shortfalls, particularly since 2008 – which in turn have led governments to engage in severe austerity measures in countries, particularly Greece, Spain, and Portugal. While some trade unions have acquiesced to austerity, others have participated in large-scale protests against cuts to services and jobs. The European Trade Union Confederation coordinated a "European Day of Action and Solidarity" on November 14, 2012, in which millions of workers from over 40 unions in 23 countries took part in the mass walk-out (Ward 2012).

Privatization

Smaller public budgets also fertilized the terrain for privatization: the outright selling off of publicly-owned assets and businesses and contracting out of public services – in some cases, via long-term leases. Privatization has hit most parts of the world as neoliberalism spread: the ideology suggests that the private sector can operate more efficiently and effectively than the public sector. Tighter public budgets make it even more appealing for politicians to sell off assets for short-term gains. In a review of privatization studies, economists Megginson and Netter (2001) wrote:

"privatization now appears to be accepted as a legitimate – often a core – tool of statecraft by governments of more than 100 countries. Privatization is one of the most important elements of the continuing global phenomenon of the increasing use of markets to allocate resources" (p. 1). They cite one study that found the cumulative value of proceeds to governments around the world raised by the sale of state-owned enterprises reached over $1 trillion by 1999.

The details of privatization stories are sometimes hard to believe. Perhaps most shocking is the large-scale privatization of the former Soviet Union assets after the fall of the USSR. Megginson and Netter (2001) write that these practices became unpopular quickly "because of the largely correct perception they were robbery by the old elite and the new oligarchs" (p. 6). But decades after the Russian case, and with mounting evidence that privatization can be a flawed policy, politicians continue to pursue privatization deals.

In 2008, Chicago Mayor Daley announced that the city was awarding a 75-year lease to its 36,000 parking meters to Chicago Parking Meters, LLC – whose chief investor is Morgan Stanley. The firm would pay $1 billion to the city upfront, but was then entitled to returns from the meters, worth an estimated $5 billion. The agreement, which included a commitment to quadruple meter rates, has many protections for the private company. For example, if the city removes a meter or blocks it off due to construction or a festival, the city must compensate the company for lost revenue. The city has already been billed almost $50 million for lost meter revenue in just two years, including $13.5 million to compensate for lost revenue from disabled parking spots. The deal even grants the private company police powers to enforce parking rules and write tickets (Dumke 2009).

Certainly not all examples of privatization are this egregious, and research suggests that in some cases, privatization did result in improved services. Yet the evidence overall shows that the claims made by privatization enthusiasts were often overstated, and public sector savings came at the expense of reduced wages and conditions for workers (Luce 2004; Chang 2008).

Trade Agreements, Trading Blocs

Another factor that impedes unions' ability to organize and protect workers today are trade agreements and policies. I discussed the WTO in chapter 2, and explained how the structure of the WTO and trade agreements work to provide rights to investors but not to workers. Bilateral and multilateral trade agreements can have the same impact. There are different kinds of trade agreements: they can range from short, simple agreements covering tariffs on a few industries and products, to complex documents with tariffs on goods and language on intellectual property rights and investor rights. The agreements follow different models, ranging from those that promote neoliberal reform, to those based in the tradition of managed capitalism, and those based on alternative principles of planned or solidaristic economies.

The neoliberal forms are best reflected by the U.S. Free Trade Agreements. The U.S. has negotiated 20 FTAs as of 2012. As mentioned in chapter 2, these agreements include investor rights, allowing companies to sue governments for expropriation, including anticipated expropriation or anticipated loss of profit. In practice, this means that once a country signs a trade agreement, a corporation can claim that any change of law is a potential threat to profit. If a country raises wages, or strengthens union rights or environmental standards, a foreign corporation engaged in trade in that country has the right to sue the respective government for potential loss of profit. Companies can also sue for other "barriers to trade," such as government subsidies to domestic firms, or policies that give preference in government contracting to local firms. In this way, these agreements lock in the status quo, making it difficult to improve laws in the future. Some agreements require countries to open up public markets to private investors. For example, Costa Rica had a public health insurance program for 85 years until the rules of DR-CAFTA (Dominican Republic-Central America Free Trade Agreement) forced the country to allow the sale of private sector insurance, paving the path to privatize health care (Clark 2011).

The agreements contain fairly solid dispute resolution

mechanisms for corporations to sue related to commercial interests, but there is no comparable protection for labor rights. NAFTA includes a labor side agreement, and the FTAs post-2006 contain stronger language relating to labor standards, but none include comparable dispute resolution mechanisms. The NAFTA side agreement provides for a complex and lengthy process that has many opportunities for governments to drop the complaints. The process is not transparent, and there is little space for democratic input from the aggrieved parties (Kay 2011). Most of the Asian trade agreements, including the ASEAN-China Free Trade Agreement signed in 2002 by China and 10 other countries, promote neoliberal reform (Arnold 2006; Wibowo 2009).

In contrast, the agreement that formed the European Union (EU) attempts to promote an upward harmonizing of labor standards. The agreement established a Commission, Parliament and Council tasked with setting labor directives for the entire EU (Compa 2006). Each EU member country must adjust its domestic laws to meet the directive. For example, one directive requires EU member countries to prohibit children under age 15 from working. Another requires companies operating in the EU to inform employees of any major changes in the company that could affect their jobs. The European Court of Justice has power to hear disputes, make rulings, and mandate countries to change laws to comply with directives.

The EU agreement also provides more parity between capital and labor by creating a single labor market. Workers are allowed to cross borders within the EU to work, unlike the NAFTA agreement that provided no rights for labor migration. However, research suggests that the EU model is not as strong as it might seem. The directives do not address all areas of core labor standards – notably absent are directives providing the right to collective bargaining. Thomson (2007) studied six labor directives and found that compliance varied, with countries resisting compliance with directives not compatible with existing domestic law.[7]

Another model that includes some social dimension is the Common Market of the South (MERCOSUR), established in 1991. It includes a Social-Labour Declaration and a permanent tripartite Social-Labour Commission, comprised of the heads of state of each of the four partner countries, business, and labor representatives. The Declaration commits to meeting fundamental labor rights, which includes the core ILO standards and more, such as rights for migrant workers. The Declaration does not link compliance with labor standards to trade sanctions, and the Commission does not have enforcement authority. However, according to Compa (2006), unions are provided greater voice than they are in the NAFTA model, and "[t]hey have seen a broadening and deepening of social dialogue, which they view as progress in the long march toward an effective social dimension in trade" (Compa 2006: 255).[8]

A different model of regional trade agreements is the Bolivarian Alliance for the Peoples of Our America (ALBA), first established in 2004 by Venezuela and Cuba. Their goal was to facilitate trade and regional economic integration in a deliberate challenge to neoliberal theory: trade should be used to reduce poverty, increase the general standard of living, and to promote the "social" aspect of economic development over profit maximization (Harris and Azzi 2006). The first stage of ALBA was a direct exchange of resources – Venezuela provided oil to Cuba, and Cuba provided doctors and health care expertise. Six countries have since signed on. The ALBA includes the creation of a new currency, the SUCRE, and in 2010, Venezuela and Ecuador signed a trade agreement that uses the SUCRE as the common currency. The ALBA appears in principle to have many features much more favorable to workers. What is less clear, however, is the role for trade unions. ALBA is governed by several layers of councils, with the Council of Presidents at the top. Unions can participate in the Council of Social Movements, but there is no other formal role for them. The ALBA currently includes no explicit chapter or language regarding trade unions.[9]

These trade models represent varying approaches to economic integration with different impacts for workers and unions. The neoliberal model, represented clearly in U.S. FTAs, poses a serious challenge for trade unions in the U.S. and partner countries. Even where the FTA negotiations have helped push forward enactment of stronger labor standards, such as in some Gulf countries, other factors set in motion by the FTAs undermine worker rights. The EU and ALBA suggest more worker-friendly models are possible, although both still contain potential challenges for unions.

Laws and Regulations

Beyond trade agreements, a host of laws and regulations contribute challenges for unions to survive and grow in the global economy. In a 1991 report, the United Nations Centre on Transnational Corporations notes that while actions taken on the international level in relation to the emerging WTO were important, the "most important foreign-direct-policy investment policy arena remains at the national level, in the efforts of policy makers to improve the overall competitiveness of their economies." Among those changes, the authors highlight deregulation, privatization, and the growth of debt-equity swaps as key. While the changes were often done to attract foreign capital to the global south, in the developed economies, the reforms were not aimed specifically at international capital, but instead were done to improve the overall business climate. In both cases, they created changes that favored corporations.

The more that countries adopted neoliberal policy, the more other domestic laws were weakened, even in areas not directly related to trade. The expansion of a globalized economy has intensified competition between firms, leading to increased pressure to avoid labor regulations – either by leaving the country or region, or by lobbying domestic governments to change the regulations and laws. Countries with stronger laws (such as a high minimum wage or strong health and safety laws) are pressured to weaken their standards, while countries with weak laws feel no pressure to improve.

There is widespread evidence that countries have, on average, weakened their labor laws, downscaled enforcement, or failed to modify laws to keep up with changing labor markets. In the U.S., Human Rights Watch found in several in-depth studies that labor laws are poorly enforced and do not protect workers who want to organize. Executive Director Kenneth Roth remarked that "[t]he cards are stacked against workers in the U.S.," as thousands of workers are fired or penalized each year for trying to organize unions, and millions more are excluded from labor laws altogether (Human Rights Watch 2000).

The International Trade Union Confederation (ITUC) conducts an annual survey of violations of trade union rights. The 2012 report noted that the economic crisis continued to have negative impacts on workers, not just via unemployment and the rise of precarious work, but also as governments moved to restrict worker rights and collective bargaining. For example, Greece, Portugal, Hungary, and Romania all adopted restrictions as part of austerity packages. Canada, New Zealand, and several U.S. states also passed measures restricting freedom of association in 2011 (ITUC 2012). While difficult to measure actual trends, the ITUC reported the persistence of poor labor law enforcement, or the lack of necessary legal protection for unionists in a wide range of countries, including use of mass dismissals and arrests to repress strikes in Botswana, Georgia, Kenya, and South Africa; and trade union repression in Mexico, Zimbabwe, and the Philippines. Trade union leaders are subject to violence and murder. In 2011, hundreds of union activists were killed in the Arab Spring uprisings, and another 76 were killed for their union activity in Colombia, South Africa, Guatemala, the Philippines, and elsewhere (ITUC 2012). Reports like these show that poor labor laws and weak enforcement continue to be a major challenge for trade unions around the world.

While the WTO has created an international court where employers can take their grievances, via national governments, there is not an equivalent system in place for the development and enforcement of international labor law. This raises the question of the ILO, to which we now turn.

The ILO and Prospects for Enforcing International Labor Law

Following World War I, the International Labour Organization (ILO) was created in 1919 as part of the Treaty of Versailles.

Labor unions argued that the world needed a global institution that could promote worker rights. The organization created was not nearly as powerful and visionary as some of its proponents had hoped, but the sentiments stated in the Preamble might seem radical today:

> 1. Whereas universal and lasting peace can be established only if it is based upon social justice;
> 2. And whereas conditions of labour exist involving such injustice hardship and privation to large numbers of people as to produce unrest so great that the peace and harmony of the world are imperiled; and an improvement of those conditions is urgently required;
> 3. Whereas also the failure of any nation to adopt humane conditions of labour is an obstacle in the way of other nations which desire to improve the conditions in their own countries.[10]

The ILO is a tripartite organization with representatives from unions, employers, and government. It was given no enforcement power and, over time, its mandate became less bold but its presence helped standardize labor law in the international arena. Legal scholar David Trubek (2006) argues that the ILO helped foster the idea that the state should be used to counter the imbalance of power between labor and capital. The global institutions were meant to mediate global economic booms and busts, thereby stabilizing domestic economies and shielding them from the extremes of the market. In theory, this would provide the protection and stability needed for countries to apply a set of domestic regulations and labor law, and redistributive social welfare. This worked for several decades after World War II, but with the spread of neoliberalism, it began to unravel. The system of international institutions and domestic laws is no longer sufficient to right the balance of power between capital and labor in a neoliberal economy. There are many who call for a new system, but there is no consensus on what that new system might look like and there are many points of contention. In the arena of laws and regulations, some key factors include the following.

First, should the ILO be granted more power? The WTO has enforcement powers, and can apply sanctions against a country. It has a system of mediation and arbitration and decisions made by WTO tribunals carry the weight of law. The ILO has no comparable power. Some scholars and activists argue that the ILO should have enforcement powers similar to the WTO, or connected to the WTO, and that dispute resolution mechanisms should be available on labor issues as well as commercial ones (Elliott 2000; Brown 2001).[11]

Critics from the Left argue that the ILO is an outdated institution, based primarily on the model of formal trade unions and collective bargaining, and rooted in more of a European "social dialogue" tradition that rests on voluntary agreements between large unions and employers. This excludes the informal sector and non-union sector, which together comprise the majority of workers in most countries. For these critics, the ILO is not sufficient as an anchor for a new system of international labor rights.

A second debate is the question of "hard law" versus "soft law" in resolving labor disputes. The U.S. has tended toward "hard law" in general, which relies on contracts that are enforceable in court and can come with penalties. In the matter of trade, this tends to mean trade sanctions. The European model has tended to favor "soft law" approaches, which prioritize voluntary cooperation and establish a framework for dialogue toward mutually agreeable solutions. "Soft law" advocates claim that sanctions can have negative side effects, such as reducing trust between countries, or that they are applied unilaterally by rich countries against poor countries. Those who favor "hard law" point out that soft law approaches only work where there are cooperative and willing parties, but in the U.S. many employers have an adversarial approach to unions and are not likely to abide by voluntary agreements on their own (e.g., Wells 2007). Some scholars call for a mix of hard and soft law approaches (e.g., Hepple 2005).

A third debate relates to the role of private actors and civil society in a new system of global governance. Already, non-state actors play some role in global governance systems. This includes corporate codes of conduct, union–employer international framework agreements, and non-governmental organization (NGO) involvement in workplace monitoring. We will discuss these topics more in chapter 8, but for now, we will point out that these raise questions about the nature of law and governance in a global economy. Some scholars argue that a globalized economy makes states less relevant, and therefore regulation is best left to private actors. But we can already see the problems with blurring the lines between private actors and states. Most global institutions regulate countries, not corporations. WTO disputes are filed by one country against another. This might make sense when the grievance involves tariffs or subsidy programs, but it does not address the complicated cases of corporations that operate in multiple countries, or cases where corporations are legally based in one country but primarily operate in another. Trade agreements such as NAFTA allow private companies to sue governments, and can order countries to pay corporations, but not vice versa. Therefore, corporations can violate labor laws without fear of major penalty. A new governance system must allow for the ability to file complaints against corporations.

A few unions and worker organizations have attempted to use existing domestic laws to hold multinational corporations accountable for international labor law violations. In the U.S., this has primarily happened via the Alien Tort Statute, which sets the parameters under which parties outside the country can hold individuals, the government, or private actors accountable for actions that violate U.S. laws or treaties. These cases were filed against corporations mostly in relation to environmental and human rights abuses, but also labor law abuses – primarily in cases of forced labor or violent suppression of trade union rights. Some examples include *Sinaltrainal versus Coca-Cola*, which argued that Coca-Cola hired paramilitary agents to kidnap, torture, and murder union leaders in Colombia (Coliver et al. 2005). The case was filed in Miami, Florida, and demanded $500 million in damages for the death of three workers. The District Court dismissed the case. A few other lawsuits have had more success – not all in the courts, but some have led to settlements. For example, activists sued Unocal for aiding and abetting a repressive government in Burma for the purposes of constructing an oil pipeline. The suit alleged that Unocal was complicit in, and had knowledge of, the government's repression against citizens and the use of forced labor. The case ended in a settlement.

Three major lawsuits were filed in California and Saipan in the 1990s, under federal laws (the Alien Tort Claims Act, the Fair Labor Standards Act, and the Racketeering Influenced and Corrupt Organizations Act), and under a state law (California Business and Professions Code), by a number of unions and worker NGOs, against over a dozen garment brands and retailers (including Gap and Walmart) (Hong 2000). The suit charged that the U.S. companies were liable for actions of their subcontractors – foreign-owned firms operating in the U.S. territory of Saipan, violating labor laws, including child labor and overtime laws (Bullard 2001). Again, this case concluded with settlements between the U.S. companies and the plaintiffs, which impacted over 50,000 workers.

Conclusion

Coming out of the 1970s recession, many companies restructured their business practices. One way to cut costs was to convert full-time jobs to part-time ones, and adopt human resource strategies that would shift the risks of employment from the company to the worker via a wide variety of "flexible" work arrangements. Employers increasingly hired anti-union consultants – first in the U.S. but then elsewhere – to break existing unions and keep new ones out. Corporations expanded their global operations, as the finance sector grew in prominence: both trends gave corporations more power to threaten workers, unions, and governments. As a result, governments cut corporate taxes and enacted a slew of policy changes to make themselves more attractive to investors – often at the expense of unions.

Unions have two additional major external challenges: the expansion of trade agreements, and the changes to domestic laws and regulations, that coincide with neoliberal reform, financialization, and corporate restructuring. While there are variations in approaches to trade regimes, and also heterogeneity in domestic laws, on average, the trend has been in the direction of favoring investors and employers over workers. In the WTO, employers have a new international entity with the power of enforcement. Even though it is set up as an agreement between countries, corporations have the right to sue governments and collect penalties. Workers have no equivalent, as the ILO can only publicize and shame a country at best.

4

Adding to Further Decline: Labor Market Changes

A second set of external challenges unions face in remaining relevant stem from major changes in global labor markets. These changes have occurred alongside corporate restructuring and, indeed, the causal direction between these is often difficult to discern. For example, corporations are more able to pursue flexibility as the labor force grows. Employers can expand global supply chains as countries push peasants off communal land and create a pool of wage laborers.

In this chapter, I discuss changes in labor markets that have impacted workers and unions around the world. The decline in union power has occurred alongside significant changes in global labor markets, which are related but distinct phenomenon. First, the size of the global labor market has dramatically increased. Second, migration within and between countries has spiked. Third, contrary to the predictions of neoclassical economists, employment in the informal sector and precarious work has grown, despite rising global GDP.

"The Great Doubling"

In the mid-2000s, Harvard economist Richard Freeman began talking about "the great doubling" – the fact that in the early 1990s, China, India, and the former Soviet Union all entered the global capitalist economy increasing the global labor force from

1.46 billion workers to 2.93 billion (Freeman 2005). Looking another way, from 1989 to 2011 the global labor force grew by 991 million people, with developing economies accounting for 885 million of those people (UNCTAD 2012). At the same time, the countries did not bring the equivalent amount of capital, thereby reducing the global capital to labor ratio by about 61 percent (Freeman 2005). The immediate effect was to shift more power to capital, vis-à-vis labor.

As a result, capital enjoyed much more freedom in the 1990s and 2000s to move in search of lower wages and a more compliant workforce. If workers tried to organize for better wages, the employer could easily threaten to move overseas, or even to a neighboring state. This increased the "threat effect" – employers' ability to threaten workers with discipline or job loss. Even if all threats were not carried out, the threats became more credible with the growing workforce (Bronfenbrenner 2009).

The impact was felt not just in wealthy countries with higher-wage workers, but also in poorer countries, that now had to also compete in a larger pool. As China entered the global economy, it made it more difficult for countries like Mexico or Bangladesh to attract investment based on the comparative advantage of cheap labor.

Whether you adhere to a neoclassical view or a Marxist view of labor markets, the greater labor supply (and reserve army of labor), particularly relative to the number of jobs, disadvantages workers and their ability to organize for higher wages.

Migration

As the labor market expanded, more people were pushed to seek wage labor – first moving within countries, often from rural areas to border cities, and then moving across borders. Neoliberal policy created some of the pressure to migrate. For example, when Mexico entered NAFTA, subsidized U.S. agribusiness was able to ship corn into Mexico and sell it at a lower price than Mexican corn. Mexican farmers were driven out of business, and forced to migrate in search of work. Many moved to Mexican cities; others to the border free trade zones to search for work in factories; others came to the U.S. (Bank Muñoz 2008). One study estimates that approximately 10 percent of the entire Mexican population is in the U.S. (Lochhead 2006).

Similarly, when countries privatize common land, subsistence farmers can no longer grow their own food, and must also move in search of work. While trade agreements and financial liberalization have created more open borders for investment and capital, they have not provided equal mobility for workers. There are some exceptions, such as the EU agreement that included free movement of people within the EU borders. But for the most part, more open borders for capital has coincided with more closed borders for people. For example, Australia, Italy, Spain, and the U.S. are among the regions that have passed stricter immigration laws in the last two decades (Williams 2010).

The link between trade, global institutions, and migration can be seen in the Philippines, which began to adopt IMF/World Bank Structural Adjustment policies in the 1980s. This included defunding social programs and education, putting many teachers and nurses out of work. Many were retrained to be "exported" as guest worker teachers or nurses (Rodriguez 2010). Other workers were trained to work overseas as domestic workers or construction workers.

Some countries have come to rely on their exported workers as a major contributor to the economy. For example, remittances account for more than 10 percent of GDP in 24 countries, and in nine countries, they make up over 20 percent of GDP – and that only accounts for remittances via formal channels (World Bank 2011).

The number of international migrants is at a historic high, at 213 million people, 3 percent of the world's population. This is almost 38 percent higher than the 1990 level (Table 4.1). About half of those migrants are workers. That number only includes those crossing borders but many more people are migrants within their own countries. In China, an estimated 200 million people move within the country to work in factories and construction

Table 4.1   Number of International Migrants, 1990–2010

Year	Estimated number of international migrants*	Migrant share of world population
1990	155,518,065	2.9%
1995	165,968,778	2.9%
2000	178,498,563	2.9%
2005	195,245,404	3.0%
2010	213,943,812	3.1%
Percent change, 1990 to 2010	37.6%	

*Estimate taken at mid-year.
Source: United Nations, Department of Economic and Social Affairs, Population Division (2009). Trends in International Migrant Stock: The 2008 Revision (United Nations database, POP/DB/MIG/Stock/Rev.2008). http://esa.un.org/migration/

each year – the largest human migration in recorded history (Miller 2012).

How does migration impact unions? U.S. mainstream labor unions have long seen immigration as a threat to their power, despite the fact that many unions were built by immigrants. Various studies show that there is no correlation between number of immigrants in a country and union density (e.g., Penninx and Roosblad 2000; Burgoon et al. 2010). However, there are competing studies on the impact of migration on domestic employment and labor unions. On the one hand, work by economists such as David Card find that immigration can have little negative impact, and even a positive impact, on regional economies and labor markets. Card pioneered some of his work in "natural experiments" by examining the impact of the Mariel boatlift from Cuba to Miami. The outcome of Cold War maneuvering, President Reagan opened the borders to Cuban refugees in 1980, and most settled in Florida – increasing the Miami workforce by about 7 percent. Neoclassical theory would predict that this would lead to increased unemployment and lower wages among U.S. workers, but Card, in comparing Miami to similar cities, found little impact, even on the low-skilled workforce (Card 1990).

Other scholars have replicated his method and findings in other places, such as studies analyzing the impacts of increased immigration from Algeria to France, the return of Portuguese colonialists from Africa after 1974, and Russians to Israel in the early 1990s (Friedberg and Hunt 1995; Friedberg 2001).

Other scholars find negative impacts of immigration on domestic workers. For example, economist Kathleen Schwartzman examined the poultry industry in five southeastern states from 1980 to 2000 (Schwartzman 2008). In the 1970s and 1980s, the workers, mostly black and female, fought employers over poor conditions, and in some places, organized unions and went on strike. Over time, black workers were replaced by Latino immigrants. Schwartzman suggests that there are various possible explanations for the transformation of the workforce. First, it is possible that black workers acquired skills and experience needed to move into better jobs. Second, it is possible that as chicken production expanded, employers could not find enough domestic workers and filled new jobs with immigrant Latino workers. The third hypothesis is that employers deliberately used strategies to replace the workforce, as a response to worker organizing, and/or a preference for immigrant workers.

Economists Richard Mines and Jeffrey Avina conducted a case study that provides evidence for the third hypothesis (Mines and Avina 1992). They studied the transition of the janitorial sector in Los Angeles, describing how it went from one-third African American and 7 percent Latino in 1970, to 61 percent Latino immigrants and only 12 percent African American by 1990. In the mid-1970s, SEIU Local 399 had over 5,000 janitorial members and contracts at almost every major building in the city. By 1990, the union had been decimated, with fewer than 1,800 members and covering only a small fraction of buildings. The causes for the transition are varied, but one was the successful efforts of a small group of employers who had been fighting the unions in the janitorial sector. These employers took advantage of opportunities to outsource work to non-union contractors. Here, the influx of Latino immigrants coincided with employers' interests, breaking the union: in 1982, union wages were approximately $12 an hour, compared to $4 an hour in the non-union sector. These studies suggest that while immigration does not necessarily have to have a negative impact on domestic workers, employers are sometimes able to use it deliberately to replace workers, break unions, and lower wages.

This can also been seen in certain occupations where employers have outsourced work to guest workers, claiming a labor shortage, such as among teachers and nurses. Labor studies scholar Gordon Lafer analyzed this trend in the U.S. and concluded that there was not a shortage of skilled and trained nurses, but that domestic nurses were leaving the profession due to stagnant wages and poor working conditions (including forced double shifts and poor nurse to patient ratios) (Lafer 2005). Rather than raising wages and hiring more domestic nurses to reduce the workload and improve working conditions, employers claimed a labor shortage and used this to fight for an increase in guest worker visas for nurses. Other scholars find similar trends in education (Ingersoll 1997). According to Shannon Lederer of the American Federation of Teachers, school districts in the U.S. are looking to bring in guest worker teachers from other countries, such as the Philippines, rather than increase domestic hiring. In some cases this has become a significant trend. For example, Lederer states that approximately 15 percent of teachers in the Baltimore school district are guest workers – a change that occurred in just five years (Lederer 2012).

Guest worker programs have been growing in the U.S., creating a challenge for union organizing because the programs create vulnerable workers with second-class citizenship (Ness 2011). Their status is dependent on their job, so if they organize and get fired, they will be deported. Guest worker programs are common internationally as well, and many countries deny guest workers the right to join unions or engage in collective bargaining. According to the ILO, migrant guest workers often are charged exploitative and illegal fees for visas, passports, and housing, leading to a situation of involuntary servitude or forced labor due to extreme debt (Plant 2008).

Certain countries have very high numbers of migrants. Almost

87 percent of the population of Qatar are migrants; in Kuwait and the United Arab Emirates, around 70 percent of the population are migrants (World Bank 2011). In all three, unions are forbidden or severely restricted (ITUC 2012). Other countries with a large share of migrant workers include some with sizeable export zone production: Jordan (about 45 percent of its population comprised of migrants), Singapore (41 percent), Israel (40 percent), and Bahrain (39 percent).

Unions have differed in their perspective on immigration. Penninx and Roosblad (2000) review case studies from Western Europe to compare how trade unions approached immigration policy in the post-World War II period. Throughout Western Europe, the postwar reconstruction was fairly successful, leading to economic growth and labor shortages. Each country had to deal with immigrant labor, but the unions varied considerably in their approach. Unions in Germany, Sweden, and the Netherlands cooperated with employer and state demands for increased immigration, but negotiated immigration flows that were regulated and controlled. On the other hand, Austrian unions were strong enough to resist massive immigration, and kept it limited to temporary workers with limited rights. But after a boom in immigration in the late 1960s and early 1970s, followed by the 1973 economic crisis, the countries all adopted more restrictive immigration policies. According to Penninx and Roosblad (2000), this was fueled in some cases by concerns about employment for native-born workers, and also by fears of greater burdens placed on the welfare state. But by the mid-2000s, several European nations renewed their interest in guest worker programs, in part to fuel economic growth, and in part to better regulate people crossing borders (Castles 2006). Germany had re-established temporary migrant worker programs in the late 1980s, allowing low-skilled workers to come for several months at a time.

Unions have a challenge in organizing not only immigrants in general, but guest workers and undocumented migrants in particular. In the U.S., there are approximately 11 million undocumented workers. While the National Labor Relations Act does not differentiate workers based on legal status, a 2006 NLRB ruling found that workers fired for trying to form a union do not have to be paid back wages or protected if they are undocumented. This increases the difficulties for organizing undocumented workers. Yet a few unions are taking innovative approaches to organizing migrants, which we will explore in more depth in chapter 8.

Informal Employment and the "Precariat"

Alongside the "great doubling," there has been an increase in the informal sector and precarious workers in the global labor force. The informal sector includes people without any work or employer, and workers employed in the formal sector but in informal relationships, such as temporary or "dispatch" work.

There is a growing body of research that attempts to define and measure the rise in precarious or contingent work. Scholars use terms such as regular and irregular, or nonregular work; or standard and nonstandard work, but the definition of precarious work put forward by Leah Vosko (2010) is useful: work that is "uncertain, unstable and insecure." Whatever term is used, there is a growing consensus that the growth in precarious work is a serious problem for much of the globe (Ross 2009). Former ILO economist Guy Standing describes this group as part of "the precariat": those "flitting between jobs, unsure of their occupational title, with little labour security, few enterprise benefits and tenuous access to state benefits" (Standing 2011). It includes the "more fortunate" slice of workers in the informal economy, while the rest are relegated to a lower status still.

Precarious work and informal sector work are not a new status under capitalism, but mainstream economists had predicted that this group would diminish with the spread of capitalism. As GDP rose, precarious work and the informal sector would shrink. That has not happened in many parts of the world. Standing notes that many workers remain trapped in agricultural work in the global south, and more workers are pushed into the "precariat" as neoliberalism spreads. These workers face a difficult existence.

Example 1: India

Naseen[1] is 36 years old. She works 8–10 hours per day, hand-rolling bidis (small cigarettes) in her small home. Naseen lives with her husband and three children. Her oldest daughter stopped going to school at 7th grade, and now works with her mother. They roll thousands of the small cigarettes all day and do household tasks in between. Naseen says that the work has been steady, as the demand for cigarettes has increased, and the work must be done by hand. She gets 27 rupees a day for her work of about 1,000 bidis, and her daughter does as well, so they make 54 rupees between them (about U.S. $1.50). At the time, the minimum wage for a home-based bidi rolling in Gujarat was about 65 rupees per 1,000 bidis, but Naseen says that if the traders had to pay that much, they would leave.

Example 2: United States

Jennifer[2] is 22 years old. She works at a chain retail store in Manhattan. She has been on the job for two years, but still only earns $9.50 an hour – not much above the federal minimum wage of $7.25. Even if she worked a full-time schedule, she would earn just $19,000 a year – far below most estimates of what it takes to meet basic living expenses in New York City. But Jennifer can't get full-time work. She was hired to work full-time, but her employer has everyone on erratic schedules. Jennifer will be scheduled for an on-call shift – meaning she has to call in the night before to find out if she should come to work. On occasion, she has shown up for a full day but been sent home after two hours – and only two hours pay, despite a state law that says she must be paid a minimum of four hours. Her schedule is unpredictable, making it hard to pick up a second job, and nearly impossible to imagine going to college. She does not get health insurance at work, so has gone without it for the past few years, and just hopes nothing serious happens.

Example 3: China

Zhang is 17 years old.[3] She is a student in a vocational school in southern China and, as part of her schoolwork, was placed as an "intern" at the Foxconn factory in Shenzhen, working on Apple products. Although the law sets limits on student work, she says the company often violates those, making her work 12-hour days, six days a week, standing, with little time for breaks. Since she is officially a student, the law says she doesn't have the same rights as do regular workers, so the employer does not have to pay health insurance or social security benefits and is allowed to pay a lower wage. Zhang says the workers are constantly monitored – on the production line, but also in the dormitories where they live and in the cafeterias. After more than a dozen Foxconn workers committed suicide in 2010, the company raised wages. But production standards were raised too and the work is now even more grueling. The company also eliminated quarterly bonuses and seniority payments, returning basic wages to a low level. The intense pace of work is hard to maintain, and the average age of the Foxconn workforce is only 21 years old. Zhang is not really gaining skills, nor saving money, so it is hard to see what her life path will bring after she finishes her "intern" experience at Foxconn.

While their conditions of work and income vary widely, they all share a level of insecurity and lack of power.

It is difficult to provide an exact estimate of the size of the informal sector, as data collection is often poor and even the definitions of employed and unemployed differ by country. For example, in the United States a worker only needs to work one hour a week to be considered "employed," when in reality many workers are involuntarily part-time and therefore in tenuous economic status. Economist Robert Pollin describes how he visited Bolivia in the 1980s to work on a UN report advising the government on macroeconomic policy. Pollin says that he met with the Ministry of Planning to discuss the unemployment problem in the country, and was told that there was no unemployment problem. Pollin asked about the people he saw selling batteries or gum on the streets; the government official replied that these people *were* employed, selling batteries or gum (Pollin 2012).

Researchers point out that the line between formal and informal is often blurred, particularly with the growth of flexible labor practices (Williams 2009). The ILO estimates that one-half to three-quarters of the non-agricultural workforce in developing countries is in the informal economy. Estimates range widely by country: for countries where data was available for 2009 or 2010,

Table 4.2 Percentage of Workers in the Informal Economy, Selected Countries, 2009–2010 (sorted by percent)

Country	Persons in informal employment, %
Paraguay	70.7
Peru	70.6
Philippines	70.1
Uganda	69.4
Vietnam	68.2
Sri Lanka	62.1
Ecuador	60.9
Liberia	60.0
Colombia	59.6
Argentina	49.7
Panama	43.8
Thailand	42.3
Brazil	42.2
South Africa	32.7
Turkey	30.6
Armenia	19.8
Serbia	6.1

Source: ILO LABORSTA Database. http://laborsta.ilo.org/informal_economy_E. html (accessed February 25, 2013).

estimates ranged from just under a third of workers in Turkey, to over 70 percent in Peru (see Table 4.2). In some cases this is due to a large informal economy, but in others, it also represents a high degree of informal employment in the formal sector – such as in Paraguay, where almost one-third of workers in the formal sector are in informal employment (ILO 2011).

This is not just a phenomenon of the global south. Rich countries have also seen an increase in informal work with globalization (Gottfried 2012). As of July 2012, 15 percent of the U.S. labor force was unemployed, marginally attached, or involuntarily working part-time (Bureau of Labor Statistics 2012). One study estimated that 16.4 percent of the labor force in seven European Union countries was in the informal sector in 1999/2000 (Vahapassi 2004). A 2007 survey of European Union workers found that 5 percent of employees working in the formal sector are paid in "undeclared wages" (Williams 2009).

Another segment of the precariat are workers misclassified as independent contractors. As part of their effort to shift costs and risks associated with employment, employers are increasingly converting regular jobs into contractor jobs because it allows them to avoid paying mandated benefits (such as unemployment insurance taxes, workers compensation, and Social Security and Medicare taxes). It also lets them avoid labor and employment laws, as contractors are not covered by minimum wage and overtime, nor do they have the right to form a union under the NLRA. One study found that about 700,000 workers, or 10 percent of the private sector workforce in New York State, was misclassified each year (Donahue et al. 2007). This is not just a U.S. problem: the ILO notes the increasing phenomenon as employers in many countries shift from formal jobs to informal jobs (Hussmanns 2004).

These workers pose a number of challenges for unions. Traditionally unions have represented workers who have an employer and workplace. With no formal employer or workplace, with whom does the union bargain for higher wages or better working conditions? In most respects, the informal sector is actually disguised unemployment, so it is not clear what the role of the union is when there is not really a job or employment relationship.

Those who hold jobs but lack security are also difficult to organize, as they may change employers on a daily basis. Unions have some experience with this model, as much of early industrial manufacturing work looked similar – as did work in construction, on the docks, and on farms. Unions developed models to control hiring, helped create employer associations with which to bargain, or passed legislation to improve conditions. Still, organizing is difficult with a transient and unstable workforce.

Unions must also revisit questions raised in chapter 2 relating to the broader goals of the labor movement. With legislation and union organizing, it is possible to bring workers from the informal sector into the formal, or to turn precarious jobs into stable ones. But is this the best strategy? At best, this might just return the labor movement to where it was a few decades ago, when there were more full-time jobs but workers and unions still lacked power relative to capital. The immense size of the informal economy and growing global precariat returns us to the question of post-capitalist visions. The labor movement must consider not only ways to find stable work and living wages for workers in the short-term, but alternative economic models where work and income is shared more evenly.

Conclusion

Labor movements face a host of challenges to their very survival, let alone their ability to revitalize and grow. In addition to the changes discussed in chapter 3, there have been significant changes in the global labor market, including a doubling of the world's labor force without an equivalent growth in capital or jobs. The result is far more people competing for relatively fewer living wage jobs, creating potential divisions between workers.

One such division is between native-born and immigrant workers. The growing labor force is accompanied by historic levels of human migration – within countries and across borders. Unions around the world have varied in their approaches to migration, with some attempting to keep immigrants out, or blaming foreign workers for job loss. This attitude is changing but it will take time, and unions must find ways to not only welcome migrants into unions and union leadership, but to address the root causes of immigration. This means confronting a neoliberal system that gives corporations and investors freedom to cross borders, but places restrictions on humans wishing to do the same.

The third major labor market change is a growing precarious workforce and informal sector. Together, the "precariat" and informal workforce comprise the majority of the world's labor force. Unions must find strategies to organize these workers – whether in traditional unions, worker NGOs, or broader social movement unions. This will not be easy. In the next chapter, we discuss some of the internal challenges unions face when trying to revitalize.

Part II

Union Response

5

Changing from Within

For the labor movement to experience a revival and become effective in a global economy, unions must confront not only external challenges, but also internal practices that limit their potential. As labor scholar Lowell Turner (2004) writes, unions cannot simply blame employers or laws for their failings. They must also address those factors over which they bear some responsibility and over which they have some control to change. In chapter 2, we discussed some of the history of the debate about the role of unions. The triumph of anti-communism created or enhanced some of the internal challenges, as it shut down broader discussion about unions' role and, in particular, their relation to the broader political economy. Many unions narrowed their focus to better wages and benefits for members, establishing or entrenching a form of "business unionism" that excluded many workers and failed to stay current with changing labor markets.

There is a larger literature on "union revitalization," or union renewal, which acknowledges that unions have lost membership and clout in much of the world, but asserts that there is a possibility for rebuilding. This chapter will review some of the major internal challenges facing unions, and discuss some of the strategies unions have been pursuing to change.

A Legacy of Exclusion

The earliest trade unions were formed as guilds among crafts. Workers joined together for mutual aid, training, and to protect their jobs. The system worked in part by limiting the supply of labor. The crafts were basically closed workplaces, and workers generally gained access by being born into them. The craftsmen trained each other in high-skilled work, and kept that knowledge to themselves, keeping the demand for their products high. The guilds gained power by keeping other workers out. This model of power through exclusion stuck with some unions for decades. In the U.S., many unions excluded whole groups of people, such as black workers and women. The Knights of Labor, formed in 1869, was an exception, in that it declared it was open to all workers – yet even they excluded Chinese workers. Some Canadian labor bodies also called for a ban on all Chinese workers around the late 1800s, and excluded them from membership (Camfield 2012).

The guild system began to break down with industrialization, which included dividing up the tasks of labor into smaller parts (Smith 1776). This division let parts of the process become mechanized and deskilled, making workers easily replaceable. Job training and apprenticeship was less necessary, and employers now had leverage to hire and fire workers. Unions could no longer easily control the labor supply and had to look for other sources of power. As the guild system waned, some unions began to expand their notion of membership beyond a specific craft or occupation and instead tried to organize all workers in an industry, as unions began to understand that they would not gain power through limiting the labor supply, but would instead try to organize more universally – through firm-wide and ideally industry-wide collective bargaining, industry-wide systems of codetermination, and also through building political parties and passing legislation. By raising the floor for all workers, through minimum wage laws and union contracts covering as many workers as possible, employers would have less incentive to fight the union or its demand for higher wages.

Still, the more universal approach – referred to in some

countries as industrial unions – was not always completely inclusionary. Unions often still fought to maintain some limits on the labor supply, keeping black workers, women, and immigrant workers out. There is extensive evidence of the ways unions excluded women – supporting labor market practices that prohibited women from working altogether or entering certain fields, or denying women membership in apprenticeships and guilds. In some cases, women organized their own unions but received little support from their male counterparts (Gottfried 2012). Early unions in many countries fought for a "family wage" for their male members, premised on the idea that men needed to earn a wage high enough to support a stay-at-home wife and child. Union leaders often accepted employer claims that women did not need high wages because they did not need to support a family (May 1985). Even when unions began to admit women as members, they were slow to accept some of the demands that women had (such as for child care), and made it difficult for women to move into union leadership (Humphries 1977; Foner 1979; Milkman 1985; Cobble 1993).

The situation was similar for workers of color who were also kept from occupations and union membership in a number of countries (Kelly 1996). Some unions excluded black, Asian, Latino, and indigenous workers altogether; in other cases they required workers of color to form their own locals. Many U.S. unions maintained segregated locals and conventions up through the 1950s and 1960s (Draper 1994). Historians note similar trends in the U.K., where trade unionists barred black workers from membership for many years (Wrench 1986).

Unions in some countries also fought for restricted immigration policy. As mentioned in chapter 4, Western European trade unions varied in their policies toward migrant workers in the twentieth century, but a number of the main unions fought to limit immigration out of concerns about labor market competition (Penninx and Roosblad 2000). Schmitter Heisler (2000) shows that in Switzerland, unions took a protectionist stance against immigration in the post-World War II era, but in the 1960s that shifted to a nationalist stance – still against immigrants. Many Latin American countries still do not allow foreign-born workers to serve as union leaders (ITUC 2012).

The issue of exclusion takes different forms in other countries. In Japan and South Korea, trade unions have predominately represented "regular" workers – those with a standard contract and often a "lifetime" commitment to one company. These are large firms that maintain "company unions." Others are relegated to "non-regular" status – part-time, temporary, or contract agency workers. Generally once a worker is on the path of "non-regular" status, it is not possible to move into "regular" status. In Japan, the size of the "non-regular" workforce has grown, alongside a sharp fall in union membership nationally. Labor unions are beginning to realize the need to organize "non-regular" workers (Suzuki 2012).

South Korea formally established their regular/irregular worker status after the 1997/1998 Asian financial crisis, through the "Dispatching Law." This created an "at-will" system of temporary worker employment similar to the U.S., allowing employers flexibility in hiring and firing. Today, over half of Korean workers are irregular status. The trade unions initially ignored the irregular workers, so irregular workers began to form their own unions (Lee 2012).

The division between full-time and contracted workers is becoming more prevalent in Latin America as well. Employers use subcontracting to keep the workforce divided as the laws protecting subcontracted workers are usually weak. For example, in Peru, temporary workers are not allowed to join the same union as permanent workers (ITUC 2012). Chile does not allow workers on apprentice contracts or temporary status the right to collective bargaining (ITUC 2012). Some unions have expanded their organizing to contracted workers, but this has been slow and had mixed results.

The challenges of organizing among temporary, part-time, and irregular workers are related to the issue of the informal sector discussed in the previous chapter. These challenges are partly an "external" issue for unions, as they are a result of changes in work, economic policy, and laws, but unions must adapt quickly if they want to remain relevant to the majority of workers. According to a report by Rutgers University professors Susan Schurman and Adrienne Eaton (2012), labor movements around the world have faced similar challenges in expanding their membership to informal sector workers. While there are a number of experiments underway, there is little conclusive evidence as to what strategies are best to deal with this segment of the workforce. We will address some of these experiments in later chapters.

Unions have attempted to increase power by limiting labor supply, either domestically or internationally, which meant that they built their solidarity on exclusion, failing to build alliances with other domestic workers, irregular or unemployed workers, or immigrant workers. While this strategy may be successful in the short run, it inevitably was undermined. Employers took advantage of the divisions in the workforce, pitting one group of workers against the other. Race, gender, and nationality are intricately intertwined with class, and a labor movement cannot thrive without a comprehensive understanding and organizing approach. By excluding groups of workers from their ranks, unions created the conditions for their own decline.

Nationalism and Foreign Policy

Unions excluded workers for protectionist reasons but also for nationalist and ideological ones. They took an exclusionary stance toward some workers within their borders, but also toward workers in other countries: domestic exclusion and nationalism are two sides of the same coin. Historian Charles Williams (2012) documents how the U.S. labor movement joined with other Left and progressive forces in the 1930s to build an alliance rooted in nationalism. Despite using broad inclusionary rhetoric relating to workers' rights and civil rights, Congress of Industrial Organizations (CIO) unions still framed their movement on nationalist ideas. For example, Walter Reuther and colleagues pushed a resolution at the 1940 United Auto Workers convention that would bar any member from union office that belonged to the

Communist Party, arguing that "the membership must be unified behind a commitment to American democratic principles and trade unionism" (Williams 2012: 499).

The decision of U.S. union leaders to fight Communists and promote American nationalism set the stage for decades of internal labor fighting over ideological issues, and for the foreign policy of the American Federation of Labor and Congress of Industrial Organizations (AFL-CIO) that worked with U.S. forces to undermine Communist-allied unions and leaders in other countries. In 1961, the AFL-CIO created the American Institute for Free Labor Development (AIFLD) to promote "free" trade unions in Latin America, over Communist-allied unions. AIFLD was funded by the U.S. State Department and worked closely with the CIA and foreign governments. Much of the AIFLD history is still kept secret, but scholars have uncovered evidence showing that AIFLD helped support coups to overthrow governments in Brazil, Chile, and Guatemala, tied into the work of the CIA mentioned in chapter 2 (Yates 2008; Scipes 2011); and some assert that the AFL-CIO has been active recently in attempted coups in Venezuela (Scipes 2011). For decades AFL-CIO foreign policy promoted American nationalist views on what trade unions should look like, and as a result, undermined and alienated potential labor allies in many parts of the world.

Similarly, economist Robin Hahnel argues that European unions and parties adhered to eurocentrist perspectives in the last century, to the detriment of international labor solidarity (Hahnel 2005). He writes that the "greatest failing of twentieth-century social democracy was its failure to effectively oppose Western imperialism and resolutely support Third World movements for national liberation" (Hahnel 2005: 127). This includes social democratic leaders and trade union leaders who supported colonialism, such as the French social democrats who supported colonial rule in Algeria, as well as Western political and union leaders that failed to support Third World national liberation struggles.

The problem was not a new one. Indeed, Marx and Engels, and Lenin, wrote of various aspects of the nature of trade union consciousness and nationalism. In the latter 1800s, Marx and

Engels asked why the labor movement had failed to build a revolutionary movement, especially in England, where capitalism had its deepest roots (Hyman 1971). They speculated that one reason was the monopoly of British capitalism. The British Empire allowed employers to earn excess profits, which they could share with workers in the form of higher wages. This meant that British workers could benefit at the expense of workers in other countries or the colonies. Marx and Engels predicted that this was only temporary, as the British economy would eventually fall to international competition.

Legal scholars Ashwini Sukthankar and Kevin Kolben (2006) provide a case study in how this played out between British and Indian workers in the late 1800s and early 1900s. They write, "Forging solidarity proved difficult in part because the perceived economic interests of many British workers were allied with the protectionist interests of British industry and the trade agenda of the imperial British state" (p. 62). British textile workers feared job loss from Indian imports, and supported restrictions on textiles produced by "sweated labor" in India, rather than working to press for higher standards and worker protections in India. At the same time, the British unions did not speak out about low wages and poor conditions in the Indian cotton plantations, as they had an interest in obtaining cheap cotton imports for British textile mills. British and Indian unions did cooperate occasionally, but those cases tended to be focused on specific legislation or union rights and did not extend to broader discussions about industrialization in India, and there was little dialogue about the history of colonialism and racism that had divided the countries. This has hindered deeper solidarity between the workers and unions of the countries, and creates challenges for future joint campaigns against common employers.

Nationalism is a problem in the same way that domestic exclusion is. It may appear to work in the short term, but it allows employers to exploit divisions between workers. While unions looked at foreign workers as the enemy, employers were moving jobs overseas, enhancing their ability to move production, break strikes, and threaten workers. Nationalism is one reason why many unions have such a poor approach to globalization today. Many union leaders assumed their interests were aligned with their employer, rather than workers overseas, leading them to see globalization as a phenomenon of country versus country, rather than worker and union versus corporation. They then blame globalization for declining union power, rather than neoliberalism.

Failure to Organize

Alongside excluding workers from membership altogether, many unions became complacent in the post-World War II era, representing only their current members, and making little effort to appeal to new workers in their industries, or expand union coverage to new occupations as industries evolved. Some argue that this is a key reason for dramatic union decline. For example, for much of the post-World War II era, many U.S. unions did not have organizers on staff and did not pursue efforts to bring new members into unions.

By the early 1980s, AFL-CIO leadership realized they needed to change that path, and convened a strategic planning meeting in 1983 to push affiliates to adopt an "organizing model" aimed at membership growth (Hurd 2004). A group of reformers took over leadership of the AFL-CIO in 1995, with John Sweeney as president. SEIU led the way by committing to spend 30 percent of its budget on organizing, and pushing other unions to do the same. Eventually, SEIU led a group of unions to break from the AFL-CIO and form their own federation, Change to Win, with a shared commitment to organizing. Change to Win unions, and others in the AFL-CIO, made attempts to organize previously excluded workers, particularly immigrants. Some unions increased their research staff and focused on strategic research to target specific industries or employers where the unions might have some leverage. The AFL-CIO enhanced efforts to work with students, community groups, and organizational partners to support unionization drives or contract campaigns.

British unions went through a similar trajectory. Facing major membership decline and a hostile political climate, the British Trades Union Congress adopted a "New Unionism" platform in 1996, and created the Organizing Academy in 1998 to train new organizers, modeled in large part on the U.S. program. The Australian Council of Trade Unions similarly created a training program, Organizing Works, in 1994, and pushed affiliates to adopt an organizing model (Carter and Cooper 2002).

The call for new organizing has had limited success. Looking at the labor movement overall, union density has continued to decline for several decades, despite the increased attention to organizing in the last 15 years. But it may not be fair to judge the labor movement overall, as not all unions made major efforts to expand. Evidence from the U.S., U.K., and Australia shows that some unions resisted change, failing to increase their organizing budget and staff (Simms et al. 2013). In the U.K., more conservative unions pushed for increased "labor-management partnerships" rather than focusing on organizing (Carter and Cooper 2002).

SEIU is among the most aggressive unions to take on the organizing challenge. Their own numbers suggest that the strategy has had some success. According to their website, the union has grown in total members from 625,000 in 1980 to over 2 million in 2012. In that same period, total union membership in the U.S. went from 20 million to just over 14 million (Hirsh and Macpherson 2013). But critics point out that the numbers are misleading. Much of the growth came through mergers, such as a 1998 merger with Local 1199 in New York, with 120,000 members, and a series of what journalist Max Fraser calls "hostile takeovers" of smaller unions between 2002 and 2009 (Fraser 2010). While the union did have some success in new organizing, leaders admit that it was not enough to match industry growth or achieve the kinds of gains they had hoped for. So far, it seems that committing more money and staff to new organizing has not been enough to turn the tide in labor's favor. It might be that not enough unions have taken up the challenge. It might also be that there has not been enough time to fairly evaluate the efforts.

However, there may be larger problems. In a comparative study of union revitalization, Frege and Kelly (2003) found that unions in the U.S. and U.K. have focused the most on new organizing – in large part due to those countries having weak labor institutions. But focusing on organizing may come at the expense of other strategies for revitalization, including labor–management partnerships, political action, reforming union structures, coalition building, and international solidarity. They argue that these strategies are interconnected. For example, new organizing may not be possible as a stand-alone strategy without rethinking political strategy. Organizing workers into unions is difficult without larger structural changes – such as revised labor law, trade policy or immigration law. It may be that unions will not see a large upsurge in membership until they build enough power to change laws at the federal and international levels. Unions cannot rebuild without focusing on new organizing. Yet organizing must be pursued as part of a larger strategy, understood in an international political and economic context.

Electoral Politics

The issue of political power is primarily an external challenge, as few unions control their own political parties or the political system in which they operate. But unions have some control in this area: they can make choices about their level of engagement with political parties and electoral work, about if and how to endorse candidates, and if and how to lobby governments for legislative change. I discuss some aspects of these decisions here, and elaborate on the question of political power in chapter 6.

Trade unions have varied approaches to the political party system, which are not necessarily mutually exclusive: creating a labor party, aligning with an existing political party, endorsing candidates or legislative issues, or little to no engagement with political parties.

Labor parties, or social democratic parties founded with labor support, have been common, particularly in Europe. Many were founded in the late 1800s or early 1900s. In some countries, the union–party alliance rose out of a common struggle for liberation or against a dictator, resulting in a long-term alliance, such as in Spain or Venezuela, or the formation of labor parties, such as the African National Congress of South Africa, founded in 1912; the Workers' Party of Brazil, founded in 1980; and the Democratic Labour Party of South Korea, founded in 2000.

The relationship between unions and political parties is complex and varies by country. The type of political system and historical legacy of labor parties has had a strong impact on the ability of unions to exert power via electoral politics and legislative change.

The U.S. is exceptional among industrialized countries in that it never had a sizable labor party. Early AFL leader Samuel Gompers advocated a strategy of "rewarding your friends and punishing your enemies," which suggested no alliance to a particular party, but instead working with any politician that supported labor's interests. While many trade unionists attempted to build radical parties, none ever gained dominant status in national politics. The Socialist Party, Progressive Party, and Populist Party had some success in winning municipal elections in the nineteenth and early twentieth centuries. The Socialist Party had over 600 mayors before World War I, and candidate Eugene Debs got 6 percent of the vote for president in 1912. However, no formal Labor Party ever gained prominence, and since the 1930s, the U.S. labor movement has strongly supported the Democratic Party. Since World War II, unions have relied heavily on political and legislative channels for building the labor movement. Some argue that reliance on political channels has increased for unions as their power to win demands via shopfloor strength has diminished at the local and national levels in the past two decades (Fine 2005).

Much has been written about the alliance between the Democratic Party and the labor movement, and most observers note that the relationship has weakened in recent decades, at least in terms of what the Democrats give to labor in exchange for their considerable support. On the one hand, national unions and both national federations continue to sink large amounts of money and resources into electoral work. For example, the Center for Responsive Politics shows that 30 unions spent over $800 million on Political Action Committees (PACs) from 1989 to 2012.[1] But

PACs only represent one form of spending – unions also give money through independent expenditures and in-kind donations (Francia 2006). While this sometimes includes Republicans, and even some third-party candidates, the vast majority of labor support goes to Democrats. Yet, most observers conclude that this investment in political activity has produced little change.

For example, U.S. unions made record contributions to the 2008 presidential race, spending more than $400 million to elect President Barack Obama and pro-labor Congress members (Maher 2008).[2] The AFL-CIO and Change to Win stated they had three top priorities they planned to address once Obama was in office: first, labor law reform, then health care reform, followed by immigration reform (Shaw 2010). But once President Obama took office, it was clear that there were not enough Democrats in Congress that supported labor law reform, so it never even made it to a vote. There was also no movement on comprehensive immigration reform throughout Obama's entire first term. The Administration did pass the Affordable Health Care Act, though in the end it included a controversial provision to tax "generous health care plans" in order to pay for the program. This provision will particularly impact union members, who have maintained some of the best health care packages to date in the private sector (Slaughter 2010).

Obama failed to come out with any real support for major union battles during his presidency. He did not support public sector unions fighting to retain collective bargaining rights in Wisconsin and Ohio or teachers' unions under attack from mayors, governors, and even some in Obama's own administration. Despite this, unions once again endorsed and campaigned for Obama's re-election in 2012, and set goals to spend another $400 million in the election (Hananel 2012).

For many unions, decisions about the electoral arena are constrained, given the political system of the country and the power of parties to enact real change in a small economy. But unions do have some control over how they spend their money and set their priorities. In the U.S., mainstream unions have been slow to move away from their relationship with the Democratic Party, and in fact seem to have increased their commitment in recent years. While it might not be realistic to form their own party, unions could take greater risks in relation to electoral politics. Granted, the two-party system makes it challenging to support an alternative party. The winner-take-all system is candidate-centered and caters toward the median voter. The role of money in elections makes it nearly impossible for labor to match the influence of corporations and the wealthy.

Still, there is room for experimentation. Some labor leaders advocate continued affiliation with the Democratic Party, but in a more strategic way: putting in place more stringent standards for candidate endorsement or targeting money toward real allies. Others advocate withholding support for candidates and instead focusing on organizing around legislative issues or general voter education. Still others support forming third parties, such as the Working Families Party that exists at the state level in New York and Connecticut. Some unions have supported municipal level political action where races are non-partisan, to sidestep some of the challenges of a two-party system.

U.S. unions spend vast amounts of money and time on an electoral system that seems clearly broken. For this reason, I raise the issue as an internal challenge. This may be most applicable in the U.S., but is relevant elsewhere. We will return to the topic of political power in the next chapter.

Government-Controlled Unions

Another challenge is the complex case of trade unions that are not independent from the government. This might be considered an external challenge as much as an internal challenge, but some debate about the nature of these unions occurs inside the unions, so I include it here.

Government-controlled unions were common in the former Soviet Union, and in some places this became a site for independence struggles. Most famously, Solidarnosc in Poland was an effort to win the right to an independent trade union. While only a few countries retain this system, one is of particular relevance: China, where the All-China Federation of Trade Unions (ACFTU) is controlled by the Chinese Communist Party. In state-owned enterprises this means that the union is structurally an extension of the employer. Workers do not have the right to establish independent unions. Recently, the ACFTU has established that workers can elect their own union leaders, but the practice is new and it is not clear yet if this will result in independent-acting unions (see Box 5.1).

Government-controlled unions exist in other countries that identify as socialist or communist, such as Vietnam and Cuba. North Korea allows freedom of association in its Constitution, but the ITUC reports, "in reality trade union rights are essentially non-existent" (ITUC 2012). In Cuba, the Central de Trabajadores de Cuba (CTC) is the only organization authorized to represent workers, and it is subordinate to the Cuban Communist Party. The law allows for collective agreements but the process is highly regulated. The law does not give workers the right to strike or protest (ITUC 2012). Views on the role of the CTC vary according to one's perspective on the validity of a one-party/one-union state. Supporters say that the CTC has been incorporated into the government and has a real voice in how the economy is run and establishing labor legislation (Lindenberg 1993; Ludlam 2009). Critics argue that the CTC does little to protect workers' rights, allowing frequent labor law violations and acting as a force of labor discipline. Some workers who have attempted to form independent unions have been persecuted and arrested (Leiva 2000).

Box 5.1: A Closer Look at China

We have touched on China in a few places but given the size and importance of the Chinese economy and labor force, and unique characteristics of its labor movement, I provide here an in-depth look at labor politics in China. In 2011, China's labor force reached 1 billion people (*The Economist* 2012). There were over 263 million migrant workers by the end of 2012, according to the National Bureau of Statistics of China (Song 2013).

Approximately 20 percent of the Chinese workforce belongs to a union – or 258 million people (Xinhua 2012). That means that the ACFTU

---

membership is almost the size of the labor force of the U.S., Japan, and Germany combined.

The country has authorized only one union – the All-China Federation of Trade Unions (ACFTU), comprised of 10 national unions and over 30 regional bodies. The ACFTU was formed in 1925 but has changed considerably over time. It was dissolved during the Cultural Revolution in 1966 and not refounded until 1978, after Mao died.

At the height of the Chinese Communist regime, there was no labor market in China – meaning employment and wages were not set through supply and demand but instead through government planning and institutions. But as China began to introduce markets in the late 1970s and 1980s, labor markets began to develop as well. The country passed the Trade Union Law in 1992 to define the role of the ACFTU, and a host of laws since then including ones that establish the requirements for collective bargaining.[3] The law distinguishes between state-owned enterprises (SOEs), and a "Sino-foreign joint venture." In the former, the law states that the union should take part in democratic management, including decisions about wages and working conditions. For joint ventures, the union has the right to make suggestions on issues relevant to workers, such as wages, but there is no requirement that management adopt recommendations or engage in collective bargaining.

Rapid industrialization and growth in China has led to a number of key debates about labor markets and labor rights, including organizing. I will review three of those here: independent trade unions, strikes and labor law reform, and global labor solidarity.

First is the question of independent trade unions. The ITUC states that workers do not have freedom of association in China because only the ACFTU is authorized to represent workers. The common practice in SOEs was that the union was a branch of management. It served more like a social work agency than an independent representative for workers' rights. In private firms, union leaders are often appointed and paid by management. Management must pay union dues, which are a percentage of total payroll.

Workers have complained that union representatives do not look out for worker rights and instead have allegiances to management. The Trade Union law gives workers the right to elect their own grassroots leaders, but the process is very top-down and must be approved by higher levels of the union. In recent years, a number of developments appear to have opened the door for discussion around greater independence. While China does not appear ready to authorize other trade unions, it has allowed discussion about the rights of workers to elect their own union leaders.

In 2008, workers at a Nestlé factory in China demanded the right to replace their management-controlled union leader with one that was elected by workers. The leader of this effort was fired (Carillo and Goodman 2012). Two years later, in the midst of a large strike wave in southern China, workers at the Nanhai Honda Motors factory went on strike. Although they were formally represented by the ACFTU they asserted that the union did not represent them, and they chose to elect 16 of their own workers as representatives in the strike negotiations. The workers eventually won significant wage increases and the right to elect their own enterprise level union officers (Chan and Hui 2012; Friedman 2012).

Due to numerous strikes, and perhaps due to some international attention to Chinese factories after stories of suicides at Foxconn, Guangdong Province officials announced that they would establish new guidelines that would provide a stable workforce. The "Democratic Management Rules of Enterprises" would create a collective negotiation mechanism for resolving disputes in the workplace – but they would focus on disputes over wages (Democracy Digest 2011; Xinhua 2012). However, the proposals never passed, but discussions about reforms continue.

Alongside these discussions were debates about reforms concerning strikes. The 1949 Constitution gave workers the right to strike, but this was removed in 1982 (ITUC 2012). The current Constitution makes no reference to strikes and Trade Union law does not use the word strike. Therefore, while strikes are not officially allowed, they are not explicitly outlawed. The recent unprecedented strike waves raise questions for employers and the government about how to contain the strikes and ease unrest. Some observers fear that reforms that legalize strikes would likely come at a cost, such as limiting the right to strike to economic, and not political, demands. This means that workers might be given the right to strike only when demanding higher wages. Strikes regarding democratic voice and representation could be made explicitly illegal. There is no resolution on this point as of 2013. In the meantime, workers continue to strike frequently – mostly for material demands, but in some cases, for political demands as well.

The third debate concerning China has to do with whether and how Western unions should orient to the ACFTU. During the Cold War period, Western labor movements did not associate with unions in socialist countries. After the fall of the Soviet Union, these divisions began to disappear, but a number of Western countries – particularly the U.S. – were reluctant to establish ties with the ACFTU due to its Communist roots. In the early 2000s, a few U.S. union leaders began to visit China and establish relations. Today, the AFL-CIO still does not formally recognize the ACFTU but has significantly reduced their resistance to relations. In fact, there have been a few meetings between high-level AFL-CIO officials and ACFTU leaders in recent years. Now the debate seems to be more about how, rather than whether, to relate. The question remains: is the ACFTU capable of making significant changes so that it becomes a vehicle for independent worker voice? Some observers note that given the immense size and geographic variation of the ACFTU, you are able to find a wide range of political opinion inside the organization. Others assert that the ACFTU is a top-down organization, controlled by the Communist Party, making it impossible to envision a peaceful path to reform.

Corruption

Another internal challenge for revitalization is union corruption. On the extreme end, some unions have been infiltrated by organized crime and the union became a vehicle for mob-controlled businesses to obtain government contracts through nefarious means (such as in waste management or construction). They also tried to control pension or welfare funds, by offering "sweetheart contracts" to employers. The most famous example in the U.S. is that of the Teamsters union, particularly under the leadership of Jimmy Hoffa in the 1950s through the early 1970s, but in some places for much of the twentieth century.

In countries with labor parties or labor influence in government, there are perceptions of, and sometimes evidence of, corruption in government–union relations, such as giving jobs or resources to unionists in exchange for political support ("clientelism"), or skimming money from public accounts. Unions have been accused of corruption for aligning with employers to take dues, but failing to represent workers or provide benefits. Less extreme but perhaps more prevalent are cases of individual corruption, where union leaders take money from union budgets directly, or indirectly in the form of high salaries and lavish perks.

Union corruption appears widespread in certain countries, such as Mexico, where "ghost unions" are prevalent. These are a form of company union: the union signs an agreement with the employer, sometimes even before a plant is built. Workers have dues deducted but the union does not represent workers' interests and the workers may not even know they are in a union (La Botz 2012).

Stories of unions under criminal control or operating on behalf of employers instead of workers can be found in many countries. But how common is union corruption? Labor historian David Witwer (2011) bemoans the lack of scholarship on the issue and calls on fellow historians to engage the topic seriously and not leave it entirely to union critics. Since the 1970s, there has been little academic investigation of corruption, leaving us without solid data beyond anecdotes. Despite the vast amount of commentary on the subject in the U.S., there are no systematic studies of union corruption and very little academic work on the topic for most parts of the world. There is no reason to believe that corruption is greater in the labor movement than in other areas, such as in the corporate world or political arena. Because unions are intended to represent workers, people are rightly more offended by union corruption than by dishonest behavior in other parts of society. But historian Joshua Freeman notes that while union corruption is worth study, it is unlikely a key factor in explaining the modern travails of the U.S. labor movement: "Maybe there is a connection between union corruption and the decline of organized labor, but timing suggests that it is at most attenuated" (Freeman 2011: 74).

At the same time, unions can take measures to meet a higher standard and reduce corruption, which tends to be greater where there are fewer mechanisms for accountability and transparency.

In unions, there is likely less corruption when there is greater rank-and-file involvement. This relates to the issue of union democracy.

Weak Union Democracy

Union democracy and rank-and-file involvement are desirable for several reasons. Not only are they likely to reduce the chances for corruption, but research shows they can build stronger unions. The Association for Union Democracy (2002) provides a list of benchmarks to assess whether a union is democratic, including: fair elections that promote participation; frequent, contested elections; access to membership lists; member ratification of contracts; regular local meetings; strike votes; access to information; and elected representatives. This list is not exhaustive but meant to provide guidelines and generate debate. Just as unions can be a way to expand democratic rights in society at large, workers need basic rights to participate in their own unions. The ILO's Freedom of Association Convention also lists some of the basic democratic rights that workers should have as union members: the right to establish and join organizations of their own choosing, elect their own representatives, write their own constitutions and by-laws, and establish and join a labor federation.

Beyond basic rights, there are qualitative aspects to union democracy that can deepen the role of members in building the union and broader labor movement. Democracy can help unions win and enforce better contracts, develop leaders and build strategic capacity. Labor journalists Mike Parker and Martha Gruelle (1999) argue "democracy is power," as a union can only be as strong as its ability to mobilize members to enforce their own contract and rights. Most labor conflict occurs daily on the shop-floor, and unions that are run by union staff will not be present to enforce the contract. Workers must be organized and educated to know their rights and enforce them regularly. Judith Stepan-Norris and Maurice Zeitlin (2002) studied collective bargaining agreements from CIO unions from 1937 to 1955, and found that left-wing unions were more likely to promote democratic functioning, as well as win contracts that gave greater power to workers, had more equality between workers, and promoted racial egalitarianism. It is not clear if there is a causal relation, but their work shows at least a strong correlation between union democracy and pro-labor contracts. Levi et al. (2009) also find that greater internal democracy and membership participation and effective contract negotiations are "mutually supportive."

A more democratic union can be more effective because internal participation encourages rank-and-file members to debate key questions facing the union: to go on strike, to accept or reject a contract, to change the bargaining priorities, or to reorient resources toward new organizing. Members who are able to articulate their own views, and then speak publicly about why they support a strike, for example, become leaders. When the Chicago Teachers Union (CTU) went on strike in 2012, they had spent more than a year educating members, training them on contract issues, and developing them as organizers and leaders. The member-organizers were given autonomy to organize their co-workers and debate issues. Mark Brenner, director of the organization Labor Notes, remarked, "Democracy is what builds the capacity to take high-stakes, risky actions like the CTU did" (Uetricht and Perez 2012). Members who are invested in the union's actions may work harder to win the fights, and are more likely to be able to explain the union's decisions to the broader community and engender support. In fact, Levi et al. (2009) found the greater democratic culture inside the International Longshore and Warehouse Union helped foster greater member interest and support for broader social and political issues.

If union democracy is so valuable, why don't we see more of it? Kim Moody (2000) writes that union leaders have too many temptations to become complacent – it is easier to cooperate with the employer than to maintain a militant stance. Union leaders have incentive to stay in their positions, which are generally much more prestigious and enjoyable, and can pay much better, than the shopfloor jobs they came from. This creates incentive to consolidate power and fight to stay in office. Union leaders may come to see union members as a threat to their own power and do not want an active rank-and-file that could challenge their leadership.

In addition, union leaders have a responsibility to protect the union as an institution, which can be a conservatizing force. For example, union leaders may decide not to take risks or engage in illegal activities (such as go on strike when striking is not permitted), as this could result in fines and other penalties. In 2005, the Transport Workers Union Local 100, representing subway and bus drivers in New York City, went on strike, violating the state's Taylor Law that prohibits public sector workers from striking. The union president was sentenced to 10 days in jail, and a judge penalized the union by taking away dues check-off. This resulted in a large drop in union dues, creating financial hardship for the union. Moody argues that since union leaders usually have a material interest in taking a more conservative stance toward union activity, militancy is most likely to happen with an active rank-and-file, as workers have fewer conflicting interests than union leaders. Of course, there is no guarantee that an active rank-and-file will be militant.

Lack of Internal Education and Training

Union democracy usually goes hand-in-hand with vibrant member education and training. Labor education has taken different forms over the decades, often coinciding with larger trends in the labor movement and social movements. For example, in the U.S. and Canada around the early 1900s, labor education programs were primarily broadly political – mostly connected with the Socialist Party or Communist Party (Taylor 2007). With the thought that revolution was in the near future, labor schools like Brookwood College were aimed at educating the working class, preparing them to be leaders of their own workers' society. After unions won the federal right to organize and engage in collective bargaining, labor education in the post-World War II era focused more on training union staff on how to handle grievances, arbitration, and other aspects of union administration. Many of these programs were run through public university's labor extension programs, but unions created their own internal education departments as well (Dwyer 1977).

According to a study by Byrd and Nissen (2003), labor education activities were more extensive in 2002 compared to the 1960s, and on average, shifted from mostly union maintenance classes to union building. But the AFL-CIO eliminated its education department altogether in 2002, and most U.S. university-based labor education programs have taken large budget cuts, and some have shut down. Even when unions have education programs, members are not always aware of them. One scholar found that while most union leaders studied in Ohio said their union had a political education program, four out of five members surveyed were not aware of such programs (Clawson and Clawson 1999).

Yet research shows that successful union revitalization often involves intensive education programs (Fletcher and Hurd 1998; Voss and Sherman 2000). Bronfenbrenner and Hickey (2004) reviewed successful organizing and concluded that membership education was one component to increasing union capacity for organizing. At least two studies found that when union leaders are trained in organizational justice issues, their members then saw the leaders as more effective and members increased their participation in the union (Skarlicki and Latham 1997). Understanding the need for education, ILO Convention 140 states that workers should have the right to paid educational leave time during regular work hours for trade union education, training, and social and civic education.

Despite the positive role that education and training can play, union leaders do not always emphasize its role – particularly its role in revitalization efforts (Taylor 2001). The programs can be costly and time-consuming, and often the pay-off may seem to be a long-term gain, while the union leadership feels it must focus on the current demands such as an upcoming contract negotiation. Some programs may be run well, but if they are not integrated into a larger strategic plan, members may not be able to use their new knowledge and skills after the training is over, and in fact they may get frustrated and burn out if they are trying to become more active in a disengaged or dysfunctional union (Needleman 2004; Weststar 2006). Member education can also be threatening to existing leaders, as well-informed members may decide to get more active and run for office. Finally, just because a union decides to provide education and training does not mean that members are interested in participating.

There are some promising examples of current union education programs, which will be discussed in chapter 7.

Conclusion

Unions face a host of challenges for survival and expansion. Some of these challenges are historic, while others are new in the face of neoliberalism. Indeed, neoliberalism destroyed the very conditions that made union growth possible in many countries in the post-World War II era.

While some of the challenges are due to actions by employers and governments, union leaders are not without agency. Some unions must confront their own legacy of exclusionary practices that may have helped them grow in the short term but undermined their long-run survival. A nationalist approach to organizing made them ill-prepared to operate in the neoliberal global economy, both logistically and ideologically. After decades of stagnation and decline, some unions have changed their strategy by putting more resources and staff into organizing new members. Yet this must be integrated with a broader program for union revitalization, including rethinking union relations to political parties and electoral work. Unions must fight internal corruption and bureaucracy, educating members and developing leaders, deepening democratic practice. In this way, they can expand their own capacity to organize and grow.

6

Union Power

Unions have relied on various sources of power throughout their history. As discussed in chapter 5, the earliest unions functioned primarily by controlling the labor supply. Craft unions and guilds did this by keeping skills of the trade relatively secret. This system began breaking down as entrepreneurs found ways to divide the labor process into pieces, and develop new methods of work and technologies to replace or reduce the need for skilled labor. With mechanization and a division of labor, an employer could more easily hire someone outside of the craft to do the work. This weakened the unions, making it harder to maintain control over their own labor, as well as their wages and working conditions.

Another form of union power came from direct organizing on the shopfloor and withholding labor power. To be effective, a union had to organize enough support to stop production, and to prevent the employer from hiring replacement workers. This was easier for workers in skilled trades, but even those in less skilled occupations had some success.

In some countries, unions quickly turned to the political process, even forming their own political parties to win gains through legislation or ensure representation in national political structures. In the coordinated market economies, unions maintained close relationships with social democratic parties, and together they functioned to represent the broader needs of the working class.

This chapter begins by reviewing the ways in which employers have gained more power relative to workers and unions under neoliberalism. I then discuss several theories of power, each offering different prescriptions for where workers and labor movements might focus their energies. From there I return for a more in-depth examination of the traditional strategies that unions have utilized, and assess the opportunities and challenges associated with relying on those strategies in the current economic environment.

Employer Power in a Neoliberal World

Neoliberal reform has greatly increased the power that employers have over workers and unions. This can be seen in a number of ways but I will list four of them: increased power to move jobs and investments around the globe; supply chains that allow firms to deny responsibility for poor labor conditions; a much larger pool of unemployed and underemployed workers; and substantial restructuring in the public sector.

First, international agreements governing trade and investment, together with technical advances in communications and computing, have reduced the costs and barriers to moving money around the globe. This makes it easier for an investor to pull money out of one company and put it into another, or even move a factory from one place to another. Liberalized financial markets make it even easier for portfolio investors to move their money from domestic investments into emerging markets. Workers do not have the same ability to move, and so their jobs may move but they cannot, giving more power to investors and employers. There are many examples of this, such as Sensata Technologies, owned by Bain Capital. Despite earning record revenue in 2011, the company announced in 2012 that it would shut its factory in Freeport, Illinois, and move the 170 high-tech jobs to China (receiving a tax break for relocating). Before losing their jobs, Sensata employees were required to train their Chinese replacements (Holland 2012). Sensata could do this in large part due to deregulation of foreign direct investment (FDI). In the past, many countries had strict regulations governing FDI, such as the 1887 U.S. Alien Property Act that prohibited foreign investors from owning land in the U.S.

territories. Only U.S. citizens and corporations could get mining and logging rights. Japan banned all FDI in vital industries before 1963, and Korea and Taiwan had strict regulations regarding FDI in non-EPZ areas. Many countries, including the U.K., France, Germany, and India limited the amount of foreign currency that could enter or leave the country. Neoliberal reform removed or reduced many of these FDI restrictions, greatly expanding the opportunities for investors to move capital overseas (Chang 2008).

Along with expanded global operations came the complex supply chains and subcontracting arrangements discussed in chapter 3. This makes it easier for a corporation to deny responsibility for labor conditions where their products are made – creating a second way in which firms gain greater power relative to workers. Recent garment factory fires and accidents in Bangladesh highlight this problem. In November 2012, over 110 women died when a fire broke out in the seven-story factory. Workers reported that they smelled smoke but were ordered to keep working; when they tried to escape they found the doors locked. The factory, Tazreen Fashions Ltd, produced garments for global corporations including Walmart, Disney, and Sears. The corporations did not accept any responsibility for the fire even though Walmart admitted that it had received an audit earlier that year labeling the factory high-risk (Alam 2012). Then in April 2013, a building containing three garment factories collapsed in Dhaka, killing over 1,100 workers and injuring over 2,500 more. This is the worst accident in garment industry history – yet the brands that had clothing produced in the factories were slow to accept any responsibility for the tragedy. Subcontractors blame corporations for paying too little for products; corporations blame subcontractors for unsafe conditions; and workers are left without power to improve their situation.

A third trend stems from the labor market changes discussed in chapter 4. The larger global labor force and high underemployment, along with a decrease in social safety net programs, create a large "reserve army of labor" – a pool of workers willing to work for low wages and in poor conditions (Engels 1973 [1845]). This gives employers more power to pit workers against one another:

threatening to fire one group when they ask for higher wages, and hire from the "reserve army" available to work. Those unions that attempt to gain power by controlling the labor supply have far less power when there is such a large supply of unemployed workers. Employers with job openings gain more power over workers. This is enhanced by increased global migration and the limited rights usually afforded to guest workers. For example, in 2009 the Hershey chocolate company laid off 600 members of its unionized workforce in Palmyra, Pennsylvania, and moved production to Mexico. In the meantime, they began hiring international students in the U.S. on a J-1 work visa to pack chocolates in their warehouse. The J-1 visa program was initially designed to create exchange opportunities, allowing students to do some small jobs while they learned about U.S. culture. Over time, employers realized they could hire the students to work for minimum wage and long hours. The case came to light when the 300 J-1 students, from China, Poland, Turkey, Ukraine, and elsewhere engaged in a one-day strike in 2011. Investigations revealed that employers were exploiting J-1 students around the U.S. (Breslin et al. 2011; Brown 2011).

A fourth way in which employers have gained power relative to workers and unions is in the public sector, via neoliberal policies that promote privatization, cut social programs, and eliminate public sector jobs. There are examples of this occurring around the world, as mentioned in chapter 3. One early extreme case was Mexico, where the number of state-owned companies went from 1,155 in 1982 to 195 in 1996. The state sold off even highly profitable companies, like the Mexican telephone company Telmex. Privatization was part of an economic agenda meant to downsize the role of government, increase the size of the private sector, and expand free markets in the hopes of generating growth. While there is some variation in the impacts of privatization, in general it led to greater concentration of capital in the hands of a few wealthy investors and large corporations, increasing inequality in the country, and increased power of employers relative to workers (Rose et al. 2000).

These four trends represent some of the ways in which

neoliberalism has enhanced the power that employers hold in the global economy relative to workers and unions. How might unions fight back?

Theories of Power

In order to assess how unions might counter employers, I now review several theories of power.

Associational and Structural Power

Sociologist Erik Olin Wright (2000) describes two kinds of power that workers could have in relation to employers. "Associational power" arises from workers' organizing together into collective organizations, including unions, works councils, political parties, or other entities that bring them together to advance their class interests. Any functioning labor union is an example of "associational power," as workers act to win gains together that they could not win on their own.

Workers can also have "structural power" based on where they are within the economic system. A worker with desirable skills in a tight labor market has more power than workers without desirable skills, or in a slack labor market. Workers located in strategic points in the production or distribution process have more structural power than other workers. These two kinds of power can be related. For example, highly skilled workers (with relative structural power) may be more likely to organize collectively (associational power) to maintain control over their skills and jobs. Wright argues that power must be understood as a relational concept, as workers' ability to realize their own interests may depend, in part, on their ability to counter the power of employers.

This suggests that workers could have power, even in a global economy, depending in part on their local labor market conditions or their position in the global supply chain. Those workers in key production or distribution sites have greater structural power, and may also be able to affect the capacity of employers to pursue their interests. Dockworkers are an example: they are in charge of loading or unloading billions of dollars worth of goods from ships. When dockworkers refuse to do their job, they exercise associational and structural power, creating tremendous economic losses for multiple industries.

Structural power relies on luck, in a sense, based on where you happen to be located in the labor market.[1] As British theorists Sydney and Beatrice Webb (1987) observed over 100 years ago, whether you can strike to withhold labor effectively depends on the industry in which you work. Certain industries had higher skill levels and workers were harder to replace. Others worked in industries that were more profitable. These workers could strike and likely win some concessions. Workers in other industries were not as lucky, and had to rely on other kinds of power, such as indirect political power – for example, winning higher wages by convincing legislators to pass minimum wage laws. Sociologist Beverly Silver (2003) expands on this idea, arguing that labor unrest has historically been greatest in those regions of the world where there was a large inflow of capital, suggesting that union power is determined not just by industry but by region.

Even within an industry, ability to exercise structural power may rely in part on luck, depending on the employer you work for. Not all employers earn a profit, or one sufficient to sustain higher wages. Under neoliberalism, we have seen a large increase in market share and power by a smaller number of companies. As mentioned before, this increased power allows the transnational corporations to push down wages, but also to push down prices they pay to contractors or suppliers. Whether you work for the more profitable brand itself, or for the less profitable subcontractor that makes the products for the brand, is somewhat about luck: where you were born, and which employer hired you.

Advocacy, Social Power and Symbolic Power

Labor organizer Steve Jenkins (2002) provides a similar but somewhat different frame for understanding worker power. "Social power" comes from being in a position to withhold labor in a way that hurts employers, or to engage in a way that *coerces* decision makers to meet your demands. Workers utilize social power when they strike and prevent the employer from producing. When social movements engage in civil disobedience and stop a city from functioning, such as when the U.S. Civil Rights movement conducted sit-ins and filled up jails, it is a form of indirect social power.

An alternative form of power, according to Jenkins, is "advocacy power." Workers must rely on advocacy power when they are not strong enough on their own to *coerce* changes from those in power; instead they must *persuade* decision makers to make changes. If employers are allowed to fire workers for striking, or can easily replace them, then workers essentially lose the power to strike. Workers with questionable legal status, who are not in a union, such as guest workers whose visas are attached to a job, may have to persuade elites to fight for their demands. For example, worker centers or NGOs can file legal cases on behalf of vulnerable workers or consumers can launch a boycott to protest the poor treatment of workers making a product. The anti-sweatshop campaign exercises advocacy power for workers who may be too weak on their own to exercise social power, given their place in the global supply chain. These kinds of campaigns can win, but they rely more heavily on technical experts (lawyers, researchers, journalists).

Jenkins says that many labor campaigns use both forms of power, but that social power is preferable to advocacy power as it is more likely to win and also is more likely to involve workers in determining their own destinies. Jenkins writes, "if a group never exercises its social power, both its capacity to act collectively and its potential power in the eyes of decision-makers may diminish" (p. 63). Furthermore, campaigns that primarily rest on advocacy power do not alter existing power dynamics. They may, in fact, reinforce them. Not only do they leave elites in power, but they also tend to bolster people in privileged positions within movements – namely those who are more likely to persuade. That means a lawyer or researcher employed by a worker center may have more power than its members. For Jenkins, exercising social power means that workers are directly involved in their struggle, and have a better chance of winning the demands they are advancing, rather than winning demands that are most palatable to supporters or elites.

On the other hand, sociologist Jennifer Chun (2009) asserts that workers without strategic power, or structural power, might be able to utilize what she terms symbolic power. This comes from the ability to appeal to the broader public and societal values. Workers have been able to win strikes by shaping public opinion and shaming "bad employers" or an employment system that denies workers their basic rights and dignity. Whereas Jenkins see this strategy of appealing to the public as a possible weakness, Chun argues that it can change traditional power dynamics in the labor movement, with the more vulnerable and disenfranchised workers gaining the power to win struggles that more traditional workers and tactics cannot.

Strategic Capacity

Another theory of power comes from social movement scholar Marshall Ganz, who says that workers can sometimes win seemingly impossible battles by employing "strategic capacity" or resourcefulness (Ganz 2009). In a study of how the United Farm Workers (UFW) were able to win against powerful agricultural employers – where the better resourced unions failed – Ganz argues that the UFW leadership created a more effective strategy for winning, in part due to three factors: motivation, access to diverse and relevant information, and "heuristic processes" – the ability to reframe the situation and devise new creative tactics. The UFW leadership and the organization itself were structured in a way that capitalized on these factors and increased their chances of winning. They redefined the labor struggle to a broader one involving community: converting a struggle over wages and the right to unionize into a larger battle for social justice and civil rights for immigrant farm workers. UFW leaders – as a part of this community – had a deeper commitment to winning the campaign than did other unions. They also had better access to important information about the work, and used that to make key decisions about strategy.

The lesson for today's labor movements is that unions need to give much thought to how they develop leaders and structure their organizations. The best leaderships are diverse, bringing in fresh ideas and varied perspectives on how to win. They are run by people who come out of the work and have a deep commitment to and material interest in success. And they are connected to workers and other relevant actors who can provide key information about the work process and industry.

Despite their varied perspectives, Wright, Jenkins, Chun, and Ganz come to similar conclusions:

1. Workers in strategic positions have greater structural or social power – though it is not automatic, and must be exercised – often through collective action (associational power).
2. Workers that have little or no structural power must look for power in other places, working collectively in unions, political parties, or other organizations that can impede employers from achieving their objectives (associational power). Unions can strategically build a leadership team and organizational structure that increases strategic capacity (strategic power).
3. Workers without structural power, and with weak social power, can still organize collectively, with allies (advocacy power) or by appealing to the broader public (symbolic power).
4. Employers have power as well, and may attempt to counter workers who use their power, thereby potentially shifting the terrain.

In addition to types of power, we must also consider tactics or strategies that are used in conjunction with different kinds of power. I have mentioned the strategy of controlling the labor supply but discussed the weaknesses associated with that approach over the long term. Here I focus on other strategies for developing and exercising power.

The traditional tactic unions have used is power on the shop-floor – the power to slow or stop production. In addition to disrupting production for specific employers, labor movements have utilized the mass or general strike to fight for (or try to stop) political reforms. Related to that, unions in some countries have worked through political parties or run independent legislative campaigns to win rights or demands. Here, we assess these traditional sources of power.

Power on the Shopfloor

Unions have often relied on their most basic structural or social power: the ability to withhold their labor, or to "down their tools." It is their work that is their most valuable asset, for without that labor, the employer cannot produce and cannot generate profit. Unionized and even non-union workers have engaged in strikes, and sometimes engaged in "wildcat" strikes – where unionized workers strike without authorization from their union leaders. Workers have also withheld their labor in other ways, by slowing down the work process or engaging in workplace sabotage, up to and including destroying machines. But with the spread of neoliberalism, workers have less power on the shopfloor. There are fewer strikes, and they are harder to win. I argue that strikes, and other forms of shopfloor power, are still relevant but unions need to be aware of their limitations and use them strategically.

The right to strike can be sanctioned by law, but in some cases, the laws governing the right to strike end up creating more restrictions than freedoms. For example, private sector workers in the U.S. won the right to join unions and engage in collective bargaining in the 1930s, but the laws do not prevent employers from hiring replacement workers during a strike. In many places, labor law prohibits workers from striking altogether. This is the case for many public sector workers, who often traded off the legal right to join unions for the right to strike. In the U.S. this varies by state. For example, in New York the Taylor Law allows public sector workers to unionize, but prohibits striking.

The ILO does not have a specific Convention on the right to strike, but its Committee on Freedom of Association has interpreted the right to strike as a general right that is part of freedom of association. Therefore, the committee has recognized the right in general in the private sector. The Committee is less clear about the rights of public sector workers, and has accepted limitations on the right to strike for workers in essential services or in unusual cases, such as a national emergency (Gernigon et al. 1998). However, the Committee did rule for the right of the New York Transport Workers Union Local 100 workers to strike, for example, and urged the New York State legislature to amend its laws so that only those public sector workers performing essential services "in the strict sense of the term" be restricted in their right to strike (Committee on Freedom of Association 2012).

In a 1998 survey of national laws, Gernigon et al. found that the principle of the right to strike is almost universally recognized, though many countries place restrictions on that right. Those may include onerous requirements, for example, providing advance notice to securing support from a mandated proportion of union members. The laws also may be generous toward employers in allowing replacement workers, thereby significantly reducing the power of workers to stop work and exercise their economic leverage.

Whether workers have a legal right to strike or not, theorists have argued that withholding labor power is historically the most effective way to unionize. Economist Gerald Friedman (2008) examines data for 13 industrialized countries and concludes that except for Australia, all countries saw their fastest unionization growth in years with the highest proportion of workers striking.

Work Stoppages

Despite their importance, strikes are on the decline.[2] Data is not comparable across countries but the overall trend is a reduction in the number of work stoppages in many parts of the world in recent decades. Workers in global north countries had steady levels of strike activity between the 1950s and 1970s but rates have declined since the 1980s as neoliberalism spread. In Western Europe, "the militant 1970s were followed by the quiescent 1980s and 1990s," according to labor scholar James Piazza (2005). ILO strike data for 40 countries shows that from 1999 to 2008, 25 experienced a drop in the number of work stoppages over the time period, with a median decline of 83 percent.[3] Table 6.1 shows the strike activity for these countries. Of course, the trend is not uniform, and some countries show wide variation, making the selection of years important. Still, the overall trend is downward.

Not only are there fewer strikes, but also it appears that unions are losing the power to win by striking. This does not mean that strikes have been rendered obsolete, but, especially in the Anglo-American countries, strikes have become harder to win. U.S. unions witnessed several high-profile defeats – such as PATCO, Hormel, and Trans World Airlines in the 1980s; Staley, Caterpillar and Bridgestone/Firestone, and the Detroit Newspapers in the 1990s; and the New York City transit strike, General Motors, and American Axle strikes in the 2000s. The U.K. saw a similar trend – including the miners' strike and steel strikes of the 1980s, and the Liverpool dockworkers' strike in the mid-1990s. Some observers note positive by-products from these strikes, such as the impact on social movement and cross-border organizing – but overall, they typically ended in weaker contracts and more embattled unions.

In addition to fewer strikes, unions are increasingly on the defensive against lockouts by the employer. *New York Times* reporter Steven Greenhouse wrote in early 2012 that while strikes were falling to record low numbers,

> Lockouts, on the other hand, have grown to represent a record percentage of the nation's work stoppages, according to Bloomberg BNA, a Bloomberg subsidiary that provides information to lawyers and labor relations experts. Last year, at least 17 employers imposed lockouts, telling their workers not to show up until they were willing to accept management's contract offer. (Greenhouse 2012a)

The frequency of lockouts reflects a shift in the balance of power toward employers in the neoliberal era.

There are several reasons why workers are striking less and winning fewer strikes. First, due to neoliberal reform, coupled with technological advances in communications and shipping, employers are able to move production easily, reducing the power workers once had at the point of production. For example, when

Union Response

Table 6.1 Strike Activity in 40 Countries and Territories, 1999–2008

Country	1999	2008	Change
Russian Federation	7285	4	−182025%
Romania	85	8	−963%
Botswana	10	1	−900%
Israel	66	14	−371%
Australia	731	177	−313%
Denmark	1079	335	−222%
Ireland	32	12	−167%
Sri Lanka	125	51	−145%
Turkey	34	15	−127%
Canada	413	187	−121%
Myanmar	13	6	−117%
Sweden	10	5	−100%
South Africa	107	57	−88%
Korea, Republic of	198	108	−83%
Mexico	257	171	−50%
Norway	15	10	−50%
United Kingdom	205	144	−42%
New Zealand	32	23	−39%
Panama	9	7	−29%
Mauritius	19	15	−27%
Brazil	508	411	−24%
Italy	753	621	−21%
Netherlands	24	21	−14%
Peru	71	63	−13%
United States	17	16	−6%
Austria	0	0	0%
Dominican Republic	0	0	0%
Singapore	0	0	0%
Isle of Man	1	0	0%
Spain	749	811	8%
Hong Kong, China	3	4	25%
Ecuador	8	11	27%
Finland	65	92	29%
Chile	108	159	32%
Hungary	5	8	38%
Switzerland	5	8	38%
Puerto Rico	1	2	50%

132

Table 6.1 *(continued)*

Country	1999	2008	Change
Poland	920	12765	93%
Estonia	0	1	100%
Slovakia	0	1	100%

Source: ILO LABORSTA. Countries that had data for both 1999 and 2008 are presented here.
* The high number of strikes in Poland in 2008 appears to be an anomaly, and possibly an error, as the total strikes for 2007 was 1,736. The ITUC Annual Report shows no widespread strikewave in Poland in 2008.

American Axle and Manufacturing workers struck at five plants in New York and Michigan in 2008, it appeared that they had significant leverage. The company was the main supplier of axles for GM light trucks and SUVs, creating a potential bottleneck in GM's most profitable segment of car and truck production. But American Axle was able to maintain production at its non-union plants in other parts of the U.S. and in Mexico, limiting the strike's impact on GM, weakening workers' leverage. This suggests that methods of corporate restructuring designed to create more extensive global supply chains has had an impact on union leverage.

Researchers concur that there is some correlation between globalization and strike activity. Piazza (2005) examined 15 industrialized countries to see the impact of increased globalization (measured as increased international trade and investment and weaker international capital controls) on strike activity since the 1970s. He concluded that globalization, on average, had an impact on strike activity, decreasing union membership and institutions, thereby making them less able to support higher levels of strike activity. However, this relationship was mitigated in some cases. Where union density was high to begin with – the Nordic countries and Belgium – globalization has had less impact on strike activity. However, even most of those countries saw a drop in strikes in the 2000s (Vandaele 2011).

Second, court decisions, weak labor laws and poor enforcement gives employers more weapons against strikes (Rhomberg

2012). In the U.S., labor law allows employers to hire replacement workers, thereby decreasing the ability of unions to stop production. In most large U.S. strikes and lockouts, employers brought in replacement workers from other facilities, or off the street. Union-busting consulting firms provide pools of "scab" workers ready to step in and work during a strike. Some countries do not allow replacement workers, but set high barriers for unions to pass in order to go on strike. In Japan, unions in some sectors must give 10 days advanced notice before a strike – the same is true for health care workers in the U.S. Workers in Nigeria must obtain permission from the police to go on strike, and strikes dealing with economic and social policy are prohibited (ITUC 2012).

Third, employers learned to work around the strike, and even take advantage of a strike to eliminate the union. The anti-union consultant industry grew rapidly in the 1980s, and led employers to take on more aggressive tactics toward labor and strikes. According to U.S. unionist Mark Dudzic (2012), "The tactics honed in easier times – the wildcat strike, militant shop-floor resistance, a strategic strike against a single plant – were worse than useless against a determined union-busting employer. The bosses actually counted on these types of responses. They were part of their game plan." Employers no longer had to compromise with unions to end a costly strike: they took advantage of weak labor law and weak union leverage to limit the economic damage and sometimes used strikes or lockouts to break unions (Rhomberg 2012).

A fourth issue is the growing proportion of public sector workers. As mentioned above, many public sector workers do not have the right to strike. For example, in Spain and Italy, strikes cannot jeopardize transportation, health care, energy, bank, and postal services. But in addition to legal restrictions, many public sector workers have ambivalent feelings about exercising the right to strike, as they see themselves working for the public, rather than a corporate boss. Public sector strikes do not impact a corporate bottom line, and instead can have an impact on the public itself, including those reliant on public sector services such as education and health care. Despite these concerns, many public sector workers do strike. Sometimes, that requires a different way of organizing, in order to build alliances with the public or those dependent on public services, as I will discuss in chapter 7.

Due to challenges exercising the power of the strike, some unionists sought new ways to fight employers.[4] United Auto Workers leader Jerry Tucker helped develop the "inside strategy" – finding ways to exercise worker power on the shopfloor without using the strike. Tucker advised, "Don't let the bastards provoke you into striking! Stay inside. Learn to 'run the plant backwards'" (Dudzic 2012). The "inside game" was not new. Workers have engaged in "inside" tactics in the past, up to and including sabotage of the production process or machinery or "sit-downs" to take over the plant and prevent production. But the tools became more developed in the 1980s and 1990s, as workers had to think creatively in order to fight against powerful global employers. This included "work to rule," where workers only did exactly what was required as spelled out in their job description or union contract; adding additional tasks such as daily in-depth safety checks of equipment; or calling in management for advice on doing any complicated task (Galpern 2005). Unionists also tried quick one-day unpredictable strikes, sometimes "rolling" from one worksite to another. For example, the flight attendants at Alaska Airlines developed the CHAOS program – Create Havoc Around Our System. They launched a series of random strikes in various cities in the 1990s targeting particular flights, resulting in a 20 percent drop in passengers for the affected airlines (Borer and Burns 2005).

Union members have tried other direct action tactics elsewhere, such as the uptick in factory occupations seen in Argentina, Ireland, Scotland, and Canada in the 2000s (discussed more in chapter 7). In an analysis of workplace dispute data, Tanguy (2013) finds that while the number of strikes lasting longer than two days decreased in France from the mid-1990s to the early 2000s, there was an increase in one-day walkouts, work to rule, collective petitions, demonstrations, and in particular, a large increase in collective refusals to work overtime.

Are Chinese Workers Moving in a Different Direction?

While strike activity appears to be on the decline in much of the Western world, there has been a marked increase in strike activity in China. Official unions, part of the ACFTU, typically do not sanction these strikes. According to China specialist Eli Friedman (2012), "it is certain that thousands, if not tens of thousands, of strikes take place each year." Chris King-Chi Chan and Pun Ngai (2009) note that it is difficult to obtain reliable data on strikes, but that "official statistics reveal that between 1993 and 2005 the number of mass incidents [large-scale demonstrations] rose dramatically from about 10,000 to 87,000 – a 20 per cent annual increase on average."

Some recent strikes have generated significant media attention, such as one at the Nanhai Honda auto parts factory in Foshan, southern China, in 2010. The initial walkout spread across the company's operations in China and then to other companies. Most workers demanded better wages and benefits, but some also demanded the right to elect their own union representatives. Many, though not all, of these strikes ended successfully (China Labor News Translations 2010). For example, workers producing parts for Toyota planned a strategic strike in 2012: for three days, they did no work and made no demands, and had no representatives. Production at the nearby Toyota plant quickly stopped. The CEO of their factory flew from Japan to meet with them, and on the third day the workers elected 27 representatives and successfully negotiated a significant wage increase (Friedman 2012). But at another Honda parts plant, striking workers were less skilled, and the company brought in replacement workers and fired some of the strikers. Eventually, the company did raise wages and benefits, and strikers returned to work – but they did not gain as much as the Honda workers in Foshan and some workers lost their jobs permanently (Bradsher 2010).

According to Friedman (2012), most of the recent strikes in China were over non-payment of wages. The strikes tended to be short, and management did not bring in replacement workers. Some recent strikes have addressed other issues. For example, as mentioned, in the Honda strike at Foshan, workers demanded the right to elect their own independent trade union leaders. In 2011, workers coordinated strikes in PepsiCo bottling plants in over 10 cities when they learned that their company was being sold as part of a merger. They demanded the right to information about the sale of the company, and that they should be able to retain their labor contract under new ownership (Zhong and Zhang 2011).

Sociologist Beverly Silver (2003) argues that it is no surprise that this strike wave is happening in China, as her research indicates that worker protest increases following substantial capital investment. Tracing over 100 years of production and protest patterns, Silver looks to China as the likely location for labor's renewal. The numbers of workers engaged in work stoppages there over the past several years is unprecedented. And while China no longer has the lowest wages in Asia, the government and employers have invested tremendously in building the infrastructure needed for innovation and competition. Therefore, employers may need to compromise with workers, and in fact, already have to some extent. This suggests a dynamism and potential for change in China that could have a ripple effect in much of the rest of the world. It is noteworthy that many (though not all) of the strikes have occurred at foreign-owned plants rather than Chinese-owned ones, and it is likely that the Chinese government is far more tolerant of strikes against foreign owners. Still, strike activity in China continues to spread and is a strong exception to the trend in other parts of the world.

Is the Strike Dead?

Neoliberalism has given more power to employers, and made it much harder for workers to engage in and win strikes. But the strike wave in China shows that strikers can still win. Elsewhere, strikes and other forms of shopfloor activism remain powerful tools for unions, if they are used strategically. Unions should focus on where they have leverage, or structural power. That might require broadening their struggles to engage allies. This is easier to envision in the public sector, where workers have overlapping interests with the public. For example, teachers' unions could build alliances with students and parents, linking the fight for better working conditions to better learning conditions. One example is the Chicago Teachers' Union, where 27,000 teachers struck in September 2012. While the union was formally striking over contractual issues like seniority and hours, they made it clear to the public that they were also fighting for more resources for classrooms (Moran 2012).

Unions have also struck an alliance with community members and human rights organizations to fight privatization of public services. Community members and human rights groups protested water privatization in Bolivia for over two years. In 2000, labor unions joined the protesters in a four-day strike against price hikes, also known as the Cochabamba Water War. The strike ended in victory, with the government reversing the privatization to return water service to public control (Public Citizen 2003).

Another example is the Canadian Union of Postal Workers (CUPW). When the CUPW went on strike in the 1970s, reporters asked the union president what he would do if the public did not support the strike. He replied, "Then to hell with the public" (Tufts 1998). But the union changed its approach over the next decade, as the Canadian Postal Corporation began cutting jobs through new technology and contracting out. In the mid-1980s the government announced plans to close rural post offices and cut back delivery services, which gave the union a chance to build an alliance with grassroots community groups upset by the closures. The alliance won some of their demands through an integrated worker/community member campaign, and built the foundation for a longer-term alliance.

General Strikes

In addition to traditional strikes over wages and working conditions at a particular employer, unions have also conducted general strikes. Theorists since Rosa Luxemburg (1906) have written about the potential of political strikes, such as "mass strikes," or general strikes that make more broad-based demands, including those calling for larger economic and political reform. Since evidence shows workplace strikes are less frequent and harder to win in recent decades, unions may be turning more to general strikes as a way to achieve gains. And, workplace-based strikes may in fact enjoy more success when integrated with broader social movements and political strikes.

The general strike as a tactic has been much more common in some parts of the world than in the U.S. The U.S. has only had a handful of these, such as in Seattle in 1919 and Minneapolis and San Francisco in 1934. Defining general strikes more broadly, W. E. DuBois (1999) asserted that African Americans engaged in a general strike on plantations in the south to help defeat the South in the Civil War. A more recent corollary came on May 1, 2006, when millions of people marched and rallied across the U.S. in the name of immigrant rights. Framed as a national boycott of work, school and commerce, the protests varied in different parts of the country. In some cities, coalitions called for a day of no work, whereas in other cities the events were framed more as rallies rather than strikes. Still, estimates show that over 1 million people participated that day in California alone, making this one of the largest "general strikes" in U.S. history (Lazos 2007; Ortiz 2013). But overall, the tactic is not common in the United States.

General strikes have been more common in Europe and parts of Latin America and Africa. The general strike was an oft-used tool in many European countries in the late nineteenth century and early part of the twentieth century, and some argue this was instrumental in establishing the broad-based social policies of many of those countries (Hamann and Kelly 2010).[5]

There is no official data on general strikes, but the organization New Unionism Network has tried to catalog some of the largest cases. They acknowledge that strike data are inconsistent, and reports about particular strikes are likely to vary. Still, they note that there have been a number of large-scale general strikes in recent years. For example, unions in India have united across sectors and regions to call for a series of national general strikes. On February 28, 2012, they held a one-day national general strike to demand better conditions for all workers, including a national minimum wage, universal social security fund, and stronger enforcement of labor laws. *The Hindu* newspaper noted the strike represented "the first time since Independence that trade unions, cutting across ideological and political affiliations, have joined hands to register their protest on a wide range of issues arising out of the liberalisation policy" (*The Hindu* 2012). There were no records of the number of workers involved in the February 28, 2012 strike. A September 2010 general strike was reported to have drawn 100 million workers, which at the time was called the largest strike in history (Hall-Jones 2010).

In recent years there have been large general strikes in Europe, where tens of thousands, and sometimes hundreds of thousands of people have taken to the streets to protest austerity measures being put in place following the 2008 financial meltdown. For example, Greek unions called for a general strike in 2009, and in 2010, unions in Portugal and Spain called for their first general strikes in decades. There have been general strikes occurring almost annually, and sometimes more often, in each of these countries since then. The same is true for Italy, France, Belgium, and Turkey – including general strikes in Turkey in support of the 2013 Gezi Park protesters. Unions in the U.K. called for a coordinated 24-hour strike for public sector workers throughout the country in May 2012. Hamann and Kelly (2010) argue that there has been a growth in general strikes in Europe since 1980, which might reflect that some unions are using the tool as a political tactic more than an economic one, as a way to strengthen alliances with supporters fighting neoliberal policy.

General strikes have been used in a number of African countries as well, including in South Africa, Nigeria, and Burkina Faso. General strikes have also been used directly, or as threats, in the democratization struggles of North Africa and the Middle East, such as in Egypt and Tunisia (ITUC 2011; Reuters 2012).

On October 3, 2012, over 2 million workers from over 700 factories across Indonesia went on a one-day strike in protest against a law that allows companies to hire temporary workers without benefits (*Jakarta Globe* 2012). Unions have been protesting the law, which has helped moved the country to one where "precarious work is the new norm," according to the ITUC. The number of permanent workers in the formal workforce went from 67 percent in 2005 down to 35 percent by 2011, and in export zones, nearly 100 percent of workers are on temporary contracts (ITUC 2012). Despite high barriers and risks for striking, workers engaged in dozens of strikes in 2012, leading up to the massive general strike in October.

While it is difficult to get official data, these stories suggest that while the number of traditional work stoppages may be on the decline in many parts of the world, the number of people involved in larger political or general strikes may be on the rise, at least in parts of Europe, Asia, and Africa. It might also reflect the ways in which public budgets and public services have been under attack in the neoliberal order, creating conditions for public sector workers and those who rely on public sector services to strike. An increase in general strikes may also reflect the large numbers of informal sector workers who do not have traditional employers against which to strike.

In any case, these trends could suggest that the odds of winning traditional strikes against individual employers are more difficult under neoliberalism, and therefore may be more successful when paired with more universal economic and social policy demands, just as the Egyptian strike wave helped catalyze the overthrow of a military dictatorship. Unions in Brazil, South Africa, and South Korea pursued this strategy, using the labor movement as an anchor for a larger political movement for universal rights and expanded democracy (Seidman 1994). That includes protests for specific legislation, but it also includes alliances with political parties.

Political Power

Another traditional source of power that unions have utilized is via the political process, engaging political parties, legislation, and the state. The relationship between unions and parties varies greatly around the world. On one end are those unions that have operated, or are operating, in a one-party socialist state, where the union does not have independence but instead operates under the authority of the government, such as in China and Vietnam.

Other countries – although not socialist – have models where the ruling party controls the unions, such as in Mexico. There, the Constitution and labor law provides workers the right to form unions, but the Federal Labor Law passed in 1931 set up a tripartite structure (government, employers, and union representatives) to oversee labor relations. This resulted in a strong role for the state in controlling union registration and authorizing collective bargaining agreements. Over time, the ruling party (the Partido Revolucionario Institucional, or PRI) developed an alliance with the main official labor federation – the Confederación de Trabajadores de México (CTM). This made it very hard for workers to establish unions independent of the CTM, particularly when the PRI was in power.

In a number of Western European countries, labor unions have strong and sometimes formal relations with political parties. Some of these are called Labor Parties, but others have different names, so I will refer to them as "labor-backed parties." Bernhard Ebbinghaus (1995) calls the working-class party and the labor union the "Siamese Twins" of Western industrialized countries. Many labor-backed parties were formed out of organizing efforts by trade unionists and socialists in the late 1800s and early 1900s (Burgess 2004). This is the case with the British Labour Party (founded in 1900), Australian Labour Party (1901), Swedish Social Democratic Party (1889), and the German Social Democratic Party, which has changed over time but originated in the 1860s. There were also labor-backed parties formed in Latin America, such as the Labour Party in Argentina (1945), the Revolutionary Nationalist Movement party in Bolivia (1941) and the Democratic Action party in Venezuela (1941). These were not founded by trade unions, but unionists participated in the broader coalitions fighting for democracy and working-class representation.

There are strong ties between political parties and unions in many Asian countries, where it is common to have different labor federations associated with each of many political parties. India currently has 11 Central Trade Union Organizations. All but two (the Self-Employed Women's Association and the New Trade Union Initiative) are affiliated with a political party. More recent parties include the Democratic Labor Party of South Korea, formed to provide a political arm for the Korean Confederation of Trade Unions.

As discussed in chapter 5, the U.S. never had a Labor Party, and since the 1930s, the labor movement has primarily supported the Democratic Party – but it has no official representation in that party. U.S. unions are also less and less able to hold Democrats accountable to a pro-labor agenda.

What accounts for the different outcomes, and what explains the cases where strong labor parties do or did exist? In some countries, unions were a driving force behind the creation of a political party. In others, unions were not as central to party formation, but due to their large size and prominence they still had significant formal voice in party program and the direction of the party (Ebbinghaus 1995). For many decades in the mid-twentieth century, there was relative socio-economic stability in Western Europe and Latin America, which allowed political parties to make commitments to unions and workers, "in the context of Keynesian demand management, limited global competition, and the Bretton Woods system of fixed exchange rates" (Burgess 2004: 17). Governments could use public money to create jobs and social programs that benefitted workers. Burgess further argues that unions could more easily organize workers in the period of geographically concentrated production, and where there was a relatively homogeneous labor force.

This all began to change in the 1980s and 1990s as many labor-backed parties adopted economic reforms that went against the interests of labor unions. In the tightening vise of neoliberal practice and ideology, labor-backed parties faced pressures to reduce the size of the state. Increased economic globalization enhanced competitive stresses for many companies, which then restructured and threatened to relocate. Governments succumbed to neoliberal policy in order to appease investors and to attract and retain capital. The welfare state was converted to the "competition state" (Cerny 1997).

This meant that there was mounting tension between unions and elected officials, even those from labor-backed parties, in at least three ways. First, governments adopted neoliberal policies that undermined their own tax base (such as reduced corporate taxes), thereby creating budget pressures forcing them to cut public employment and curtail public services. Second, even in times of budget surplus, politicians were pressured to cut public spending to show they were "business friendly." Third, trade unions were losing members in many countries and experiencing a decline in their power. These trends hurt the parties as well as the unions, but in the relationship of the "Siamese Twins," the balance of power tilted toward the parties. For the most part, party leaders attempted to shore up their political base to remain politically viable by shifting their policies rightward. This was made easier by a fourth trend: the growth of conservative political movements. Neoliberalism was not only an economic theory but also an ideological perspective. Many of its tenets appealed to voters, including union members, who were pulled to the right. Union leaders did not pose credible alternatives, and instead at times played into a nationalist, protectionist response – thereby fueling the growth of conservative political movements and a general rightward shift for many political parties.

As a result, unions felt betrayed by the labor-backed parties. In some cases this resulted in a formal split, such as in Spain. The Spanish Socialist Workers' Party (PSOE) and the General Workers' Union (UGT) had been in alliance since the 1880s. But when the PSOE came into power from 1982 to 1993, they were one of the early European nations to adopt neoliberal reform. The unions were strong enough to extract some concessions early on, but eventually, the relationship came to an end. By 1988, the UGT called for a general strike against the economic and social policies of the PSOE, which ended without concessions from the ruling party. The next year, the UGT did not support the PSOE candidates running for positions in the European Parliament – the first time the UGT did not support the PSOE since the end of fascism in Spain (Burgess 2004).

There were official splits, increased tensions, or strained relations between unions and labor-backed parties in many other countries in this period, including Britain, New Zealand, Argentina, Bolivia, Poland, South Africa, Germany, Sweden, and Austria. The result is that for the most part, union ties to these labor-backed parties weakened over the last 20 years (Levitsky 2003; Burgess 2004). Labor-backed parties have also suffered loss of clout, but some have reoriented politically, such as the "New Labour" Party of Tony Blair that adopted neoliberal policies in the 1990s.

An increasing amount of research suggests that countries with strong labor parties and representative political systems may have been able to delay and mitigate the impact of neoliberalism, but none seem capable of escaping it. Even some of the best cases – Germany, Sweden, and Portugal – have witnessed a weakening of union/party relations, and a decline in union power relative to the power of capital via the state. The evidence seems clear that labor movements have lost power around the world in the last several decades in terms of relationships with labor-backed or labor-allied parties.

What options do today's unions have? First, they can look to form new parties. This has occurred in a few places where labor movements worked with democratization movements against military dictatorships. Two notable examples are Brazil, where trade unions launched the Workers' Party (PT) in 1980, and in South Korea, where the Korean Confederation of Trade Unions helped form the Democratic Labour Party in 2000. Syriza, a coalition of left groups in Greece, was formed in 2004, and registered as a formal party in 2012 after experiencing a major growth in support, including among many trade unionists not allied with the Communist Party (Mason 2012; Wainwright 2012).

Another strategy is to focus on issues rather than parties or candidates. A few U.S. unions have pledged to adopt this strategy, promoting policies like the minimum wage and campaign finance reform rather than focusing on electing individuals. However, there are constraints to this approach, as unions still operate in a candidate-centered, "winner take all" system and often feel compelled to help elect candidates who make promises to unions or who are "the lesser of two evils."

A third strategy is to retreat from electoral politics altogether. This is rare for organized labor movements, and more likely to occur among social movements. A recent example is the *indignado* movement in Spain. Since 2011, activists have engaged in various forms of protest against inequality and injustice in Spain. Also referred to as the 15-M movement, the protests began in dozens of cities on May 15, 2011, and continue in various forms today. This is not a traditional labor movement, and in fact there is not a clear linkage between unions and the movement. Yet protesters and Spanish unions have a common diagnosis of the country's economic problems, including high unemployment, cuts in public services, growing inequality, and economic stagnation. A key part of the *indignados* approach is to reject the current political parties and system and, in fact, it called on people not to vote for either of the two major parties in the Fall 2011 election, even though there was a good chance that the center-right People's Party would oust the ruling Socialist Party. In the end, the People's Party did win, bringing in more austerity and neoliberal reform. But the *indignados* saw the Socialist Party as part of the problem (Gleave 2011). They argued that existing political parties, including many traditionally allied with labor unions, are not capable of addressing the global economic crisis and challenges of neoliberalism, succumbing to austerity rather than promoting alternatives in the interest of the majority of the country's population. The anger against formal political parties is growing in other parts of the world as well, among social movements and potential union allies, including the unemployed, precarious workers, the Occupy movement, and within anarchist/autonomista movements in Latin America. This suggests that a broader labor movement may need to explore alternative forms of political representation in addition to alternative economic models.

Conclusion

Neoliberalism has greatly weakened labor movements, giving employers far more power relative to workers. The traditional strategies for union power each have limitations, and these limitations have grown sharper in recent years. Exercising power on the shopfloor is more difficult as neoliberalism and technological changes have provided employers with more tools to shift production and break strikes. Workers with greater structural power – such as those who are highly skilled or located in strategic positions – will have more chance of success, but employers have power of their own and will use it.

Workers without structural power have to rely on other strategies, such as building alliances with political parties and other social movements. One tool that these alliances have used is using their social power in a way to disrupt "business as usual," such as with a general strike. Where union density is low, the ability to engage in a general strike is lower, but alliances with community groups and other movements can help. Workplace strikes can also be effective when integrated into a larger struggle for worker rights and universal social benefits, and workers may rely on symbolic power to make their struggle seen as a broader fight for social justice.

Unions have also historically relied on alliances with political parties to win their demands. Here too, neoliberalism has had an impact, as politicians must rely on wealthy investors more than ever. "Business-friendly" policy is now the common sense. Even labor-backed parties have pulled back from a pro-worker agenda, leaving relations between unions and parties frayed or destroyed. Unions are struggling to find new models of political participation and representation.

Each of these traditional sources of union power has limitations, but still has potential to contribute to building a broader and more effective labor movement. But unions cannot rely only on traditional methods. Increasingly, union leaders are looking to access new sources of power, and revitalize and rebuild their movements. In the next chapter, we discuss some of these efforts.

7

Rebuilding the Movements

Labor movements are still relevant, and indeed, have a crucial role to play in the global economy. But neoliberalism has rendered traditional sources of union power less effective. Strikes are harder to win as reforms and trade agreements have made it easier for employers to move investment and jobs. Policymakers are more reluctant to pass pro-worker policies when investors can threaten to move their money out of the city or country. As a result, unions have been turning to other sources of power, such as building labor–community coalitions and working with other social movements. As sociologist Dan Clawson (2003) argues, union growth comes in upsurges, when unions utilize new tactics and organizational forms, and redefine the concept of a labor movement.

In this chapter I discuss some of the innovations and areas of growth for unions. I begin with strategies that unions are using to expand their membership and power – including organizing models, labor–community coalitions, community unions, labor education and universal social policies. I then examine non-union organizing approaches, including worker centers and NGOs, and worker cooperatives.

Union Organizing

As mentioned in chapter 5, unions in the LMEs, particularly in the U.S., U.K., and Australia, started focusing on organizing as a strategy for revitalization earlier than other countries, as the CME unions focused more on unionization via political engagement and centralized collective bargaining. A handful of unions in the LMEs adopted an "organizing model," which included increasing the portion of their budget spent on organizing non-union workers, hiring new staff to organize full-time, conducting research on potential workplaces and industries to target, and employing a range of tactics such as building shopfloor committees and conducting house visits with potential union members (Milkman and Voss 2004).

As these efforts progressed, union leaders encountered major obstacles in unionizing new workplaces – in particular, employers who were gaining power to avoid or break a union. U.S. unions began employing "corporate campaigns" (or "comprehensive campaigns") designed to pressure companies from many different angles, including from their workforce, consumers, and stockholders. These campaigns typically conduct strategic research into corporations' holdings and its board of directors, and then implement media campaigns, legal actions, consumer boycotts, and other creative and escalating tactics (Bronfenbrenner and Hickey 2004). Labor organizer Ray Rogers ran the first U.S. "corporate campaign," working with the Amalgamated Clothing Workers of America to organize the large textile company J.P. Stevens. The campaign succeeded in unionizing 3,000 workers at 10 plants in hard-to-organize southern states (Jarley and Maranto 1990).

U.S. unions face extreme employer opposition during the official union election and decertification processes overseen by the National Labor Relations Board (NLRB). As a result, more unions turned to "non-board" strategies: working to win without conducting an NLRB election (Eaton and Kriesky 2009). Of the 400,000 workers organized into private sector unions in 2008, only 70,000 were organized through the NLRB process (Warren 2010). One non-board approach is neutrality and/or card check agreements: unions use pressure to extract an agreement from employers that they will not intervene in the election process. The employer might also agree to forego the election, and simply recognize the union if 50%+1 of workers signs an authorization form stating that they want the union to represent them. "Card check," or variations of it, is already a common path to unionization in many countries, and in the United States, 12 states mandate card check for at least some employees (Gely and Chandler 2011).[1] Economist Chris Riddell (2004) conducted a quasi-natural experiment when the province of British Columbia, Canada, changed its labor laws in 1984, by introducing mandatory elections, and then in 1993, by converting to card-check procedures. Examining union certification data for 1978–98, he found that unionization rates fell by an average of 19 percent during the election period, and rose by the same amount during the card-check period, suggesting that card-check makes it much easier for workers to unionize.

New organizing is not limited to the LMEs, however. Germany, once thought of as a union stronghold, has seen a steady decline in union density since the 1990s as well as the growth of anti-union employers. The German industrial relations model had focused on non-adversarial social partnership between unions and employers, but a handful of unions have adopted some variation of U.S.-style confrontational organizing. This includes a successful effort by a union to organize against the anti-union drugstore Schlecker, and the on-going campaign against the discount supermarket Lidl, launched by the union ver.di (Gajewska and Niesyto 2009; Turner 2009).[2] But German unions are still utilizing traditional structures to organize as well. Behrens (2009) argues that while U.S.-style tactics have had some success in Germany, works councils still have a useful role in union organizing. In a 2005 survey, Behrens found that almost half of works councils were involved in union membership recruitment, and, in fact, "[w]orks councils have done the lion's share of membership recruitment on behalf of unions." Behrens argues that unions should not abandon the works council model, and instead work more closely with works councils to expand union organizing.

Unions are also pursuing organizing via a few new strategies or variations of older ones, including labor–community coalitions, community and regional unions, deeper visionary labor education, and innovative policy.

Community and Regional Unions

Community and regional unions are organized around a geographic identity rather than a specific employer or workplace. The term is used to describe a variety of labor models, but here I focus on cases where unions or regional labor councils have opened their membership up to individuals regardless of where they work, or whether they work at all. According to Simon Black, the term "community union" was first used in the U.S. in the 1960s to describe the challenge that unions would face with long-term unemployment and deskilled work. Jack Conway of the United Auto Workers saw that traditional trade union models would not work for organizing the urban poor or migrant farm workers. Activists needed a new model to organize people around common grievances, such as against abusive landlords, access to services or the need for job creation (Black 2005). These formations go beyond a labor–community coalition, in that the organization itself integrates demands relating to work and community.

Japanese activists began creating community unions in the mid-1980s, and the national labor federations Rengo and the left-wing-led Zenroren adopted the concept of regional unions in 1996 and 2002, respectively. By 2009, Rengo had 15,500 members in regional unions (Takasu 2012). As of 2010, Zenroren had 152 regional unions, representing 11,338 members, ranging from a handful of members to as many as 400. Members can join as individuals, as full or associate members. They affiliate directly to the local Zenroren federation and pay dues. Zenroren provides labor counseling centers and mutual aid funds. Only 41 percent of affiliates had full-time staff, but Zenroren hires retirees and dismissed workers also on a part-time basis (Takasu 2012). Community and regional unions in Japan have been growing, particularly among women, migrants, and young workers (Lee 2012). In some cases, the community unions engage in collective bargaining with employers on behalf of workers. They also engage in direct action tactics.

A form of regional unions exists in South Korea as well, where there are three general unions representing three different regions of the country (Lee 2012). These three unions (B General Union, CH Regional Union, and KN General Union) organize workers in enterprises but also allow individuals to join, including unemployed and dismissed workers. The unions organize around workplace issues as well as broader issues, such as poor public service provision. Suzuki (2012) suggests that this form of unionism is perhaps easier to establish in countries where the legal requirements for union formation are relatively minimal, as is the case in Japan and South Korea. For this reason, similar strategies have been pursued in other countries, but often without the legal status of a trade union. I discuss these efforts below, in the non-union organizing section.

Labor–Community Coalitions

Another strategy for revitalizing unions and building power is through building alliances with other organizations, such as community groups, consumers, students, environmentalists, and housing activists – I will use the term "labor–community coalition" as shorthand for these approaches. This concept encompasses everything from ad hoc alliances to support a strike to deeper long-term coalitions with shared programs, but it also overlaps with "social movement unionism" and "community unionism." These strategies all share the goal of working on issues beyond wages and working conditions, looking for common interests between workers and community members, and enhancing union power via electoral work or direct action. The concept is not new, but as neoliberalism has made it harder for unions to win on their own via strikes, unions have been looking to increase their power via community alliances. The strategy has had some success when done well and strategically, but it is not always easy to do, and can be subject to some pitfalls.

Labor leaders have highlighted the need for community support for much of the past century (Craft 1990). But in the U.S., the community programs established by unions to garner popular support, starting as early as the 1940s and 1950s, were primarily aimed at providing services to union members and non-members, and avoiding broader, sometimes divisive, community issues such as fair housing or school integration. This began to change in the late 1970s, as unions faced difficulties organizing new workers. They saw they needed to deepen their relations with the community, viewing community groups as potential allies. Unions without structural power may turn to allies to help strengthen their capacity to exercise social power in other ways, such as through voting or mounting multi-faceted pressure campaigns against employers. In fact, even before the 1970s, some unions partnered with community groups in organizing drives. A well-known example is the alliance between the American Federation of State, County and Municipal Employees and civil rights groups that worked together to ensure public sector workers had the right to join a union and engage in collective bargaining in a number of cities, including Memphis, Tennessee.[3] But the potential for partnerships increased in the 1970s because the number of community organizations also grew, as elements of the social movements of the 1960s and 1970s became institutionalized into non-profit organizations that were self-sustaining, via member dues, donations, and grants. This helped create the groundwork for building alliances, as some of the organizations worked with the same populations as unions, particularly in the low-wage service sector.

Some alliances run deeper than coalitions. Social movement unionism is a term first applied to unions that operated primarily in South Africa and Brazil, fighting against authoritarian governments (Suzuki 2012). These unions or federations, COSATU in South Africa and the CUT in Brazil, built alliances that were deeper than instrumental coalitions. They fought for workers' rights and community issues in an integrated way, as part of a broader movement for democratic rights (Seidman 1994; Moody 1997). In wealthy countries, social movement unionism looks more like an alliance between weakened unions and civil society organizations. But according to Moody, the common characteristics include a focus on union democracy, involvement of the rank-and-file, and strong alliances with social movements (Moody 1997).

Research on coalitions suggests that there are some potential pitfalls and advantages to this strategy for building worker power.

For some, coalitions signal labor's weakness. Unions are unable or unwilling to organize their own members or new members, and have diluted their class orientation by turning to community partners – meaning that instead of focusing on workers' demands on the shopfloor, unions concede power to employers and instead focus on community issues that might be easier to win but less likely to alter employer power (Suzuki 2012). Labor–community coalitions can sometimes do more harm than good, if unions attempt to bypass their own members in the work, focusing just on leader–leader relations (Luce 2012). Unions might also take an instrumental ad hoc approach to the coalition (Tattersall and Reynolds 2007; Tattersall 2010). For example, activists in the faith-based community have talked about the attitude of unions to "rent-a-collar" – forming a quick relation with a pastor or priest to speak at a union rally or hearing, but not really building deep mutual relations. This might achieve a short-term goal but in the long run, but may undermine alliances and trust.

When done well, however, labor–community coalitions and social movement unionism can lead to increased union strength as well as broader working-class victories. Amanda Tattersall (2010) developed a typology of four kinds of coalitions, ranging along a scale of integration from ad-hoc to deep coalitions. She argues that deep coalitions integrate mutual interests and present a broad vision for workers and communities rather than just focusing on specific workplace demands. Interestingly, unions that attempt to maintain tight control over the coalition gain little from it; those that concede control to coalition partners are more likely to increase their power. In a case study of the Canadian Auto Workers, Michael Schiavone (2007) argues that by using a social movement unionism approach, the union organized proportionally more new members and obtained a better collective bargaining agreement than it would have under a more traditional union model.

Labor Education to Challenge Neoliberalism

In chapter 5, I argued that labor education is one of the internal challenges unions must address in rebuilding, as few unions make serious efforts to provide education and training to members, or to integrate education into a broader organizing or political strategy. Many existing labor education programs emphasize basic union skills, such as filing grievances or dealing with contract negotiations. While important, these skills alone are not enough to give union members the broader understanding of neoliberalism and its impact on workers. To fulfill the potential roles that unions have – including countering corporate power, expanding democracy, and exploring alternative economic models – unions must dramatically expand the reach and depth of their education programs. There are some promising examples.

The National Confederation of Metalworkers (CNM/CUT) in Brazil launched the education program *Programa Integrar* in 1996 (Fischer and Hannah 2002; Mello n.d.). The union decided it needed to provide education not just to their members, but also to the broader working class and activists from other movements. The program is influenced by the Brazilian educator Paulo Freire and his perspective that education should be explicitly conscious of power and the roles of students in social change. Because illiteracy is high and the public education system has been under attack in Brazil, *Programa Integrar* is a way to expand the skills of the working class and combat social exclusion. Courses include basic skills such as reading and math, but they are taught within a political context, based in workers' life experiences and premised on the notion that education leads to action. The program also includes group work, directed study, and the development of "economic solidarity" projects where workers learn to generate alternative sources of income. The union views the program as a way to expand their capacity as a union and build a larger labor movement that can influence public policy and fight for universal working-class interests in opposition to neoliberalism.

Another example is the Canadian Union of Postal Workers (CUPW), which won in contract negotiations the formation of a member education fund in 1992. CUPW states that the purpose of education is "developing the knowledge, will and confidence of the membership to defend their rights and the rights of others;

. . . recognizing shop floor, picket line and community activism as significant educational experiences; . . . [and] developing the awareness and confidence that can change the world." To that end, the union provides a four-week program that focuses on a wide range of social justice issues, including an explicit analyses of neoliberal globalization and the ways in which the ideology of the free market hurts workers and unions. Any member in good standing is allowed to participate, and the Union Education Fund pays lost wages, meals and accommodation, travel expenses, and child care and elder care expenses (http://www.cupw.ca/index.cfm/ci_id/1165/la_id/1.htm; Taylor 2007).

Labor unions in South Korea and South Africa also place a high value on member education, and have established extensive programs. COSATU educates members on a broad range of issues, including international political economy, organizing, and women's leadership. In South Korea, the regional union, B General Union, demands in collective bargaining that employers provide space for education and time off each month for members to attend classes (Lee 2012).

Novelli (2004) describes how a public sector union in Colombia (SINTRAEMCALI) went from one focused narrowly on members to a social movement union active in a broader labor–community coalition with international allies using what he calls a "strategic learning" education process. When the union was threatened by impending privatization in the early 1990s, a group of rank-and-file members started pushing for more union activity, and used informal educational activities to gain support within the union. After building a base of cadre, the members took over in the union and established an extensive program of applied education: learning about privatization and the neoliberal logic behind it, studying the public entities slated for privatization, and working with local communities to develop an alternative plan for running the utilities better while keeping the services public. This laid the groundwork for a successful effort to block privatization and implement their own plan.

Universal Policy Approaches

Industrial relations scholars have concluded that one of the main factors influencing union density is the presence of the Ghent system, currently in operation in Denmark, Finland, Iceland, Sweden, and partially Belgium. First implemented in Ghent, Belgium in 1901, the system gives labor unions power to distribute government subsidized unemployment insurance benefits. The insurance is voluntary, and workers usually belong to the union in order to be eligible for the benefits depending on the country.[4] The Ghent system gave workers strong incentives to join the union for the benefits, and it can also maintain high unionization even during high unemployment (Western 1993).

While it may seem far-fetched that unions could implement a Ghent system in other countries,[5] there is in fact a modified form of this now in place in Argentina. As mentioned in chapter 2, the country established a national workfare program in 1996, *Plan Trabajar,* to address high unemployment. Under the plan, municipal governments were required to work with local NGOs to develop public projects that would employ local residents. The program eventually resulted in the creation of on-going community projects, from soup kitchens to worker-run manufacturing. The projects are run by local associations that use general assemblies to decide which activities to support and how to distribute resources. Residents have to be members of the associations to participate in decision making and in the projects (Garay 2007). The program has not necessarily increased union density in the traditional sense, but laid-off union members and labor organizers have played a key role in the creation of *Plan Trabajar* and the formation of the two large unemployed workers' associations. Through protest and organizing, the groups have been able to win higher levels of resources from the government, and use that to create jobs for unemployed workers, who are members of growing *piquetero* organizations (Benclowicz 2011).

Another policy strategy that could provide universal benefits to workers and possibly increase the capacity of labor movements is the basic income guarantee (BIG) (also known by other names, such as basic income grant). Based on the concept that societies are healthier when all citizens have their basic needs met, the BIG proposal would provide all citizens, regardless of need or status, a minimum income to cover the basics of survival. Proposals vary, but most call for a payment in cash, to individuals, with no restrictions on how it is spent and no work requirement.[6]

The BIG differs from the Ghent system in that you do not need to be a member of a union or community organization to be eligible, and therefore some unions see BIG programs as detrimental to unionization. In fact, although one of the main advocates of BIG is the Belgian philosopher Philippe Van Parijs, the Belgian unions have opposed the idea because they believe it would make it more difficult to negotiate wages with employers and further encourage precarious work (Vanderborght 2006). On the other hand, unions in Namibia and Brazil supported efforts to implement BIG plans in those countries. The Namibian Union of Namibian Workers was one of the four main anchors of a two-year pilot program in the town of Otjivero-Omitara. The final assessment of the program showed the BIG resulted in increased economic activity and unemployment dropped from 60 to 45 percent (Basic Income Grant Coalition 2009).

There is much to debate about BIG and other universal policy proposals that unions might support. The Ghent system suggests that those programs that allow an official role for labor unions, and incentivize union membership, are closely linked to high union density. However, there are reasons to believe other forms of policies could strengthen labor movements by increasing the capacity of unions and allied organizations, and raising the floor for all workers, thereby generating increased economic activity and employment.

Non-Union Worker Organizations

Not all workers have the legal right to join a union, and some workers do not have regular employers – whether they work in the informal economy, are employed as "independent contractors," do temporary work, or hold multiple part-time jobs. In some cases, unions can organize these kinds of workers and regularize the work. But in other cases, these non-standard workers have been ignored by unions or unable to join. Instead, they are forming alternative worker organizations – some that are membership-based, and some that are staff-driven advocacy NGOs. In addition, while not new, worker cooperatives have become more prominent in the past decade as more workers confront a turbulent global economy in capitalist firms.

Worker Centers and New Forms of Worker Organization

As union density fell, non-union worker organizations have filled some of the void. In the U.S., these are now called "worker centers" – non-profit membership-based organizations of mostly low-wage workers. Many, but not all, focus on organizing immigrant workers and most are based in a geographic community (Fine 2006). The first generation of worker centers developed in the late 1970s/early 1980s – the Chinese Staff and Worker Association in Chinatown, New York City; La Mujer Obrera in El Paso, Texas; and Black Workers for Justice in Rocky Mount, North Carolina. In 1992 there were only five known worker centers, but by 2007 there were 160 (Fine 2007). These vary in focus and population served, but most combine organizing, advocacy, and service work. There are also national networks emerging that unite worker centers sectorally, such as the National Day Labor Organizing Network (NDLON), and the National Domestic Workers Association.

Worker centers have had varying relations with unions. Some formed outside of, and to some extent in opposition to, unions they saw as bureaucratic, corrupt, conservative or exclusionary, racist, and nationalist. Other worker centers work closely with unions in some sectors (and a few centers were even founded by unions), but there are some tensions as well. Worker center expert Janice Fine (2007) points out structural, cultural, and ideological areas where the two forms can be "mismatched." Most U.S. unions are closed to members, with a fairly narrow definition of who can join and be in the leadership. Some worker centers are membership organizations and some are not, but most are much more open about who can join and get involved. Unions raise money from dues, and worker centers mostly from foundations, which gives unions more independence over their funds. Fine notes, "Not surprisingly, many worker centres experience local unions as top-down, formulaic and disconnected from the community; many unions view worker centres as undisciplined and unrealistic about what it takes to win" (p. 345).

Due to weak U.S. labor laws, worker centers have some advantages over unions. For example, the Taft-Hartley provisions of labor law make it illegal for unions to engage in "secondary boycotts" that picket or boycott one employer in an effort to win demands against another employer; or "sympathy strikes" where unions go on strike in support of another union. Unions have a fairly rigid set of guidelines governing when and how they can picket or protest. Other kinds of organizations have no such restrictions, and much more latitude for protest.

The Restaurant Opportunities Center (ROC) is a worker center for restaurant workers, formed first in New York City. ROC-NY picketed outside several restaurants that they claimed were engaging in wage theft and discriminatory practices. Three restaurants filed charges with the NLRB, but the General Counsel issued a memo declaring that ROC-NY was not a "labor organization," and therefore not subject to Taft-Hartley/NLRB provisions. A "labor organization" (union) would have been potentially liable for damages (Lynd and Gross 2008; Naduris-Weissman 2010). The restaurants also filed petitions to the Department of Labor requiring that ROC-NY be subject to complex financial disclosure requirements under the Labor Management Relations and Disclosure Act (LMRDA), but this also failed. Given the restrictions of U.S. labor law, non-union worker organizations may have more power to act as unions than actual unions.

Non-union worker organizations are common in other parts of the world, often referred to as worker NGOs and sometimes also straddling the line between traditional union and non-union organizations. Some are membership-based and others are small organizations of staff that advocate for worker rights.

Some non-traditional worker organizations organize the self-employed (or "own account") workers, such as street vendors. While they are self-employed in the technical sense, workers tend to be in precarious positions financially and in relation to the state or police (such as vendors working without a permit). One of the best-known organizations of this kind is the Self-Employed Women's Association (SEWA) in India, founded in 1972. SEWA is formally registered as a trade union, but also operates as a worker cooperative. According to Ela Bhatt, a founder of SEWA: "We wanted to be a union and not an NGO, because we wanted to change the economy. We felt we wanted to play an important role in the national economy – that is why we chose to be a trade union and a cooperative as a model, from the start" (Bhatt 2004). Some critics challenged the idea that SEWA is a union, as many of their members did not work for an employer, but instead were self-employed. But SEWA argued that the workers were still working for someone – and that the work itself was essentially the same whether done in a factory or in the home. For that reason, SEWA argued that the same laws should apply to home-based informal economy workers. SEWA has protected street vendors from police harassment, provided job training, and provided safety equipment and health training for certain occupations. The group has started projects and sister organizations to provide services for members, including a bank, education center, child care and health services. SEWA says it is both an organization and a movement that intersects the labor movement, cooperative movement, and women's movement (http://www.sewa.org/).

Worker NGOs are also growing in prominence in China. The initial groups were based in Hong Kong where there was more political space to engage in worker organizing. The Chinese Working Women's Network formed in 1996 to support Chinese migrant women, working in four areas: labor rights, feminist consciousness, occupational safety and health, and alternative socio-economic life. Other worker NGOs have developed in Hong Kong, playing different roles to support workers, including research and educational programs for worker rights organizing.

In recent years, worker NGOs have formed in mainland China as well, particularly in the south. These most commonly take the form of legal assistance centers, run by "shopfloor lawyers" – workers who have learned how to work with labor law (Friedman 2009). They take on cases for workers who have experienced problems at work such as health and safety violations or non-payment of wages. The lawyers represent workers and charge a fee, which funds the centers. The number of such NGOs has grown rapidly, but in 2012, Guangdong Province stepped up its scrutiny of worker centers, even shutting some down. The NGOs have been on tenuous ground in China, as the government has been reluctant to allow the formation of independent civil society organizations. While these NGOs could provide a safety valve function for dealing with labor unrest, the government has engaged in regular crackdowns against worker NGOs, seeing them as a political threat – and 10 were shut down in Shenzhen in 2012 (Davis 2012). Worker NGOs exist in part because workers do not have the right to form independent trade unions, and the ACFTU is not effective in protecting worker rights. However, experience from other parts of the world suggests that even if independent unions were allowed, there would likely still be a need for worker NGOs.

Worker Cooperatives

Another form of worker organization is worker cooperatives. As Ness and Azzellini (2011) state, the concept of worker control is "as old as capitalism itself" (p. 11). Workers built cooperatives during the industrial revolution as a counter to growing capitalist models of production. They were an alternative to both the harsh conditions of the industrial factory, but also an attempt to make work more secure amidst the booms and busts of markets. In the U.S., the labor organization the Knights of Labor promoted worker and consumer cooperatives in the 1860s and 1870s. France legalized worker cooperatives in 1848, and in 1871 workers took over Paris and established the Paris Commune for 10 days.

One of the best-known and most successful examples of worker cooperatives is the MONDRAGON Corporation in Basque Country, Spain. A Catholic priest, José María Arizmendiarrieta, created a technical college in the 1940s after the Spanish Civil War. He and the students created a small business to build heaters in 1956, and named it after their town of MONDRAGON. The cooperative operates according to 10 basic principles that are designed to create democratic control over work. The company was successful and the cooperative soon expanded into other areas of production, and then services, including their own bank. By 2012, over 100,000 people worked in 256 MONDRAGON businesses.[7]

Worker co-ops often grow during times of economic instability (Dickstein 1991). In the 1970s and early 1980s, recession in Western Europe led to a large increase in unemployment and industrial restructuring, provoking a small surge in worker ownership (Birchall and Ketilson 2009). Another wave of worker cooperatives emerged recently in Argentina in the aftermath of the early 2000s economic crisis. Argentina has implemented new policies and programs designed to encourage their formation as a source of job creation. These have led to the formation of 7,315 worker cooperatives as of 2011 (Vuotto 2012).

While hard numbers are not available, it appears that worker cooperatives are increasing in other parts of the world as well. While small by comparison to other countries, the U.S. Federation of Worker Cooperatives estimates that there are over 300 worker cooperatives in the U.S., which employ over 3,500 people.[8] In addition to worker cooperatives there are also producer, consumer, and purchasing cooperatives; altogether the International Cooperative Alliance estimates that there are over 1 billion members of cooperatives, and 100 million people employed in the cooperative sector globally.[9]

Worker cooperatives appear to be more successful, on average, than capitalist firms in certain respects. A study by the ILO found that worker cooperatives are more resilient than other firms during an economic crisis (Birchall and Ketilson 2009). In their study of worker co-ops in the plywood industry, Craig and Pencavel (1995) come to similar findings: when faced with economic downturn, co-ops are more likely to adjust their pay in order to avoid lay-offs. They also find that worker co-ops are between 6 and 14 percent more productive than conventional firms. In a study of four co-ops in Argentina, Atzeni and Ghigliani (2007) found that the cooperative structure allowed for greater worker participation via assemblies and meetings. Workers have more rights, such as the right to require the management councils to call a mass meeting. They write, "The absence of the capitalist, of hierarchy, of intermediate managerial layers and forms of direct control, expel the despotic rationality of capital from the sphere of production and open a new space for workers' intervention" (p. 667).

On the other hand, worker cooperatives are constrained by the conditions in which they operate. One major constraint is access to capital and credit, as in a mostly capitalist economy firms must have access to capital to function. Financial institutions have historically been much more reluctant to lend to worker co-ops (in part because groups of workers tend to have little collateral; also it seems they prefer to lend to firms with a small number of managers rather than large numbers), and the average group of workers is unlikely to have enough capital free to invest in a business – particularly because starting a business is risky (Craig and Pencavel 1995). Case studies of Argentine cooperatives shows that although there are a growing number of co-ops in that country, the average co-op must still function within a market economy which reduces the space for collective and democratic control. For example, because they must compete to sell products on a timely basis, a worker cooperative cannot always take the time to engage in democratic deliberation about the terms or conditions of a sale. Worker co-ops still need to find and maintain clients or suppliers who operate under capitalist models of competition, and this pulls cooperatives to function more like their capitalist counterparts, separating production workers from managerial and sales workers (Atzeni and Ghigliani 2007).

Workplace Occupations

Many of the Argentine cooperatives were started via worker occupations – a strategy used by unions and sometimes non-union workers to defend their jobs or take over production entirely. After a severe economic crisis hit Argentina in the early 2000s, employers abandoned workplaces and workers occupied factories and started production themselves. Estimates vary, but a 2010 survey reported 205 occupied workplaces, employing approximately 10,000 people. Over 95 percent of these were constituted as cooperatives, and they include manufacturing facilities as well as health care clinics, hotels, and schools.

While not a widely used tactic in most countries, plant occupations of various forms have been used persistently for over 100 years in labor struggles, including the famous Flint sit-down strikes of 1936–7, the 1919–20 Biennio Rosso period of social unrest and factory occupations in Italy, and the 77-day occupation of the SsangYong auto company in South Korea in 2009. Reports suggest a recent uptick in occupations since the 2008 crisis, including in Canada, Ireland, and Scotland (Cullinane and Dundon 2011; Gall 2011), and cases of occupations in Egypt, France, India, Turkey, Serbia, South Africa, and Spain (Hattingh 2009). There have even been instances of workers occupying their factory and holding their bosses hostage in Bangladesh, China, France, and Nigeria.

The wave of factory occupations took off in Argentina leading up to and in the wake of their 2001 financial crisis, inspiring others. When the 2008 global crisis hit the U.S., one of the first occupations was in Chicago, Illinois, at the Republic Windows and Doors Factory. The Republic Windows workers were members of the United Electrical workers (UE), showing that worker occupation is not only a tactic for non-union workers. On December 2, 2008, Republic Windows announced it was shutting its doors in three days, and would be laying off the 260 workers – despite the federal WARN Act which mandates that companies must give 60 days' notice for mass layoffs. The company said it could not continue operations because Bank of America would not extend its line of credit – despite the fact that the Bank had just received a generous bailout from the U.S. government. On December 5, 200 workers decided to "sit down" at work in protest of the closure. They stayed in the factory for five days, garnering support from around the world, including from president-elect Barack Obama. Eventually Bank of America agreed to negotiate, and the parties worked out a settlement to pay the workers the wages they were owed.[10]

In the midst of mass austerity and high unemployment, a factory owner in northern Greece stopped paying his workers in May 2011. The workers began taking shifts in the factory to make sure no equipment was removed, and they started holding general assemblies in the workplace. Eventually, they decided to permanently "occupy" and start up production themselves as a cooperative. In February 2013 they started the Vio.me factory under worker control.

Consumer Campaigns and Corporate Social Responsibility

In addition to labor–community coalitions, unions and non-union worker organizations have worked together to utilize consumer power to leverage gains for workers. By encouraging consumers to abstain from specific products, unions can cause a company economic hardship, and ideally force them to concede to workers' demands. This tactic is perhaps best exemplified in the U.S. with the case of the United Farm Workers' (UFW) grape boycott. The boycott, which began in 1966, was started to support striking farm workers in central California, who demanded to be paid the federal minimum wage (agricultural workers were excluded from the Fair Labor Standards Act which established the minimum wage). After a strike and a march to the state Capitol failed to win higher wages, the union called for a boycott of table grapes.[11] The boycott gained national support, and after four years, the UFW had signed agreements with many growers, winning significant gains.

Consumer boycotts have been a common strategy for hundreds of years. Adam Hochschild (2005) argues that one of the first consumer boycotts was a form of labor struggle: the sugar boycott launched in England in the 1700s, in protest against slave labor. Unions have linked with consumer campaigns for at least 100 years.

One shortcoming of consumer boycotts is that unions have employed them in a nationalist or xenophobic fashion against imported goods – used to gain leverage for domestic union-made goods but utilizing exclusionary strategies. Labor historian Dana Frank (1999) explains that the "Buy American" concept goes back to before the revolutionary war, and consumer power has often been mobilized in this country around political goals, particularly during hard times. Frank tells a fairly negative story of how unions launched campaigns to blame imports for job loss in the 1970s and 1980s, calling on consumers to buy domestic-made products (especially garments in the 1970s and cars in the 1980s). The International Ladies Garment Workers Union (ILGWU) worked with the AFL-CIO to push the Foreign Trade and Investment Act of 1972, which would have imposed quotas on imports and cut tax incentives for U.S. businesses operating overseas, among other things. The bill did not pass, but the ILGWU launched a large-scale multi-year campaign to promote American-made products. This was followed by an effort by the United Autoworkers (UAW) to promote American-made cars in the face of rising imports, particularly from Japan. The UAW resorted at times to nationalist, even racist, anti-Japanese rhetoric. Consumer power has been used in other labor struggles, both domestic and international. Frank notes some of the negative aspects of the campaigns, but in other cases, consumer movements have had a positive impact on labor struggles and built broader labor solidarity.

Consumer boycotts are still a common tactic used to support worker rights. The anti-sweatshop movement picked up attention in the 1990s when a few activists highlighted the growing problem of large multinational corporations sourcing goods produced under very poor wage and working conditions, primarily in Asia, but also other parts of the global south. The issue caught wider attention, leading the U.S. Department of Labor to take measures to examine and expose abuses. By the latter half of the 1990s, student and consumer groups formed across the U.S. and in Europe, to focus on sweatshops in the global garment industry.

At the same time, a number of garment corporations responded by attempting to address the issue internally. Over 1,000 companies established their own "corporate code of conduct" and some hired external auditors, such as PricewaterhouseCoopers or the non-profit Verité, to evaluate the labor conditions of their suppliers (Vogel 2006). Some, such as Nike, established corporate social responsibility (CSR) departments, which has a CSR budget of $25 million a year, and a staff of over 200 people (Palmquist 2010).

Despite the resources, many analysts have concluded that the CSR approach has had little impact in improving labor standards. Sociologist Jill Esbenshade (2004) found that corporate-driven CSR is deeply flawed – even when the companies hire third-party monitors. Often, monitors give advance notice to factory owners before they conduct inspections, allowing owners to hide problems. Investigations are limited, often excluding workers' input. Monitors issue reports, but those reports are kept internal to the brand so the public has no way to find the results of the investigation. Furthermore, the third-party monitors tend to rely heavily on the contracts from the brands as a revenue source, which would suggest that they have little incentive to produce damaging or critical reports.

Anita Chan (2009) evaluated a more promising effort on the part of Reebok, which helped facilitate elections for independent unions in some of the factories it sources from in China. Reebok negotiated with suppliers to allow for independent union elections at five of its factories in China. After considerable effort, the elections happened at one factory, and led to some initial bargaining between workers and management. However, Chan noted that despite what she believes were good intentions on the part of Reebok, the local challenges of organizing for worker rights in China made the effort ineffective. This includes the absence of an independent trade union culture in China, the complex relationship these independent unions had with the ACFTU, and the failure of the union (or Reebok) to insist on collective bargaining and financial independence from management. Chan concludes that even in this better-case scenario, the options for CSR-driven labor reform are extremely limited. Barrientos and Smith (2007) studied codes of conduct and concluded that they have led in some cases to changes in outcomes, but little in terms of process changes or increased rights for workers.

Activists recognized early that corporations could not be trusted to improve conditions themselves and so they continued to push for change from the outside. They formed membership organizations like the United Students against Sweatshops (USAS), and NGOs like the International Labor Rights Forum, Clean Clothes Campaign, Ethical Trading Initiative, No Sweat, and others.

These groups worked on a number of fronts. First, they attempted to influence the purchasing practices of large buyers, such as universities. Student groups held rallies and sit-ins on many campuses and got their administrations to agree to a code of conduct that would commit to purchasing university-logo apparel from sweat-free factories. This required students to confront the challenge of monitoring such codes of conduct, which led them to form the Worker Rights Consortium (WRC) – a non-profit organization with representatives from universities and colleges, USAS, and independent labor rights experts. Since its formation in 2001, the WRC has established procedures to help oversee college purchasing contracts. As of 2013, 180 colleges and universities are affiliated with the group. The WRC worked with brands to obtain lists of factories, and then attempted to certify factories as sweat-free. Unfortunately, the scope of the project was far too great, and there was no real way the WRC could do more than investigate factories after hearing of problems.

The WRC and USAS have had victories, where they were able to launch an investigation into alleged abuses, send in monitors, issue a report, and direct enough pressure on the factory and brand to extract gains for workers. One example is the Kukdong factory in Puebla, Mexico, where workers went on strike in 2001 in protest against poor working conditions and abuses, and for the right to form an independent union. The case garnered international support and assistance from USAS, the WRC, and many others, which pressured Nike – one of the main brands using the factory – to help ensure improvements. After a nine-month strike, the workers won many of their demands (Compa 2008).

Unfortunately, the victories were few and far between. And furthermore, even some of the victories were fleeting, such as the BJ&B hat factory mentioned in chapter 1. After workers won their demands at BJ&B, including unionization, Nike and Reebok dropped their contracts and moved the work to non-union factories. BJ&B shut its doors and left the country, leaving the workers without jobs (Greenhouse 2010). The union at the Kukdong factory, now called Mexmode, has suffered continuing problems. For example, in 2008 the WRC released a report documenting that a union affiliated with the PRI has engaged in physical violence against union leaders in the workplace (Worker Rights Consortium 2008).

This has led early sweatshop activist Jeff Ballinger to proclaim that almost two decades of work against sweatshops "has come to naught." Ballinger acknowledges a few short-term victories but notes that workers in Mexico are earning the same, or possibly less, per garment in 2012 compared to 1992 (18 cents for every university sweatshirt retailing for $38) (Ballinger 2009).

USAS and the WRC realized the limitations of the strategy, and in 2005 developed the concept of the Designated Supplier Program (DSP). They understood that a factory that raised standards would be penalized in the market, because the profit margin is so tight in apparel, it is not possible to pay living wages and provide benefits and remain in business. The WRC figured that it could help good employers stay in business if they could provide steady work. If universities were willing to sign onto long-term contracts, guaranteeing a minimum payment, it would enable a factory to commit to its workers. The factory would need to be certified according to certain criteria to become a "designated supplier" for those university contracts. The WRC launched the program in 2011, and as of 2012, 45 universities have signed onto the DSP program (http://www.workersrights.org/; Nova and Hensler 2011).

Related to this development, Knights Apparel bought the

former BJ&B factory in the Dominican Republic, with the intention of creating a high-standards apparel factory named Alta Gracia (which is also the name of the town in which it is located) (Greenhouse 2010). The WRC studied the cost of living in the town, and Knights agreed to pay a living wage (which amounts to about three and a half times the prevailing wage in the area), as well as to create better, safer working conditions. Workers established their own union and elected their own leaders without interference from management (Drier 2011). USAS has been working to get universities to place orders with the company as part of the DSP program. Duke University, the first campus to adopt an anti-sweatshop code of conduct in 1998, became the first to place an order with Alta Gracia in 2010. By 2012 over 400 universities were purchasing products from the factory (Lloyd 2012).

The Coalition of Immokalee Workers (CIW) also employs the consumer-based model to achieve gains for workers. From 2001 to 2005 CIW called for a boycott of the fast-food chain Taco Bell until the company agreed to pay a higher price for tomatoes picked by CIW members. The boycott involved students, key consumers of fast food. After several years, Taco Bell agreed to CIW's demand to pay a penny per pound of tomatoes, with the increase going directly to wages. The Hong Kong-based Students and Scholars Against Corporate Misbehavior (SACOM) uses consumer pressure against companies like Apple and Disney in an effort to improve conditions in their factories in China.

Some activists criticize not only the corporate-driven CSR, but also the consumer campaigns coming from NGOs, for several reasons. First, critics argue that some of the consumer campaigns have been motivated by protectionism rather than solidarity. For example, economist Naila Kabeer raised serious concerns about the U.S. effort to ban child labor in the Bangladesh garment industry. She critiques the 1997 Sanders-Harkin bill to outlaw imports made with child labor, as she believes the U.S. was attempting to protect U.S. jobs, and that supporters of the legislation made no effort to collaborate with workers in Bangladesh, or to consider the consequences on Bangladeshi families of getting the U.S. to stop purchasing from the country. She writes: "Protectionist

171

lobbies have benefitted enormously from public support as a result of their growing sophistication in linking their demands to genuine humanitarian concerns. The issue of child labour is perhaps the issue par excellence in this strategy" (Kabeer 2000: 367).

A second critique is that the consumer strategies are, if not protectionist, then paternalistic – treating workers as passive victims who cannot speak for themselves (Seidman 2007). Historian Daniel Bender (2004) points out that the paternalist approach is not new. In the early 1900s, U.S. union leaders and anti-sweatshop activists used similar paternalistic language when fighting against the garment sweatshops of the day, using language that presented women as weak workers and ambivalent union members. To this end, the paternalism toward women was intertwined with a form of protectionism – of male trade unionists fighting to keep the garment jobs for men.

Kabeer (2000), Seidman (2007) and Pun (2005) all argue that the modern anti-sweatshop movement has elements that discount the agency of women garment workers. This is not only misleading but potentially harmful, particularly as paternalistic approaches to monitoring workplaces *on behalf of* women are not effective. This is because a focus on consumer power can sidestep or avoid the question of worker power. This may be deliberate in cases where workers seem to have very little power of their own, because they live in countries where there is substantial violence against union members or where independent unions are not allowed. But a consumer power approach cannot be a solution to the lack of worker power. Even if consumers are able to win concessions from a factory or corporation, the likelihood that the victory will translate into an enforceable standard is not high if workers have no power on the shopfloor.

A third critique is that the consumer or CSR model is a voluntarist approach. It pushes the corporations to behave better, out of altruism or fear of negative publicity. This may promote the side-stepping of government regulation if it leads to the attitude, "We don't need more laws – we just need corporate responsibility." Many activists and scholars say that CSR is a neoliberal approach to raising labor standards, as it coincides with deregulation and privatizing the functions once performed by governments (setting labor standards, workplace inspections, and enforcement of laws) (Esbenshade 2012).

On the other hand, some critics are concerned about the flip side of this dynamic: relying too heavily on the state to pass legislation governing the workplace. This could also be problematic, as passing legislation is no guarantee that governments will enforce the legislation. These issues all raise questions about the role for workers, unions, governments and employers in establishing and enforcing labor standards. Is there a role for each, and if so, what is the proper balance?

Despite the weaknesses, consumer power has the potential to build union power, particularly when it is integrated into a broader strategy for revitalization and growth. Workers must be central to the campaign, and there must be clear coordination between workers and consumers. Without worker involvement, the campaigns are only relying on "advocacy power" and do not make use of other forms of worker power. Furthermore, involving workers as leaders can increase the strategic capacity of the campaign, as worker leaders will have greater motivation to win and better knowledge about the work process.

Conclusion

Unions around the world are looking for ways to rebuild or enhance their structural power, or to access other forms of power by turning to community allies to build coalitions that can pressure employers and legislators. Unions must expand their vision and develop deep and on-going alliances with community organizations to build a broader social movement that fights for more universal working-class demands. Their very survival may depend on their ability to build these alliances (Muncks 2002). This strategy, when done well, can help unions move to a more comprehensive revitalization program.

Workers without structural power might also ally with consumer groups, as has been done with United Students Against

Sweatshops. Consumer boycotts can lead to change, but there are numerous potential pitfalls to this strategy. Workers must still be involved as leaders of the efforts, as they increase the strategic capacity of the union. Consumer boycotts and variations of CSR have led to some gains for workers, but they by no means can, or should, replace unions. Just as it takes unions to enforce basic labor laws as mentioned in chapter 2, unions are needed to make any code of conduct real. Unions should support consumer activism, but consumers must support union organizing as well.

8

New Directions – Going Global

Unions must rebuild in the U.S. as well as internationally. Neoliberalism has brought a host of new challenges and intensified existing ones, requiring labor leaders to think strategically and creatively about how to take advantage of opportunities to organize. Increasingly, unions and non-union worker organizations are working together on global organizing strategies. These include solidarity efforts between unions and global labor federations, strategies to expand the rights of migrant workers and women workers, and organizing along supply chains. Labor organizations are building new forms of collective bargaining beyond the workplace and even beyond national borders. They are testing ways to use trade law to their benefit. With advances in technology and communications, activists can connect campaigns around the world – allowing unionists in the global north to learn innovative tactics from those in the global south. This chapter discusses these new efforts and concludes with some prospects for global unionism in the era of neoliberalism.

The ITUC, Global Unions and International Framework Agreements

In the post-World War II period, two international union federations were formed – the International Confederation of Free Trade Unions for unions in Western countries, and the World

Confederation of Labor for unions from socialist countries. In 2006, these organizations merged to form the International Trade Union Confederation (ITUC). Parallel to the ITUC, unions also participate in global union federations, now called Global Unions, coordinating along sectoral lines. Currently there are 10 Global Unions, including education workers, transport workers, and building and woodworkers. Global Unions engage unions in different countries in campaigns against common employers, or around common problems.[1] Global Unions have been critiqued as underfunded, ineffective, and dominated by unions from wealthy countries, yet they fill an important void, and several campaigns have shown their potential (Evans 2010).

For example, Global Unions have utilized a tool called international framework agreements (IFAs) for global organizing. IFAs are an agreement between a union or Global Union and a transnational corporation, setting basic terms of employment for workers in the company's supply chain. Unlike unilateral corporate codes of conduct, IFAs are negotiated between two parties. The initial IFAs were established in Europe in the 1990s, but there were only five in place prior to 2000; by 2011, there were 83 IFAs (Fairbrother and Hammer 2005; McCallum 2011). IFAs follow in the European tradition of social partnership: They are non-binding, or "soft law" agreements, designed to provide a "win-win" outcome for both parties. For unions, the IFAs promise adherence to labor standards and worker rights on the part of employers. Employers, in turn, get a strike-free workplace.

There is some disagreement about the effectiveness of IFAs. For instance, Stevis and Boswell (2007) review several dozen IFAs and conclude that they are limited in what they can accomplish, as they have no real enforcement mechanisms, limiting their effectiveness in cases of real dispute. Still others find examples where IFAs have had a positive impact, most notably the agreement between the UNI global alliance for service sector workers, and G4S, the largest private security firm in the world (Hoffman 2011; McCallum 2011). That IFA was signed in 2008, after a five-year battle waged by UNI and its U.S. affiliate SEIU against the company. The IFA covered 600,000 G4S workers in 112 countries, including 20,000 in South Africa. Three years prior to the agreement, SEIU began working with the South African Transport and Allied Workers Union (SATAWU) to organize security guards. SATAWU had experienced rapid membership decline from 2000 to 2006, and was struggling to rebuild. They worked on the campaign to get G4S to sign the IFA, but initially were skeptical that it could accomplish much. Eventually UNI got G4S to pressure its local management in Pretoria to accept the IFA and allow SATAWU to enter worksites to talk to workers. It also granted paid leave to a few union members to do full-time union work. The union worked with UNI staff to map the industry and launch organizing drives in several cities. After 15 months, 3,000 guards had joined the union – a 40 percent increase in the number of security guard members in SATAWU. This is still far from where the union wants to be, but the case demonstrates the positive impact an IFA can have on organizing. The process involved a Global Union, a large transnational employer, a U.S. union, a South African union, and a combination of global and local organizing work.

Dick Blin (2011) from the Global Union representing industrial workers writes that the history of implementation of the 15 IFAs they have negotiated is mixed.[2] However, he says the experience is improving, and cites the example of an IFA signed in 2005 with Rhodia, a French chemical company. Rhodia bought a small non-union chemical company in Illinois in 2009, and in 2010, workers there began organizing, working with the United Steelworkers. At first, management resisted the union and engaged in anti-union activity. The steelworkers worked with the Global Union to contact the French company and make sure that the managers in the Illinois plant respected the neutrality language in the IFA. The Rhodia CEO co-signed a letter with the head of the Global Union, explaining the unionization process, which plant managers were instructed to distribute on the shopfloor. Anti-union activity stopped, and two weeks later, the union won their election with an 86 to 14 percent vote.

Transnational Migrant Rights

As mentioned in chapter 4, migration has been rising in recent decades. This includes workers moving from one section of a country to another (such as the mass migrations from western to eastern China, or southern to northern Mexico), as well as workers crossing national borders with guest worker status, work visas, or without documentation. In 2004 the ILO adopted a Multilateral Framework on Labor Migration, setting up an action plan for member countries to pursue a healthy balance between economic growth, migration, and worker rights. It also produced a manual on migrant rights for trade unions in 2010. In 2006 the UN established the annual Global Forum on Migration, Development and Human Rights, which is a space for non-binding dialogue by policymakers and civil society groups to share experiences and best practices on migration issues.

Migrant worker rights organizing falls into several categories. First are those efforts to try to win greater legal rights, enforce existing laws, and improve wages and working conditions for migrant workers. There are thousands of organizations fighting for migrant rights in global north countries but also in global south countries too. These groups fight to enforce existing laws (including wage enforcement), to protect workers from immigration raids and deportations, and to provide services such as language classes and credit access (Milkman 2011).

A second, and sometimes overlapping, group is those working to organize migrants into unions or worker organizations, including groups of migrants who are self-organizing. These efforts go beyond providing services or legal protections and attempt to create on-going organizations. For example, the Farm Labor Organizing Committee (FLOC) is a U.S. union affiliated with the AFL-CIO. FLOC led a five-year boycott of Mt. Olive pickles in North Carolina in an effort to win a collective bargaining agreement with the company and cucumber growers in the state. They pressured the North Carolina Growers' Association, a farm-labor contractor supplying guest workers to more than 1,000 growers, to remain neutral in their effort to organize H-2A visa guest workers (Hill 2010).[3] The campaign succeeded, and in 2004 FLOC signed up thousands of workers, winning union recognition and a contract with Mt. Olive and the North Carolina Growers' Association. The agreement covered 8,500 guest workers (Reyes 2004; Hill 2010). Through direct organizing and lawsuits, FLOC won back wages for over 30,000 guest workers who had illegal deductions taken from their paychecks in North Carolina. In addition, a federal judge ordered the growers to pay for the visa and transportation expenses of the guest workers they hired (Mattson 2007).

In addition to organizing in the U.S., FLOC began organizing in Mexico as well, and hired organizers to work there, helping people fill out their H-2A applications and getting them to sign a union card at the same time. FLOC let workers know about the legal agreement that prohibited recruiters from charging fees to participate in the H-2A program. FLOC had some initial success, but tragically, in 2007, one of their organizers based in Monterrey, Mexico, was murdered. Despite this, FLOC continues efforts to organize in Mexico (Hill 2010).

Another innovative example comes from Canadian United Food and Commercial Workers (UFCW) Local 832, which represents food-processing workers at the Maple Leaf meat processing plant in Brandon, Manitoba. The company began hiring hundreds of workers, mostly from Mexico and El Salvador, through the federal Temporary Foreign Worker Program (TFWP). The TFWP began in 2002, and allowed for participants in the program to eventually apply for permanent residency status. The union decided to negotiate for increased rights and benefits for these workers, and won groundbreaking contract language mandating the company file all the necessary paperwork for migrant worker members applying for permanent residency status. The union also negotiated for and won the right to a translator whenever needed by foreign workers, funded by the employer; employer funding for translation of the agreement and employee handbook for any language where there are more than 100 members for whom English is a second language; and an expedited arbitration process for any foreign worker whose contract is terminated. The agreement gives the workers the right to stay in Canada until their case is resolved.[4]

In the U.S., the American Federation of Teachers (AFT) has been working with teachers' unions in the Philippines to establish relationships and mutual organizing activities. The AFT is working to bring guest worker teachers into the union, finding ways to help integrate them into their locals and the national union. The AFT also helped 350 guest worker Filipino teachers in Louisiana file a class action suit under the federal Trafficking Victims Protection Act. Starting in 2007, school boards in Louisiana began to bring in guest workers via labor contractors. Many teachers had borrowed up to $16,000 to pay fees to the contractors, obtaining the loans directly from the contractors. Teachers also had to sign an agreement promising to give 10 percent of their second year salaries to the contractors. The contractors held the teachers' passports to make sure the teachers repaid the loans (Rockwell 2011). The lawyers first had to win their argument that coercive conditions were not only due to physical threats, but also to economic ones. They succeeded, setting a precedent for future trafficking cases. In December 2012 a federal judge ordered the contractor to pay $4.5 million to the teachers (American Federation of Teachers 2012). Shannon Lederer of the AFT International Department says, "If you want to advocate for worker rights for migrants, it is almost too late when they get here. There was already so much damage done in the recruitment process" (Lederer 2012). To that end, the AFT is attempting to address abuses on the international level via the Education International Global Union and via the International Labor Recruitment Working Groups, which bring together sending and receiving countries to develop serious and systematic proposals for organizing and reform projects.

In response to these problems, legal scholar Jennifer Gordon has proposed a system called transnational labor citizenship (TLC) to connect workers to unions and labor rights organizations when they migrate (Gordon 2009). Gordon's goals are to provide more protection for migrants, opportunities for migrant self-organization, and redistribution of some of the benefits of migrant labor from employers and recruiters to workers and their countries of origin. Currently, most migrant workers come into the U.S. via a labor contractor or recruiter, and their visa is tied to a specific employer. In Gordon's model, a migrant worker would join an organization near their home community and obtain a "TLC visa," providing the right to work for any employer hiring in the U.S. The visa would mean the worker is entitled to full labor rights, and an eventual path to citizenship. The visa would also allow for free movement between the U.S. and home country for the worker and their family. In return, the worker would belong to the organization in their home country, but also in the community where they worked. The worker would commit to report any employers who violated labor and employment laws. The local organizations would be connected through a Transnational Worker Justice Collaborative, which would monitor and coordinate the program internationally.

The model may sound far-fetched, but Gordon notes several current experiments reflect elements of this proposal. First, there are some bilateral agreements on migration that include protections for migrants. For example, the Philippines has bilateral agreements with 14 countries to which it sends migrants. The Philippines–Malaysia agreement includes a standard contract for domestic workers setting a minimum monthly wage and guaranteeing one day off per week (Gordon 2009). An agreement between Mexico and Canada requires Mexico to send a "liaison officer" with groups of seasonal agricultural workers to monitor their labor conditions while in Canada. Second are unilateral programs that a handful of countries have established to monitor migrant recruitment and placement. For example, rather than leaving migration up to individual workers and recruiters, in some countries the government regulates and even directly acts as the recruiter. The Philippines has a new law that makes recruiters jointly liable for violations that are committed by the employer. Gordon (2011) also points to EU regulations that allow lower-skill workers from Central and Eastern Europe to enjoy more rights and some benefits relative to other migrants into the EU, and the United Kingdom in particular. The lessons are complex, but Gordon argues that the EU case shows it is possible to increase labor mobility and rights across countries without negative employment effects, and with opportunities for increased career mobility for some migrants (Gordon 2011).

Gordon states that her model could benefit not only migrant workers, but also some of the migrant-sending countries that experience domestic pressure to ensure worker rights. For example, the Philippines began relying heavily on migrant workers and remittances as early as the 1970s, but in 1995, a Filipina migrant worker was executed in Singapore, leading to huge social protests in the Philippines. Under pressure, the government developed new laws and public agencies to protect migrant workers, and began pursuing bilateral migration agreements that would place some of the burden of enforcement of rights onto the receiving countries (Gordon 2009).

Organizing Women Workers

Some new models of organizing, as well as theoretical justifications for rebuilding the labor movement, come from feminist scholars and activists. Within the last decade, women became the majority of all workers migrating to developed countries, and almost half of global migrant workers (Ghosh 2009). Women also comprise the majority of the workforce in many of the world's sweatshops and export zones. In addition, women play a key role in the informal sector – both in their role as employees (domestic workers and nannies), and as caretakers for children, the elderly and infirm.

Feminists have long argued that labor organizing must have a gender analysis. In the U.S. women played a key role in some of the early industrial unions, particularly in the clothing industry and in some craft unions like teaching and nursing. Women were also instrumental in efforts to expand unions to the public sector, and of course, women are overrepresented in today's growing low-wage service sector.

There are different schools of thought on organizing women workers. One school says that women have, on average, a different attitude toward labor unions, and prefer a collaborative rather than confrontational approach to dealing with management. Labor organizer Kris Rondeau states that this non-adversarial approach was the key to successful organizing drives amongst clerical workers at Harvard University (Hoerr 1997). Others see some weaknesses in Rondeau's non-confrontational model (Leary and Alonso 1997). First, it relies on a two-way relationship, and so if management is not willing to treat workers as equals, the model is less effective. Second, while it is beneficial to focus on issues such as dignity and respect, which Rondeau says are key, they might leave too many crucial issues off the table. Other scholars argue that many women workers are not so different than men, in terms of willingness to engage in confrontational and militant action. Furthermore, some of the feminist approaches to organizing advocated by Rondeau, such as one-on-one meetings, have been used extensively by male organizers in other settings.

The economist Naila Kabeer argues that most importantly, outsiders should not see women as passive victims (Kabeer 2000). Kabeer studied Bangladeshi Muslim women doing garment work in London and Dhaka. She found that while they shared the same gender, nationality, and religion, the context of the work was key to understanding the different ways in which the women and their families and communities understood their work. Not all women viewed their work in the same way, and some were able to resist or organize in ways that improved their conditions.

Because women have been at the forefront of some of the frontiers of "globalization," such as in their work in garment factories or as migrant domestic workers and nannies, there have been a number of useful studies on women workers, including books on garment workers or domestic workers in Sri Lanka, China, the Philippines, Thailand, Indonesia, Mexico, and even in global north countries including the U.S.[5] Most of the studies highlight common patterns: women are brought into factories or domestic work in their teens, sometimes at odds with domestic child labor laws. They have a range of experiences, but for the most part wages are low and working conditions are poor. For some women, the experience gives them a freedom they would not otherwise have had, because they get to leave their home villages and live in the cities and earn their own money. They can live in dorms with friends, and delay or avoid marriage. Some maintain independence and remain in the cities. Others send most of their money back to their families and are eager to return home. Again, as Kabeer points out, it is not helpful to generalize experiences to all women workers, and the women themselves may have contradictory or conflicted feelings about their work.

At the same time, there are some common material realities facing women workers. The United Nations made gender equality and women's empowerment one of their eight Millennium Development Goals because women are more likely to experience poverty than men, and less likely to have access to primary or secondary education (United Nations 2012). The ILO has several conventions relating to gender equality, including two of the core standards that prohibit discrimination and call for equal pay for equal work. Despite this attention, women, on average, still earn less than men around the world. According to the *OECD Factbook 2013*, "across all countries and all levels of education, women earn less than men, and that gap actually increases with more education" (OECD 2013: 256). The 2012/2013 Global Wage Report showed that the gender pay gap had closed in some places, but mostly "for the wrong reasons," such as stagnating or declining pay or hours worked for men (ILO 2013). Even in countries with a relatively strong women's movement, occupational segregation remains high in certain fields. Women face many barriers moving up career ladders and into positions of higher pay and authority.

Not all labor NGOs that organize women consider their models to be feminist, but many address women's needs. This includes work against sexual harassment in and outside of the workplace, opposition to forced pregnancy tests by employers, and promotion of employer-provided child care for those women with children.

Women also face challenges as workers in global supply chains. Barrientos et al. (2003) show in a study of fruit and horticultural supermarket suppliers that the global south workers are predominantly women, and predominantly in the informal sector. Even when there are corporate codes of conduct in place for supermarkets, the codes do little to address many of the issues relevant to these women workers. They suggest that there is a gendered value chain of products that rests on a "gender pyramid," with reproductive work at the bottom, informal employment in the middle, and formal employment at the top. Codes primarily address formal employment, where men form the majority of employees – in part because women's primary responsibility for reproductive work constrains their ability to work in the formal sector. The codes may even encourage employers to subcontract further, pushing more work into the informal and unregulated sector.

Moreover, as primary caregivers, women are also part of a "global care chain," as described by Arlie Hochschild (2000). Part of what has enabled massive numbers of women to enter the paid formal labor force in much of the world in the last few decades has been the availability of other women who could step in to take care of children and the elderly. The phenomenon of women hiring other women to do care work is not new, but this is increasingly a global trend, with women leaving their home countries to live for extended periods, often many years, elsewhere. These chains can involve multiple links, as women migrants often leave behind their own children or elderly parents who must be cared for by other women.

Clearly, unions need to develop ways to organize women workers. This is already happening to some degree, through worker NGOs, migrant organizing, and union revitalization efforts mentioned in chapter 7. Other efforts include new experiments in collective bargaining and in supply chain organizing, which are not exclusively organizing women, but may provide ways to address some of the key challenges for organizing women workers.

Expanding Collective Bargaining

Trade unions have historically relied on collective bargaining as a means to win better wages and working conditions for members.

But as unions have been under attack, so too has the right to engage in collective bargaining. At the same time, unions and worker organizations have attempted to expand the issues covered by collective bargaining in order to keep up with the changing economy and labor market, such as the efforts to cover migrant workers.[6] They are also experimenting with new strategies for bargaining that might be more effective when dealing with the informal sector or precarious workers, or with global employers and supply chains.

Bargaining is done differently according to industrial relations systems, and in some countries, it plays a minor role because conditions are more likely established through other channels (such as co-determination, national agreements, or legislation). As unions attempt to work together more across national borders, they will need to experiment with models that take account of different national practices, as well as models that could work in the global economy.

Unions can pursue a "voluntarist" model of bargaining – meaning that they directly pressure employers to bargain, and the parties agree to a contract.[7] Another model relies on the state to intervene by setting laws governing the collective bargaining process, or by playing a role in bargaining via tripartite structures. In addition, the state can play an active role, creating the structures that allow for bargaining such as authorizing or pushing to create a formal employer of record, or employer association. For example, in the U.S., many home care workers work in private homes, and while they work for a client or patient, they are ultimately paid through the state. However, in most cases, the agency that issues their paychecks does not have the authority to bargain with the workers. The SEIU helped pass legislation in several states that creates a bargaining authority, so that workers could join a union and engage in collective bargaining (Delp and Quan 2002).

These models may have important lessons for expanding bargaining to a global labor force that is increasingly precarious and where employer–employee relations are unclear. For example, the tripartite system of bargaining is what SEWA in India has used to raise wages for home-based workers. Employment relations differ for different types of work, but the three largest trades of SEWA members are bidi rollers, garment workers, and street vendors. The first two can be considered "dependent producers" meaning they work for a local shop, or for a contractor who then supplies to a small local producer. In both cases, the work is primarily done as home-based piecework. SEWA uses a range of organizing strategies, one of which is their trade-based approach. Members elect representatives to serve in the Trade Council (for three-year terms). There are also Trade Committees for the major trades that SEWA members work in. The Trade Committees work to improve conditions in the trade, much like a union might do. For example, the Trade Committee may push to raise piece rates and benefits, or establish a minimum wage for the industry. In some cases, this involves tripartite negotiations between the Trade Council, local government, and employer associations. Founder Ela Bhatt explains the challenges in organizing their members, who were not even initially considered to be workers under the law. In a 2004 interview she remarked:

> There are schedules for trades, and we demanded that they make schedules for our trade. For example, bidi [cigarette] workers had a schedule, but only for factory work. But 95 percent of bidi work was home-based, and of those 95 percent are women. We demanded that the minimum wage should apply to the home-based bidi work as well. We struggled to get them declared as workers, then covered by the minimum wage. We won that. Then slowly we got the wage raised – very slowly. Just now, after so many years are the wages rising.

SEWA won higher piece rates for bidi rollers from employers and contractors, and works to enforce the 1972 Bidi Workers Welfare Cess Act that provides services and benefits to workers paid for via a tax (or "cess") on bidis. SEWA also fights to make sure that employers contribute to worker funds, as mandated by the 1952 Employees Provident Fund Act (Cohen and Chen 2001). In this way, SEWA functions like a union, bargaining for workers who are "independent own account workers," such as street vendors. Even though the vendors have no employer, the police and local government affect their conditions of work. SEWA operates as a union, negotiating for the right to vend and securing protection from harassment.

These models might also be used where there are global employers. For example, union researcher Eric Dirnbach (2008) suggests that lessons from the early 1900s garment industry could have value today. He explains how garment workers had similar problems to those facing many home-based and informal sector workers today: the lack of clarity about who the employer was, and the need for power to extract better wages and working conditions from small contractors who themselves were constrained by their power vis-à-vis larger brands or retailers. The workers had to unionize, but also to force the establishment of an employers' association that set working conditions across the industry. This helped create an agent with which to bargain contracts, and set up a structure that allowed the union to bargain at the level where the most profit resided. Dirnbach argues that a similar strategy is necessary today on a global scale, to help unions bargain with employers' associations in the global garment industry.

In this vein, the Asia Floor Wage (AFW) campaign is an effort to unite unions and worker organizations across countries to pursue a range of strategies for improving wages and working conditions. One of the potential strategies is to develop multi-partner, multi-country collective bargaining. Small subcontractors in many global south countries usually do not have the resources to pay a higher wage to their workers, due to their position in global supply chains. Workers at the very bottom of this chain have little chance to improve their conditions unless some organized party is negotiating for fairer prices paid by the retailers and brands to their contractors. The AFW has explored avenues for bargaining directly with brands, pushing them to pay higher prices to select suppliers where there are unions or worker organizations in place to ensure the higher price translated into a higher wage. In 2011 the AFW announced that it was beginning discussions with Puma about implementing a pilot project in suppliers in three or four countries (Bhattarcharjee and Merk 2011).

In another example from Asia, a number of countries that send large numbers of migrant workers to the Gulf States have negotiated bilateral labor agreements to establish a minimum wage. Most Gulf States have no minimum wage laws, but are major importers of foreign labor. India and the Philippines were among the first countries to negotiate wage levels for domestic workers, and Nepal negotiated rates to cover all workers in the Gulf (Glass 2008; Ministry of Overseas Indian Affairs 2008). In 2012, India established an alliance with Bangladesh, Nepal, and Sri Lanka to coordinate wage rates together. A representative from the Manila-based Migration Forum Asia remarked, "Collective bargaining is a worker's right, so let's start it collectively from sending countries" (Joshi 2012). These agreements have weak enforcement mechanisms, but they suggest the potential collective action on behalf of migrant countries of origin vis-à-vis improving labor standards.

Supply Chain Organizing

Another avenue of new organizing that can connect workers across borders in common campaigns, including migrant and guest workers, is via supply chains – within a particular firm, or more broadly to supply chain relationships between several firms in an industry or industries.

Perhaps the largest example of organizing along the supply chain of a firm is Walmart. A number of organizations have built networks to pressure Walmart to improve wages and conditions for its direct employees and those working it its vast supplier and logistics network, linking workers in different countries and places in the supply chain. This includes coordinating efforts to block Walmart's expansion plans, as well as pushing Walmart to obey labor and employment laws for direct employees, and take responsibility for safe and legal working conditions for the subcontractors who produce for Walmart or transport and warehouse goods for the retailer. The network includes the following:

- The Warehouse Workers for Justice (WWJ) formed in 2009, as an independent worker center representing warehouse and logistics workers in Illinois. The United Electrical workers' union formed WWJ after their successful plant occupation at the Republic Windows and Doors factory. WWJ represents workers in a range of workplaces, some of which include warehouses that store goods for Walmart stores.

- The Change to Win labor federation formed Warehouse Workers United (WWU) in southern California in 2009, also to represent warehouse workers, including many who worked indirectly for Walmart.
- In 2011, Walmart associates in the U.S. formed OUR Walmart to demand better wages, working conditions and treatment for employees.
- The National Guestworkers Alliance (NGA), based in Louisiana, represents guest workers in a range of industries and sectors, including some seafood-processing workers employed by a Walmart subcontractor.
- The Bangladesh Center for Worker Solidarity (BCWS) was formed in the 1990s as part of an effort to form the first trade union in a factory producing garments for global retailers. The Center does not focus exclusively on Walmart, but over the years has been appealing to Walmart and other corporations to improve wages and working conditions in the companies they subcontract with in the country. Walmart is the largest single buyer of clothing from the company so has received particular attention.

In 2010, workers working for Walmart subcontractors approached the BCWS to request assistance fighting for better wages and conditions. The subcontractors then filed criminal charges against three BCWS leaders (Kalpona Akter, Babul Akhter and Aminul Islam), who were arrested and tortured for 30 days. Allies in the U.S., particularly the International Labor Rights Forum and Jobs with Justice, began pressuring Walmart to get the subcontractor and Bangladeshi government to drop the charges, and more than 110,000 people worldwide signed a petition in support of these demands. After they were out on bail, Kalpona Akter visited the U.S. and attended a Walmart shareholder meeting, hand-delivering the petitions, and calling on the company to end relations with two subcontractors (Claeson and Foxvog 2011).

In 2012, these organizations participated in various actions aimed at Walmart over several months. In June, the NGA worked with a small group of guest workers at C.J.'s Seafood, a company in Louisiana that packaged crawfish for Walmart. The workers, mostly from Mexico, were required to work long hours, sometimes shifts lasting 24 hours, without overtime pay. Managers occasionally locked workers in the facility and threatened to beat workers if they took more than five-minute breaks. The workers contacted NGA to fight back, and together, filed complaints with the U.S. Department of Labor, which led to a full investigation by the Worker Rights Consortium. On June 30, several workers travelled to New York City and held a 24-hour protest outside the home of a Walmart board member's apartment (Garza 2012). In July, the Department of Labor ordered C.J.'s to pay workers $76,608 in back pay for wage and hour violations, plus approximately $170,000 in fines for violations, including serious safety issues and "willful H-2B violations" (Greenhouse 2012b). The NGA released a list of 644 federal violations at C.J.'s and 12 other Walmart suppliers. Walmart announced it would drop C.J.'s as a supplier, which would threaten the workers with deportation – but the federal government granted them special U-visas, used for victims of serious crimes. With the new visas, the former C.J.'s workers joined NGA organizers to visit labor camps across the Gulf Coast to meet with other Walmart supply chain workers (Patrick-Knox 2012).

In September 2012, warehouse workers took strike action in southern California. This group is employed by Warestaff, a temporary labor agency working on a contract with NFI – a logistics company that operates warehouses for Walmart goods. Workers went on strike over low wages, poor benefits, and dangerous working conditions (Jamieson 2012). Walmart initially declined any responsibility in the case, but after a 15-day strike and a six-day 50-mile march by strikers, Walmart announced that they would develop a mechanism to conduct random inspections at subcontractors, and review contract reviews. In addition, the employer agreed to improve safety standards.

At the same time, another group of warehouse workers, employed by Walmart-contracted Roadlink Warehouse Solutions in Elwood, Illinois, filed a lawsuit against their employer for wage theft. The company retaliated, and fired two workers, including one of the plaintiffs in the case. The workers went on strike claiming unfair labor practices. After 21 days, the employer agreed to stop retaliation, rehire those that were fired and to give back pay to striking workers. They also won some improvements in working conditions, such as ceiling fans and shin guards (Bradbury 2012).

The strikes spread, and by October, warehouse workers in 12 states had gone on strike (Greenhouse 2012b). In addition, retail workers at the stores went on a one-day strike too. Warehouse strikes continued through the fall, and on the day after Thanksgiving (known as "Black Friday"), OUR Walmart called a one-day nationwide walkout at stores. Pickets of workers and labor and community supporters took place in 100 cities (Eidelson 2012).

The day after Black Friday, a large fire broke out in a garment factory in Bangladesh, killing 112 workers. The factory produced for a number of large retailers, including Walmart. Walmart activists went into action calling on the retailer to take responsibility for the safety standards in the plant. On December 6, 2012, activists created an informational picket line in Port Elizabeth, New Jersey, in an attempt to stop workers from unloading a ship carrying garments produced for Walmart in Bangladesh. Although the cargo was unloaded, the action raised awareness of the fire in Bangladesh and connection to the U.S. Two days later, a similar picket was held in Charleston, South Carolina, when the same ship reached that port. In that case, rank-and-file members of the International Longshoreman's Association honored the picket line, refusing to enter the port to unload cargo for over two hours (Longshore and Shipping News 2012).

In May 2013, Walmart retail workers launched a period of "prolonged strikes" and a caravan of workers from 30 cities converged at the shareholders meeting in Bentonville, Arkansas. There, a striking worker and an activist from Bangladesh addressed the shareholders to raise issues of worker rights in the U.S. and abroad (Eidelson 2013).

In addition to this activity, organizations also collaborated in 2010 and 2011 to support trade unions in South Africa that were attempting to block the country from approving Walmart's entry into the country via a merger with a domestic retailer. The United Food and Commercial Workers helped coordinate international support from unions and labor experts in Argentina, Chile, Germany, and the U.S. to provide testimony to the South African Competitions Commission. In the end, the Commission allowed the merger, but the organizations were able to strengthen ties through this work, and the Commission ordered that 503 workers laid off in the merger be reinstated. Similarly, groups worked together across borders in an effort to block Walmart from entering India. Opponents engaged in protests in 2011, resulting in a temporary reprieve. But in the fall of 2012, Prime Minister Manmohan Singh announced that the country would allow foreign investors to hold a majority share of businesses in the country, setting the stage for Walmart to enter. On September 21, 2012, activists called a national strike, and thousands of small shopkeepers closed their doors in protest (Badkar 2012; *Washington Post* 2012).

An example of supply chain organizing more broadly in an industry can be seen with food workers. The U.S.-based Food Chain Workers Alliance was formed in 2009 by nine organizations, including ROC United, the International Labor Rights Forum, Coalition of Immokalee Workers, the Center for New Community, el Comité de Apoyo a los Trabajadores Agrícolas, and the Northwest Arkansas Workers' Justice Center. A number of other organizations, including a few labor unions, have since joined. All members represent farm workers, food warehousing or transportation workers, or food service employees. According to the Alliance, about 20 million people work in the food system in the U.S. While these are primarily U.S.-based groups, many represent immigrant workers, and some also work with international partners. According to their mission statement, "The Alliance works together to build a more sustainable food system that respects workers' rights, based on the principles of social, environmental and racial justice, in which everyone has access to healthy and affordable food" (Food Chain Workers Alliance n.d.). The Alliance works to provide leadership training, engage in policy efforts (such as fighting for minimum wage enforcement and increases), and support specific campaigns.

There are also efforts to engage in food worker supply chain organizing outside of the U.S., such as the campaigns mentioned earlier to target the relations between suppliers and the "big four" grocery stores in the U.K., and relations between other EU grocery chains and suppliers of meat, produce, and flowers in Africa and Asia. Activists and unions pushed EU commissions and politicians to address the issue, and in 2008, the EU Parliament passed a declaration calling on the European Commission to address the "abuse of power" exercised by large supermarkets (Vander Stichele and Young 2009).

In India, coalitions of activists have protested the passage of an India–EU Free Trade Agreement on a number of grounds, including concerns that the FTA would have a negative impact on both small-scale food producers in India, and the ability of the Indian state to enact and enforce legislation to guarantee all citizens the Right to Food (Ganesh 2011). Labor unions have joined with civil society organizations, NGOs and other activists to promote the campaign. Their view is that providing the right to food for all Indians is not only a matter of domestic concern, but relates to the larger trends of neoliberal reform that have exacerbated poverty and worsened conditions for small farmers.

Using Trade Law to Promote Worker Rights

Most of the neoliberal free trade agreements have little protection for worker rights, and those that do have only weak protections. But there are some cases where preferential trade agreements have been used to improve or enforce labor standards. For example, the U.S. established the US-Cambodia Bilateral Textile Agreement in 1999. Unlike most trade agreements, this one allowed Cambodia to increase its quotas of garment exports to the U.S., based on making progress improving labor standards. Working with the AFL-CIO and the union UNITE, the United States Trade Representative's (USTR) office created an agreement that would reward Cambodia for making improvements in certain areas of labor rights. The ILO inspected factories based on a set of criteria, and then certified those that participated and passed the expectations. Factories that were certified were eligible for increased quotas. After a few years, unions grew in the garment sector, and average wages increased. However, the program ended in 2005, when WTO rules ended the preferential quotas. The program has re-emerged as the Better Factories Cambodia program. While there are no longer preferential quotas, the ILO and U.S. continue to give resources to fund ILO inspectors, conduct worker rights trainings, and certify factories that participate in the program.

U.S. unions and NGOs have also worked in collaboration with unions in Central America to use U.S. trade law as a form of leverage to get labor laws enforced. The United States Trade Act establishes a Generalized System of Preferences (GSP), which allows the U.S. to designate particular countries as a beneficiary developing country, thereby allowing that country reduced or no tariffs on selected items. Countries can be ruled ineligible for the program for a variety of reasons, including if a "country has not taken or is not taking steps to afford internationally recognized worker rights to workers in the country (including any designated zone in that country)."[8] If a country is believed to be in non-compliance, organizations can file a petition with the USTR calling for suspension or removal of the GSP status.

In 1999, Bandegua, a Del Monte subsidiary in Guatemala, notified 900 banana plantation workers that they were being laid off due in part to pressure from large buyers like Walmart to reduce costs. The workers were members of the union SITRABI, which protested the layoffs as a violation of their collective bargaining agreement. The union enlisted the support of the ministry of labor, but the company refused to negotiate. A few weeks later, 200 armed men came and surrounded SITRABI leaders in the union office. They threatened to kill the leaders if they didn't resign and leave the area. The leaders left and made an urgent appeal for international solidarity, including contacting the AFL-CIO and an NGO called USLEAP, which connected U.S. and Guatemalan unionists.[9] The AFL-CIO filed a GSP petition focused on the SITRABI case and the USTR scheduled a hearing on the case. The Guatemalan government responded by scheduling a trial for 24 people accused of involvement in the violent intimidation, and promising to provide heavy security for witnesses in the trial. When the trial took place, 22 of the 24 accused were found guilty. Likely due to various forms of international pressure, including the GSP, the union leaders returned to their positions, 650 of the workers got their jobs back, and the union fought most of the wage and benefit cuts (Luce 2005).

Not everyone supports the GSP strategy, as some claim U.S. unions have used it unilaterally for protectionist reasons.[10] The AFL-CIO states that it learned from its past mistakes and now only files GSP petitions where there is a partner organization that wants to work with them in the other country (Luce 2005). The Guatemala case came after at least 10 years of building trust and relations between Guatemalan and U.S. unions and NGOs. Similar relations were built with unions in other Central American countries, and the GSP was one tool used in cross-border solidarity efforts.[11] The GSP no longer applies to Guatemala after passage of the Central American Free Trade Agreement (CAFTA), though it still applies to dozens of other countries.

Some scholars feel the U.S. trade model, even with labor standards, is not the best way to improve conditions for workers in global south countries for reasons listed in chapter 3. For example, a number of studies find that developing countries experience more positive impacts on a number of indicators through trade with other developing countries (south–south trade), than they do from trade with global north countries (Dahi and Demir 2012; Dutt 2012). In this case, constructing a fair and effective trade agreement between southern countries may be a far more effective way for them to create jobs and improve labor standards than inserting worker rights in north–south trade agreements.

Moving Forward: The Need to Experiment

Most of these new directions are relatively embryonic, and have yet to make a significant impact on the labor movement. Some are within the bounds of traditional trade unions, but many move into new territory. Which ones will succeed? It is not clear, but what is important is the need to expand the experiments. Indeed, a growing number of scholars see these sorts of efforts as key to labor's revival.

For example, historian Dorothy Sue Cobble (1997) studied the early days of the AFL and the CIO to show how labor organizations experimented with types of expansion. In the late 1800s and early 1900s, the AFL worked on both the national and local levels. While continuing to build itself as a federation, AFL organizers were encouraged to enroll members directly into new Locals that were not affiliated with an International, but chartered directly with the AFL. Any group of seven or more workers were allowed to petition for a federal union charter, including many who self-organized. This greatly lowered the bar to unionization that many workers would have faced trying to organize through existing Internationals, where they faced strict jurisdiction or membership requirements. From its formation in 1886 to the merger with the CIO in 1955, the AFL chartered approximately 20,000 of these directly affiliated Locals. Similarly, the CIO experimented with different structures as it developed, with craft union models existing side-by-side with new industrial union models for about 20 years, from 1933 to 1955. Cobble argues that both the AFL and CIO grew more rapidly in the periods in which they were more open to experiments and flexible structures. She asserts that such flexibility is necessary (though not sufficient) if unions want to grow again, and that unions do best "when every part of the union structure – International, local, central body, and federation – was empowered to become a center of organizing and innovation" (Cobble 1997: 441).

Sociologist Dan Clawson makes a similar argument regarding the notion of "upsurges" in the labor movement. Clawson (2003) asserts that new models must be a fusion of different kinds of social movements, including the labor movement, women's movement, immigrant rights, and others – transforming each of these in the process, resulting in a qualitative shift in what a labor movement does and is. This will take much experimentation, and will result in lots of failure – but ideally, organizers can turn these into what political scientist Eve Weinbaum (2004) terms "successful failures": campaigns that may lose their immediate objectives but build the foundation for a larger movement and more sweeping victories.

The way that the labor movement will revitalize in the next decade will require experimentation with different forms of organization, deep collaboration with other social movements, and flexibility of current union leaders, including knowing when to step aside to let independent and grassroots movements flourish. When union members and community activists flooded the Capitol building in Madison, Wisconsin in 2011 to protest impending legislation by Governor Scott Walker, they did so without first consulting national union or political party leaders. AFL-CIO president Richard Trumka himself noted that the members were ahead of the leadership, and the best thing for union leaders to do would be to get out of the way (Luce 2011). That is not to suggest that union leadership has no role in transforming today's labor movement. Indeed, Cobble's work shows that the periods of growth in the early AFL and CIO days included aggressive organizing projects led by the national federations. The challenge is to balance different experiments in a way that is complementary. Sociologist Peter Evans argues that neoliberalism has created new structural opportunities for labor organizing, but there is not one key strategic response. Rather, organizers must build interconnected approaches at the national and international levels, linking traditional unions and federations that are more vertical, with networks of NGOs and civil society organizations that are more horizontal and flexible (Evans 2010). In a promising development, the AFL-CIO approved at its 2013 Convention a proposal to allow non-union workers to join its ranks.

The Prospects for a More Inclusive Global Labor Movement

The world has changed dramatically in the last 30 years. Corporations have more power and workers have less. Labor unions still have a crucial role to play, as they are one of the few forces able to counter the impacts of neoliberalism and employer power. But to do this, they must address a host of internal problems and be more strategic in order to increase their capacity to address external challenges.

Historically, many unions won gains for members through excluding others and controlling the labor supply. This was easiest to do when they had access to scarce skills or were functioning in a tight labor market. But with neoliberalism, employers have more power to move jobs between regions and countries. Even when jobs cannot be moved easily, such as in education or health care, employers have more power to bring in new workers, using guest worker programs or "flexible arrangements" with independent contractors.

Unions must reframe their struggles as broader movements for civil rights or democracy, as the UFW did in California or as labor movements did in South Africa and Brazil. An inclusionary movement representing vulnerable or marginal workers may have less structural power, but may find other avenues to win – either by connecting with other unions that do have structural power, or building alliances with segments of society who can exercise social power and impede employers or politicians from carrying out "business as usual." Broader inclusionary worker movements might also rely on advocacy power – working with allies who have the power to persuade elites to make changes.

While these kinds of power can win gains, movements must be vigilant to keep workers in the heart of any campaign. Just as Ganz found with the UFW, having leaders from the affected community increases access to salient information, leverage, and the motivation to win. When workers are true leaders, they increase the capacity of their organization to engage in militant action and enforce any gains they might achieve.

We cannot discount the role of allies in struggles, as they can bring new resources and capacity to a movement. And where possible, unions should reframe their own workplace issues as broader societal issues. Unions must work to organize women and people of color, not just to increase membership but because a divided workforce hurts all workers. Consumers should worry about sweatshop conditions in garment factories not just for moral concerns, but because when corporations are allowed to profit off of workers, social well-being is diminished. Unions reduce inequality and make economies more stable; they can also lead to more transparent and effective government. If corporations have enough power to break unions and violate labor laws in one country, it enhances their power and makes them more likely to do the same in any country.

A renewed focus on union organizing is not enough. This is an important step but must be pursued within a broader strategy of building power in the global economy. That means finding ways to directly curtail the growing power of corporations, not just from a union perspective, but also from an international labor movement perspective. For example, the "great doubling" means that there are far more people in the labor force relative to the number of living wage jobs. Labor movements must fight to create new paid employment *and* reduce people's reliance on jobs for survival. With historic levels of migration, unions have made progress in fighting for fair immigration policy and opening their doors to immigrants, but they need to address the root causes of migration, including the role of destructive foreign policy. Labor movements must focus on job creation and economic development in all countries so that workers have the right *not* to migrate: the right to stay in their home communities and find living wage work. Unions cannot only focus on the way in which exports and trade agreements affect jobs at home: they must also fight the entire logic of neoliberal trade agreements that aim to deregulate markets and downsize the public sector. With an expansion of their global operations and supply chains, employers have more power to shift production quickly from plant to plant, thereby weakening workers' power on the shopfloor. Unions must build strategic alliances across corporate supply chains, even across borders, and learn to see that their own powers, and interests, are intertwined.

Financialization has strengthened the hand of investors, giving them more leverage in the tug-of-war with policymakers over regulatory constraints. Labor movements must try to counter these trends by supporting the reregulation of finance, perhaps financing investment and capital formation through a different model altogether. Dan Clawson (2003) asserts the most effective strategies will be those that challenge the boundaries of existing laws and regulations. In most countries, and certainly in the international arena, laws are not set up to favor worker organization or rights. Challenging those regulations and fighting for new ones most certainly will involve breaking through today's legal limitations.

The challenge may seem insurmountable, but history shows that prior movements have succeeded in winning long-term global campaigns for worker rights against even greater odds. Perhaps the best example is the international movement to abolish the transatlantic slave trade in the 1700s and 1800s. That movement involved a wide range of actors exercising various forms of power and pursuing a wide range of strategies. One key ingredient was the constant resistance from enslaved people themselves, both on a daily basis but also in coordinated uprisings – most notably in St Domingue (now Haiti), where a revolt began in 1791 against France, then Britain and Spain. The war was brutal but ultimately successful in ending slavery and establishing independence for the new country in 1804.

The fight against slavery also involved a 50-year consumer boycott in England of sugar harvested by slave labor. Abolitionists in England, the U.S., France, and Russia used petition drives, education and speaking tours, and political rallies to pressure legislatures to outlaw the slave trade. They wrote letters to their own governments and pressured rulers of other countries. Religious groups, particularly the Quakers, preached the moral sins of slave labor. Abolitionists and former slaves travelled across borders to coordinate campaigns and build support for their movement, and they brought the issue to the international diplomatic meeting, the Congress of Vienna, in 1814–15, where they secured agreement from all participating governments to abolish the slave trade (Klotz 2002; Hochschild 2005). The movement involved reformers and revolutionaries, trade unionists and enslaved workers, the "organized" and the "unorganized." Some abolitionists were concerned only about slavery; others tied the issue to universal suffrage, democratic reform, racism, and human rights. There were endless debates about tactics and strategy, many ups and downs in the movement, and hundreds of thousands of people lost their lives. In some moments, the struggle was a basic fight for freedom for an enslaved worker. In others, it was a global debate about the nature and morality of economic systems.

Today, the slave trade has been abolished but we still are debating the morality of our global economic system. Three global economic crises of the last 100 years each opened space for intensified debate about the economic and political model that should serve as the foundation for our societies. Workers have been part of those debates in the past, and need to be part today. Unions represent one of the most likely vehicles for highlighting workers' voices and asserting that worker rights, equality, and economic justice are central components of a new model or models. Employers are organized and attempting to assert their own vision; unions have been slow to step in.

On the other hand, workers have been resisting neoliberalism from its early days. Recently, protests have intensified around the world: the Arab Spring, students in Chile and Montreal, anti-austerity fights across the EU, teachers' strike and occupation in Mexico, and Occupy Wall Street or Occupy-like movements in Brazil, Turkey, and elsewhere. While there is great variation in the context and demands, these protests share some common themes: the call for greater democracy and less inequality, greater political transparency and accountability on behalf of the public good. Defeating neoliberalism is a necessary – if not sufficient – prerequisite to achieving these goals.

Unions have joined these protests in some places, and occasionally played a key role. But they must do more to integrate into a broader movement for democracy and equality. Unions must renew old debates about their role in society, and take seriously the need to build post-capitalist economic and political models. This might require rethinking work altogether, so that people are not dependent on a job for survival. Unions cannot survive if they stick to a narrow self-definition of raising wages for themselves, or continue to understand globalization as a competition between nations. Indeed, globalization itself is not the problem, and can in fact bring great benefits to workers. A global economy requires a global labor movement, and the time to build one is now.

Notes

1. Introduction

1 The informal economy consists of self-employed workers, who work in small, unincorporated enterprises, as well as people who are employed in formal enterprises but in an informal relationship. See Hussmanns (2004) and Chen and Vanek (2013) for a fuller discussion of the definition of the term.

2 Extreme poverty is measured as equivalent to earning less than U.S.$1.25 per day. Poverty is earning less than U.S.$2.50 per day.

3 There are challenges to data collection. Countries have different ways of measuring union membership. In some, union density refers to total union members as a share of the total workforce. In others, density is membership as a share of those workers eligible to join unions. In a number of countries, there is a large difference between the number of workers who belong to a union, and the number of workers covered by a union contract or union-negotiated standards. In countries with a large informal sector, union density as a share of the formal workforce may grossly overestimate the reach of unions.

4 The authors caution against generalizing their findings too broadly, as it is difficult to isolate the impacts of labor standards and bargaining from other macroeconomic effects. In addition, they note that the effects of collective bargaining systems may have been stronger in the 1960s and 1970s but have weakened since the 1990s.

5 Economist Ha-joon Chang has described how rich countries became rich through a variety of government interventions, including the kinds of high tariffs and "infant industry" protections that Argentina practiced. In modern times, the rich countries have enacted trade agreements and regulations that attempt to prohibit poor countries from employing these same strategies, on the grounds that they are anti-free market and free trade (Chang 2008).

6 For example, Panitch and Gindin (2012) write that U.S. financial markets in fact remain "almost certainly the most highly regulated markets in history, if regulation is measured by volume (number of pages) of rules, probably also if measured by extent of surveillance, and possibly even by vigour of enforcement" (p. 267).

7 Cook (2010) observes that the increase in formal labor rights, alongside a weakened labor movement in practice, is true for most of eastern and central European countries. The exception is Slovenia. On the other hand, Burgess (2010) examines Latin American countries and finds no correlation between flexibility and standards. Many countries have increased de facto flexibility, even though the laws in place vary quite a bit and are good in some places.

2. A Role for Unions?

1 Since 1983, membership rates for men have been cut in half, from 24.7 percent to 12 percent. For women, density in that same period fell from 14.6 percent to 10.5 percent (Bureau of Labor Statistics 2013).

2 For 2012, the union density rates by race and gender were: black men 14.8%; black women 12.3%; white men 11.9%; white women 10.2%; Hispanic men 10.1%; Hispanic women 9.6%; Asian men 8.9%; Asian women 10.4% (Bureau of Labor Statistics 2013).

3 The Network offers several words of caution about their data: the definition of union member varies by country; some data is out of date; some countries do not collect or report this data. See http://www.newunionism.net/State_of_the_Unions.htm#notes.

3. Why Unions Decline: External Challenges on the Macro Level

1 California then passed a law outlawing the use of public monies on union-busting activities (Logan 2006).

2 Data is from UNCTAD Global Investment Reports for 1994 (the first year with available data) and 2012. The total number of companies and affiliates represents the totals reported in the report, but the total is comprised of the most recently available data for each country.

3 The proportion of employees employed by these firms as a percentage of the global non-agricultural labor force has dropped from 10 percent in 1994 to about 6 percent in 2011. This is due to the massive increase in the labor force in Asia in this period.

4 From 1973 to 2004, the Multi Fibre Arrangement (MFA) governed trade in textiles and garments. It established trade quotas for countries in an effort to assure developing countries access to global markets. With the creation of

the WTO, the MFA was eliminated, on the grounds that it provided special treatment to developing countries. As the MFA was phased out, manufacturers were able to consolidate – particularly in China.

5 Firms can also exercise monopsony power as the single purchasers of labor. Labor economist Alan Manning (2003) has argued that today's retail markets are dominated by a few large firms that have the power to set wages in labor markets (as opposed to a labor market where wages are set through supply and demand).

6 There are many difficulties in getting consistent data on global financial activity, as this requires adjusting for prices, exchange rates, and balance of payments between countries, in addition to the usual challenges of inconsistent measures across countries. See Dunning and Lundan (2008).

7 The six directives are: the Employment Contract Directive of 1991, Pregnant Workers Directive of 1992, Working Time Directive of 1993, Young Workers Directive of 1994, Parental Leave Directive of 1996, and Part-time Work Directive of 1997.

8 Another model is the Caribbean Community (CARICOM), created in 1973. In 1994, the participating nations passed a Charter of Civil Society which provides for a fairly strong commitment to human rights, including worker and trade union rights. The Charter creates a dispute mechanism that allows anyone to file a complaint against a state or a private actor, though it relies on a model more similar to the ILO: moral pressure and public shaming to obtain compliance.

9 Another alternative is the Alternatives to Neoliberalism in Southern Africa Initiative, established by South African and Zimbabwean unions and labor organizations in 2003. Not an official trade agreement, this "non-partisan facilitation project" promotes regional collaboration designed specifically to challenge neoliberal models of development in the quest for "human-centered development" (Makanza 2011).

10 http://www.ilo.org/global/about-the-ilo/history/lang--en/index.htm.

11 The AFL-CIO has lobbied for such dispute resolution mechanisms in the U.S. FTAs.

4. Adding to Further Decline: Labor Market Changes

1 Not her real name. This example comes from a visit by the author to Ahmedebad, India. This interview took place on December 28, 2004.

2 Not her real name. This example is a composite of several workers interviewed in New York City in October 2012. Details of the study are provided in Luce and Fujita (2012).

3 This example is a composite of experiences documented by Pun Ngai and other researchers who wrote a study on the Foxconn factory. This material is based on a presentation by Pun Ngai on October 16, 2010.

5. Changing from Within

1 http://www.opensecrets.org/orgs/list.php?order%BCA.
2 An independent fact-checking group, PolitiFact.com, tried to verify what the unions actually spent in the election. They were not able to confirm an exact amount, although the $400 million number was widely reported in the press. www.politifact.com/truth-o-meter/statements/2011/mar/15/republican-national-committee-republican/rnc-said-unions-raised-400-million-obama-2008.
3 See Chang Hee Lee and Liu Mingwei (2011) for more on labor laws passed since 1992.

6. Union Power

1 Some activists have made deliberate choices to enter jobs in strategic sectors, such as groups of activists that "industrialized" in the 1970s, taking jobs in key sectors with the goal of building political movements amongst their co-workers. These activists had a theory that politicizing rank-and-file union members could revitalize the labor movement and turn it in a more progressive direction (Moody 2000).
2 There is not a consistent source of data on strike activity, and countries differ in the type of data they collect – even within country. For example, in the U.S., the Bureau of Labor Statistics collects data on "work stoppages" involving 1,000 workers or more, lasting at least one shift. Therefore, there is no data on strikes in smaller workplaces. Furthermore, the data does not distinguish between strikes and lockouts. Canada reports stoppages affecting 500 workers or more. Data from Mexico is only for strikes, but with no size limit.
3 Four countries show no change over the time period. The remaining 11 countries or territories show an increase in activity, with a median increase of approximately 38 percent.
4 Some unionists in the 1980s and 1990s attempted to develop labor–management partnership programs, to cooperate with employers in a way that would ideally bring benefits to both sides: higher productivity for employers and job security for workers. Some of these efforts continue today, although research shows that for the most part, the benefits from cooperative programs accrued primarily to employers. Mike Parker and Jane Slaughter (1995) term the programs "management-by-stress" as they often resulted in speed-up, deskilling and increased managerial surveillance.
5 There was considerable political debate about the purpose and use of the general strike, with anarchists advocating that the general strike would be a way to overthrow capitalism, while some socialists and social democrats argued the general strike could be used for wining reforms.

7. Rebuilding the Movements

1 These include California, Connecticut, Illinois, Iowa, Kansas, Maryland, Massachusetts, New Hampshire, New Jersey, New York, North Dakota, Oregon, and the District of Columbia. For some states, this only covers teachers, and in Oklahoma it only covers municipal employees (Gely and Chandler 2011).

2 Schlecker filed for bankruptcy and closed all its German stores in 2012.

3 Dr Martin Luther King Jr. was in Memphis when he was assassinated; he was there to lend support to sanitation workers striking for the right to unionize and collectively bargain.

4 There is some evidence that union density is declining in some countries as the Ghent system erodes, as with Finland, where new independent unemployment insurance programs have developed since the 1990s (Böckerman and Uusitalo 2006). But the relationship between Ghent systems and unionization still appears strong.

5 Legal scholar Matthew Dimick (2012) argues that since the U.S. Social Security Act provides states enough power to run their own unemployment insurance programs, and the language of the Act is flexible enough to allow such a program, U.S. unions could pursue a strategy of implementing a Ghent system under a progressive state government.

6 The proposals emphasize payments to individuals rather than households on the assumption that this provides greater independence for women, who otherwise may be subject to men's decisions about how to spend the money.

7 http://www.mondragon-corporation.com/language/en-US/ENG.aspx.

8 There are other forms of cooperatives, such as producer and consumer cooperatives, which are far more extensive than worker cooperatives. http://usworker.coop/about/what-is-a-worker-coop

9 http://ica.coop/en/what-co-op/history-co-operative-movement.

10 Within a few weeks, the company was sold to Serious Materials, and some of the workers got their jobs back. But four years later, Serious announced it would close too. Workers engaged in another occupation and got the company to stay open for another 90 days. In the meantime, the workers raised funds to form a unionized workers' cooperative.

11 The boycott first began as a boycott of the Schenley Liquor Company – the largest landholder in the San Joaquin Valley. The boycott worked, and Schenley signed a collective bargaining agreement with the union. The union then expanded the boycott to all table grapes.

8. New Directions – Going Global

1 The Global Unions were previously called International Trade Secretariats (ITSs). With the development of the WTO and a growing global economy and international campaigns in the 1990s, unions felt the need to restructure, and in 2000, the ITSs were revitalized into GUFs, and then into Global Unions (Fairbrother and Hammer 2005).

2 Blin was with the International Federation of Chemical, Energy, Mine and General Workers Union (ICEM). In 2012, the ICEM merged with two other GUFs to create the mega-Global Union IndustriALL.

3 The H-2A visa is issued to temporary or seasonal agricultural workers. Employers must meet several requirements to hire workers under the H-2A program. They must show that they made an active effort to hire U.S. citizens first but could not find enough workers. They must also agree to pay prevailing wages and provide housing. See http://www.foreignlaborcert.doleta. gov/h-2a.cfm for more information.

4 UFCW press release, http://www.ufcw.ca/index.php?option=com_content& view=article&id=674&catid=5&Itemid=99&lang=en.

5 For example, Chang (2000), Parreñas (2001), Pun (2005), Hondagneu-Sotelo (2007), Lynch (2007) and the edited volume by Ehrenreich and Hochschild (2004).

6 Hayter et al. (2011) conducted a survey of unions and collective bargaining agreements in over 30 countries and confirmed that the scope of issues covered under bargaining has expanded.

7 For example, the Swedish industrial relations system is built on a "voluntarist" framework (Hayter et al. 2011).

8 United States Trade Act. United States Code Online via GPO Access. http://frwebgate.access.gpo.gov/cgi-bin/getdoc.cgi?dbname=browse_usc&do cid=Cite:+19USC2462 (accessed September 30, 2008).

9 At the time, USLEAP was known as US/GLEP – U.S./Guatemala Labor Education Project.

10 This is also true for other measures to address labor standards. In particular, the Child Labor Deterrence Act of 1993, also known as the "Harkin Bill," established a ban on imports to the United States from countries that use child labor. This Bill received wide criticism in Bangladesh because it didn't address the root causes of child labor – poverty and poor schools. Instead, it ended up forcing children out of work with no options for them or their families (e.g., Rahman et al. 1999).

11 However, the AFL-CIO, along with 14 industrial unions, has filed numerous unilateral petitions against China, under Section 301(d) of the Trade Act, claiming the country engages in unfair trade due to violations of labor and human rights. This approach has been criticized heavily by Chinese labor scholars such as Anita Chan, who see it as misguided and damaging to international labor solidarity (Chan 2010).

References

Ahn, Pong Sul. 2010. "The Growth and Decline of Political Unionism in India: The Need for a Paradigm Shift." ILO DWT for East and South-East Asia and the Pacific. Bangkok: International Labour Organization.

Aidt, Toke and Zafiris Tzannatos. 2002. *Unions and Collective Bargaining: Economic Effects in a Global Environment*. Washington, DC: The World Bank.

Alam, Julhus. 2012. "Bangladesh Factory Fire: Disney, Sears Used Factory in Blaze that Killed More Than 100 Workers." Associated Press, November 28.

Alarcón-González, Diana and Terry McKinley. 1999. "The Adverse Effects of Structural Adjustment on Working Women in Mexico." *Latin American Perspectives* 26(3): 103–17.

American Federation of Teachers. 2012. "Recruiting Firm that Brought Filipino Teachers to Louisiana Ordered to Pay \$4.5 Million in Damages for Exploitive Practices." Press Release, December 18. http://www.aft.org/newspubs/press/2012/121812.cfm

Anker, Richard. 2011. "Estimating a Living Wage: A Methodological Review." Conditions of Work and Employment Series No. 29. Geneva: International Labour Organization.

Applebaum, Richard and Nelson Lichtenstein. 2006. "A New World of Retail Supremacy: Supply Chains and Workers' Chains in the Age of Wal-Mart." *International Labor and Working-Class History* 70(1): 106–25.

Armbruster-Sandoval, Ralph. 2005. *Globalization and Cross-Border Labor Solidarity in the Americas*. New York: Routledge.

Arnold, Dennis. 2006. "Free Trade Agreements and Southeast Asia." *Journal of Contemporary Asia* 36(2): 195–216.

Associated Press. 2002a. "German Union Starts Two-Day Strike at Wal-Mart Stores in Germany." July 26.

Associated Press. 2002b. "Wal-Mart Sells Milk & Butter Below Cost Hurts

Competition: German Court." November 12. http://www.mindfully.org/ WTO/Wal-Mart-German-Court12nov02.htm

Associated Press. 2012. "Half of Recent College Grads Underemployed or Jobless, Analysis Says." April 23. http://www.cleveland.com/business/index. ssf/2012/04/half_of_recent_college_grads_u.html

Association for Union Democracy. 2002. "AUD's Union Democracy Benchmarks." Updated August 12, 2002.

Atzeni, Maurizio and Pablo Ghigliani. 2007. "Labour Process and Decision-making in Factories under Workers' Self-Management: Empirical Evidence from Argentina." *Work, Employment and Society* 21(4): 653–71.

Baccaro, Lucio. 2008. "Labour, Globalization and Equality: Are Trade Unions Still Redistributive?" International Institute for Labour Studies. Geneva.

Badkar, Mamta. 2012. "Huge Protests Erupt in India over Latest Economics Plan." *Business Insider*, September 20. http://www.businessinsider.com/ indian-protests-fdi-wal-mart-fuel-subsidies-23-billion-2012-9

Ballinger, Jeff. 2009. "Finding an Anti-Sweatshop Strategy That Works." *Dissent* 56(3): 5–8.

Bank Munoz, Carolina. 2008. *Transnational Tortillas: Race, Gender and Shop-floor Politics in Mexico and the United States*. Ithaca, NY: Cornell University Press.

Barrientos, Stephanie and Sally Smith. 2007. "Do Workers Benefit from Ethical Trade? Assessing Codes of Labour Practice in Global Production Systems." *Third World Quarterly* 28(4): 713–29.

Barrientos, Stephanie, Catherine Dolan and Anne Tallontire. 2003. "A Gendered Value Chain Approach to Codes of Conduct in African Horticulture." *World Development* 31(9): 1511–26.

Basic Income Grant Coalition. 2009. "Making the Difference! The BIG in Namibia. Basic Income Grant Pilot Project Assessment Report." Namibia NGO Forum. http://www.bignam.org/Publications/BIG_Assessment_report_08b.pdf

Behrens, Martin. 2009. "Still Married after All These Years? Union Organizing and the Role of Works Councils in German Industrial Relations." *Industrial and Labor Relations Review* 62(3): 275–93.

Benclowicz, José Daniel. 2011. "Continuities, Scope, and Limitations of the Argentine Piquetero Movement: The Cases of Tartagal and Mosconi." *Latin American Perspectives* 38(1): 74–87.

Bender, Daniel E. 2004. *Sweated Work, Weak Bodies: Anti-Sweatshop Campaigns and Languages of Labor*. New Brunswick, NJ: Rutgers University Press.

Berg, Andrew G. and Jonathan D. Ostry. 2011. "Inequality and Unsustainable Growth: Two Sides of the Same Coin?" Research Department, International Monetary Fund, April 8.

Bhatt, Ela. 2004. Interview with the author. Ahmedebad, India, December 28.

Bhattacharjee, Anannya and Jeroen Merk. 2011. "Road Map to an Asia Floor Wage: 10 Steps Brands and Retailers Can Take Toward Implementing a

Minimum Living Wage." Report on behalf of the Asia Floor Wage Steering Committee, May.

Birchall, Johnston and Lou Hammond Ketilson. 2009. "Resilience of the Cooperative Business Model in Times of Crisis." Sustainable Enterprise Programme. Geneva: International Labour Organization.

Black, Simon J. 2005. "Community Unionism: A Strategy for Organizing in the New Economy." *New Labor Forum* 14(3): 24–32.

Blin, Dick. 2011. "Global Framework Agreements: Compliance." *International Union Rights* 18(2): 3–4.

Blodget, Henry. 2012. "Well, It May be Time to Face the Fact that We Need Labor Unions . . ."*Business Insider*, June 8.

Böckerman, Petri and Roope Uusitalo. 2006. "Erosion of the Ghent System and Union Membership Decline: Lessons from Finland." *British Journal of Industrial Relations* 44(2): 283–303.

Borer, David, and Joe Burns. 2005. "Flight Attendants Wreak Havoc." In Jane Slaughter, ed. *A Troublemaker's Handbook 2: How to Fight Back Where You Work and Win*. Detroit, MI: Labor Notes.

Bradbury, Alexandra. 2012. "Walmart Warehouse Workers Return to Work with Full Back Pay." *Labor Notes*, October 9.

Bradsher, Keith. 2010. "With Concessions, Honda Strike Fizzles in China." *New York Times*, June 13.

Braunstein, Elissa. 2003. "Tax Cuts and the Recession in the Massachusetts Fiscal Crisis." Political Economy Research Institute Working Paper 66. Amherst, MA: University of Massachusetts Amherst.

Breslin, Colleen P., Stephanie Luce, Beth Lyon and Sarah Paoletti. 2011. "Report of the August 2011 Human Rights Delegation to Hershey, Pennsylvania." September 2. http://www.guestworkeralliance.org/wp-content/uploads/2011/09/Human-Rights-Delegation-Report-on-Hersheys-J-1-Workers.pdf (accessed March 20, 2013).

Bronfenbrenner, Kate. 2000. "Uneasy Terrain: The Impact of Capital Mobility on Workers, Wages and Union Organizing." Cornell University ILR School.

Bronfenbrenner, Kate. 2009. "No Holds Barred: The Intensification of Employer Opposition to Organizing." Briefing Paper No. 235. Washington, DC: Economic Policy Institute.

Bronfenbrenner, Kate and Rob Hickey. 2004. "Changing to Organize: A National Assessment of Union Organizing Strategies." In Ruth Milkman and Kim Voss, eds. *Rebuilding Labor: Organizing and Organizers in the New Union Movement*. Ithaca, NY: Cornell University Press/ILR Press.

Brown, Drusilla K. 2001. "Labor Standards: Where Do They Belong on the International Trade Agenda?" *Journal of Economic Perspectives* 15(3): 89–112.

Brown, Jenny. 2011. "Hershey's Walkout Exposes J-1 Guestworker Scam." *Labor Notes*, August 25.

References

Brutents, K. N. 2010. "Colonies and Colonial Policy." *The Great Soviet Encyclopedia*, 3rd edn. (1970–1979). Farmington Hills, MI: The Gale Group.

Bryson, Alex. 1999. "Are Unions Good for Industrial Relations?" In Roger Jowell, John Curtice, and Allison Park, eds. *British Social Attitudes: The 16th Report.* Aldershot: Ashgate.

Bullard, Madeline Grey. 2001. "Child Labor Prohibitions Are Universal, Binding, and Obligatory Law: The Evolving State of Customary International Law Concerning the Unempowered Child Laborer." *Houston Journal of International Law* 24(1): 139.

Bureau of Economic Analysis. 2013. "Summary Estimates for Multinational Companies: Employment, Sales and Capital Expenditures for 2011." Washington, DC: U.S. Department of Commerce. http://www.bea.gov/news-releases/international/mnc/2013/_pdf/mnc2011.pdf (accessed September 9, 2013).

Bureau of Labor Statistics. 2012. Table A-15. "Alternative Measures of Labor Underutilization." Washington, DC: US Department of Labor. http://www.bls.gov/news.release/empsit.t15.htm (accessed August 7, 2012).

Bureau of Labor Statistics. 2013 and various years. "Employment, Hours, and Earnings from the Current Employment Statistics Survey." Washington, DC: US Department of Labor.

Burgess, Katrina. 2004. *Parties and Unions in the New Global Economy.* Pittsburgh, PA: University of Pittsburgh Press.

Burgess, Katrina. 2010. "Global Pressures, National Policies, and Labor Rights in Latin America." *Studies in Comparative International Development* 45(2): 198–224.

Burgoon, Brian, Janice Fine, Wade Jacoby and Daniel Tichenor. 2010. "Immigration and the Transformation of American Unionism." *International Migration Review* 44(4): 933–73.

Byrd, Barbara and Bruce Nissen. 2003. "Report on the State of Labor Education in the United States." Berkeley, CA: Center for Labor Research and Education Institute of Industrial Relations.

Camfield, David. 2012. "Solidarity or Exclusion? British Columbia Unions and Chinese Mineworkers." *New Socialist Webzine*, November 23.

Cammett, Melani and Marsha Pripstein Posusney. 2010. "Labor Standards and Flexibility in the Middle East: Free Trade and Freer Unions?" *Studies in Comparative International Development* 45(2): 250–79.

Card, David. 1990. "The Impact of the Mariel Boatlift on the Miami Labor Market." *Industrial and Labor Relations Review* 43(2): 245–57.

Card, David. 2001. "The Effect of Unions on Wage Inequality in the U.S. Labor Market." *Industrial and Labor Relations Review* 54(2): 296–315.

Carillo, Beatriz and David S. G. Goodman. 2012. *Peasants and Workers in the Transformation of Urban China.* Cheltenham: Edward Elgar Publishing.

Carter, Bob and Rae Cooper. 2002. "The Organizing Model and Management of

Change: A Comparative Study of Unions in Australia and Britain." *Industrial Relations* 57(4): 712–42.

Casale, Daniella and Dorrit Posel. 2011. "Unions and the Gender Wage Gap in South Africa." *Journal of African Economies* 20(1): 27–59.

Castles, Stephen. 2006. "Guestworkers in Europe: A Resurrection?" *International Migration Review* 40(4): 741–66.

Cerny, Philip G. 1997. "Paradoxes of the Competition State: The Dynamics of Political Globalization." *Government and Opposition* 32(2): 251–74.

Chan, Anita. 2009. "Challenges and Possibilities for Democratic Grassroots Union Elections in China: A Case Study of Two Factory-Level Elections and Their Aftermath." *Labor Studies Journal* 94(3): 293–317.

Chan, Anita. 2010. "American Chicken Feet, Chinese Tires, and the Struggle for Labor Rights." *New Labor Forum* 19(3): 57–63.

Chan, Chris King-Chi and Elaine Sio-leng Hui. 2012. "The Dynamics and Dilemma of Workplace Trade Union Reform in China: The Case of the Honda Workers' Strike." *The Journal of Industrial Relations* 54(5): 653–68.

Chan, Chris King-Chi and Pun Ngai. 2009. "The Making of a New Working Class? A Study of Collective Actions of Migrant Workers in South China." *The China Quarterly* 198(June): 287–303.

Chang, Grace. 2000. *Disposable Domestics: Immigrant Women Workers in the Global Economy*. Cambridge, MA: South End Press.

Chang, Ha-joon. 2008. *Bad Samaritans: The Myth of Free Trade and the Secret History of Capitalism*. London: Bloomsbury Press.

Charlwood, Andy. 2003. "Why Do Non-Union Employees Want to Unionize? Evidence from Britain." *British Journal of Industrial Relations* 40(3): 463–91.

Chatterton, Paul. 2004. "Making Autonomous Geographies: Argentina's Popular Uprising and the 'Movimiento de Trabajadores Desocupados' (Unemployed Workers Movement)." *Geoforum* 36: 545–61.

Chen, Martha and Joann Vanek. 2013. "Informal Employment Revisited: Theories, Data & Policies." *The Indian Journal of Industrial Relations* 48(3): 390–401.

China Labor News Translations. 2010. "The Nanhai Honda Strike and the Union." July 18. http://www.clntranslations.org/article/56/honda (accessed June 21, 2013).

Chun, Jennifer Jihuye. 2009. *Organizing at the Margins: The Symbolic Politics of Labor in South Korea and the United States*. Ithaca, NY: Cornell University Press.

Claeson, Bjorn and Liana Foxvog. 2011. "Bangladesh Labor Leaders Win One Case; Ten More Cases Still to Go." Sweatfree Communities. http://laborrightsblog.typepad.com/international_labor_right/2011/06/-bangladesh-labor-leaders-win-one-case-ten-more-cases-still-to-go-.html (accessed January 7, 2013).

References

Clark, Mary A. 2011. "The DR-CAFTA and the Costa Rican Health Sector: A Push Toward Privatization? *The Latin Americanist* 55(3): 3–23.

Clawson, Dan. 2003. *The Next Upsurge: Labor and the New Social Movements.* Ithaca, NY: Cornell University Press.

Clawson, Dan and Mary Ann Clawson. 1999. "What Has Happened to the US Labor Movement? Union Decline and Renewal." *Annual Review of Sociology* 25: 95–119.

Cobble, Dorothy Sue. 1993. *Women and Unions: Forging a Partnership.* Ithaca, NY: ILR Press.

Cobble, Dorothy Sue. 1997. "The Next Unionism: Structural Innovations for a Revitalized Labor Movement." *Labor Law Journal* 48(8): 439–42.

Cohen, Monique and Martha A. Chen. 2001. "Managing Resources, Activities, and Risk in Urban India: The Impact of SEWA Bank." Washington, DC: Management Systems International.

Coliver, Sandra, Jennie Green and Paul Hoffman. 2005. "Holding Human Rights Violators Accountable by Using International Law in U.S. Courts: Advocacy Efforts and Complementary Strategies." *Emory International Law Review* 169(Spring): 19.

Committee on Freedom of Association. 2012. Case 2741. Geneva: International Labour Organization. http://www.atu.org/atu-pdfs/ILO-CFA-Decision-re-Taylor-Law.pdf

Compa, Lance. 2006. "Labour Rights in the FTAA." In John D. R. Craig and S. Michael Lynk, eds. *Globalisation and the Future of Labour Law.* New York: Cambridge University Press.

Compa, Lance. 2008. "Corporate Social Responsibility and Workers' Rights." *Comparative Labor Law and Policy Journal* 30(1): 1–10.

Competition Commission. 2008. "Groceries Market Investigation, Final Report." London: Competition Commission, April 30. http://www.competition-commission.org.uk/rep_pub/reports/2008/538grocery.htm

Cook, Linda J. 2010. "More Rights, Less Power: Labor Standards and Labor Markets in East European Post-Communist States." *Studies in Comparative International Development* 45: 170–97.

COSATU. 2003. "Consolidating Working Class Power for Quality Jobs – Towards 2015: Programme Arising from the COSATU 8th National Congress." October 9. http://www.cosatu.org.za/docs/policy/2003/2015plan.html

Craft, James A. 1990. "The Community as a Source of Union Power." *Journal of Labor Research* XI(2): 145–60.

Craig, Ben and John Pencavel. 1995. "Participation and Productivity: A Comparison of Worker Cooperatives and Conventional Firms in the Plywood Industry." Brookings Papers, Washington, DC.

Craner, Lorne W. 2002. "Trade Unions Are Key to Sustaining Democratic Gains." Remarks to Worldwide Labor Officers' Conference, July 18, Washington, DC.

Cullinane, Niall and Tony Dundon. 2011. "Redundancy and Workplace

Occupation: The Case of the Republic of Ireland." *Employee Relations* 33(6): 624–41.

Dahi, Omar S. and Firat Demir. 2013. "Preferential Trade Agreements and Manufactured Goods Exports: Does it Matter Whom you PTA With?" *Applied Economics* 45(34): 4754–72.

Davidsson, Johan Bo and Patrick Emmenegger. 2012. "Defending the Organisation, not the Members: Unions and the Reform of Job Security Legislation in Western Europe." *European Journal of Political Research* 52(3): 339–63.

Davis, Bob. 2012. "Labor NGOs in Guangdong Claim Repression." *The Wall Street Journal*, July 28.

Delp, Linda and Katie Quan. 2002. "Homecare Worker Organizing in California: An Analysis of a Successful Strategy." *Labor Studies Journal* 27(1): 1–23.

Democracy Digest. 2011. "China: Worker Militancy Yields New Labor Rights." January 6. http://www.demdigest.net/blog/2011/01/china-worker-militancy-yields-new-labor-rights/

Department for Business Innovation and Skills. 2013. "Groceries Adjudicator to Have New Power to Fine Supermarkets." January 27. http://news.bis.gov.uk/Press-Releases/Groceries-Adjudicator-to-have-new-power-to-fine-supermarkets-68464.aspx

Dickstein, Carla. 1991. "The Promise and Problems of Worker Cooperatives." *Journal of Planning Literature* 6(1): 16–33.

Dimick, Matthew. 2012. "Labor Law, New Governance, and the Ghent System." *North Carolina Law Review* 90(2): 319–78.

Dirnbach, Eric. 2008. "Weaving a Stronger Fabric: Organizing a Global Sweat-Free Apparel Production Agreement." *Working USA* 11(June): 237–54.

Donahue, Linda H., James Ryan Lamare and Fred B. Kotler. 2007. "The Cost of Worker Misclassification in New York State." Ithaca, NY: Cornell University ILR School.

Drake, Bill. 2001. "Marketing Implications of Retail Food Industry Consolidation." Distance Education Program, Food Industry Management, Cornell University.

Draper, Alan. 1994. *Conflict of Interests: Organized Labor and the Civil Rights Movement in the South, 1954–1968*. Ithaca, NY: ILR Press.

Drier, Peter. 2011. "Is the Perfect Factory Possible?" *The Nation*, November 7.

Drucker, Peter. 2013. "An Alternative to the Troika." *International Viewpoint*, February 18.

DuBois, W. E. 1999. *Black Reconstruction in America: 1860–1880*. New York: Free Press.

Dudzic, Mark. 2012. "Remembering Jerry Tucker." *Labor Notes*, October 23. http://labornotes.org/2012/10/remembering-jerry-tucker (accessed October 24, 2012).

References

Dumke, Mick. 2009. "IVI-IPO Sues the City over the Parking Meter Deal." *Reader*, August 19.

Dumont, Isabelle and Bernard Harcourt. 2003. "Women in Trade Unions: Making the Difference. Research on Women and Decision-Making in Trade Union Organisations." European Trade Union Confederation. http://www.etuc.org/IMG/pdf/genre_an_080403.pdf (accessed March 12, 2013).

Dunning, John H. and Sarianna M. Lundan. 2008. *Multinational Enterprises and the Global Economy*. London: Edward Elgar Publishing.

Dutt, Amitava Krishna. 2012. "South-South Issues from a North-South Perspective." UNCTAD and South Centre. Background Paper 2. http://unctad.org/en/PublicationsLibrary/ecidc2012_bp2.pdf

Dwyer, Richard. 1977. "Workers' Education, Labor Education, Labor Studies: An Historical Delineation." *Review of Educational Research* 47(1): 179–207.

Eaton, Adrienne and Jill Kriesky. 2009. NLRB Elections vs. Card Check Campaigns: Results of a Worker Survey. *Industrial and Labor Relations Review* 62(2): 157–72.

Ebbinghaus, Bernhard. 1995. "The Siamese Twins: Citizenship Rights, Cleavage Formation, and Party-Union Relations in Western Europe." *International Review of Social History* 40(S3): 51–89.

Ehrenreich, Barbara and Arlie Hochschild, eds. 2004. *Global Woman: Nannies, Maids, and Sex Workers in the New Economy*. New York: Holt Paperbacks.

Eidelson, Josh. 2012. "The Great Walmart Walkout." *The Nation*, December 19.

Eidelson, Josh. 2013. "Striking Worker and Bangladesh Activist Address Thousands at Walmart Shareholder Meeting." *The Nation*, June 7.

Elliot, Kimberly Ann. 2000. "The ILO and Enforcement of Core Labor Standards." International Economics Policy Briefs Number 00-6. Washington, DC: Institute for International Economics.

Engels, Friedrich. 1973 [1845]. *The Condition of the Working Class in England in 1844: From Personal Observation to Authentic Sources*. Moscow: Progress Publishers.

Epstein, Gerald A. 2005. *Financialization and the World Economy*. London: Edward Elgar Publishing.

Esbenshade, Jill. 2004. *Monitoring Sweatshops: Workers, Consumers and the Global Apparel Industry*. Philadelphia, PA: Temple University Press.

Esbenshade, Jill. 2012. "A Review of Private Regulation: Codes and Monitoring in the Apparel Industry." *Sociology Compass* 6(7): 541–56.

Estlund, Cynthia L. 2002. "The Ossification of American Labor Law." *Columbia Law Review* 102(6): 1527–612.

European Commission. 2012. *Taxation Trends in the European Union*. Eurostat. Luxembourg: Office of the European Union. http://ec.europa.eu/taxation_customs/resources/documents/taxation/gen_info/economic_analysis/tax_structures/2012/report.pdf

References

Evans, Peter. 2005. "Counter-Hegemonic Globalization: Transnational Social Movements in the Contemporary Global Political Economy." In Thomas Janoski, Robert R. Alford, Alexander M. Hicks, and Mildred A. Schwartz, eds. *The Handbook of Political Sociology: States, Civil Societies, and Globalization.* Cambridge: Cambridge University Press.

Evans, Peter. 2010. "Is it Labor's Turn to Globalize? Twenty-First Century Opportunities and Strategic Responses." *Global Labour Journal* 1(3): 352–79.

Fairbrother, Peter and Nikolaus Hammer. 2005. "Global Unions: Past Efforts and Future Prospects." *Industrial Relations* 60(3): 405–31.

Fine, Janice. 2005. "Community Unions and the Revival of the American Labor Movement." *Politics and Society* 33(1): 153–99.

Fine, Janice. 2006. *Worker Centers: Organizing Communities at the Edge of the Dream.* Ithaca, NY: Cornell University Press.

Fine, Janice. 2007. "A Marriage Made in Heaven? Mismatches and Misunderstandings between Worker Centres and Unions." *British Journal of Industrial Relations* 45(2): 335–60.

Fischer, Maria Clara Bueno and Janet Hannah. 2002. "(Re)-Constructing Citizenship: The Programa Integrar of the Brazilian Metalworkers' Union." *Compare: A Journal of Comparative and International Education* 32(1): 95–106.

Fletcher, Bill and Richard Hurd. 1998. "Beyond the Organizing Model: The Transformation Process in Local Unions." Cornell University ILR School. http://digitalcommons.ilr.cornell.edu/articles/322

Foner, Philip S. 1979. *Women and the American Labor Movement: From the First Trade Unions to the Present.* New York: Free Press.

Food Chain Workers Alliance n.d. "Mission & History." http://foodchainworkers.org/?page_id=38 (accessed September 12, 2013).

Francia, Peter. 2006. *The Future of Organized Labor in American Politics.* New York: Colombia University Press.

Frank, Dana. 1999. *Buy American: The Untold Story of American Nationalism.* Boston: Beacon Press.

Fraser, Max. 2010. "The SEIU Andy Stern Leaves Behind." *The Nation,* June 16.

Freeman, Joshua. 2011. "Corruption's Due (Scholarly) Reward." *Labor: Studies in Working-Class History of the Americas* 8(2): 71–75.

Freeman, Richard. 2005. "The Great Doubling: Labor in the New Global Economy." Georgia State University. Usery Lecture in Labor Policy.

Freeman, Richard B. 2007. "Do Workers Still Want Unions? More than Ever." EPI Briefing Paper #182. Washington, DC: Economic Policy Institute.

Frege, Carola M. and John Kelly. 2003. "Union Revitalization Strategies in a Comparative Perspective." *European Journal of Industrial Relations* 9(1): 7–24.

Friedberg, Rachel M. 2001. "The Impact of Mass Migration on the Israeli Labor Market." *Quarterly Journal of Economics* 116(4): 1373–408.

References

Friedberg, Rachel and Jennifer Hunt. 1995. "The Impact of Immigration on Host Country Wages, Employment and Growth." *Journal of Economic Perspectives* 9: 23–44.

Friedman, Eli. 2012. "China in Revolt." *Jacobin*. Issue 7–8. http://jacobinmag.com/2012/08/china-in-revolt/ (accessed October 25, 2012).

Friedman, Ellen David. 2009. "U.S. and Chinese Labor at a Changing Moment in the Global Neoliberal Economy." *WorkingUSA* 12(2): 219–34.

Friedman, Gerald. 2008. "Labor Unions in the United States." In Robert Whaples, ed. *EH.Net Encyclopedia*, March 16. http://eh.net/encyclopedia/article/friedman.unions.us

Gajewska, Katarzyna and Johanna Niesyto. 2009. "Organising Campaigns as 'Revitaliser' for Trade Unions? The Example of the Lidl Campaign." *Industrial Relations Journal* 40(2): 156–71.

Gall, Gregor. 2011. "Contemporary Workplace Occupations in Britain: Motivations, Stimuli, Dynamics and Outcomes." *Employee Relations* 33(6): 607–23.

Galpern, Pamela. 2005. "Telephone Workers Pressure Verizon from Within." In Jane Slaughter, ed. *A Troublemaker's Handbook 2: How to Fight Back Where you Work and Win*. Detroit, MI: Labor Notes.

Ganesh, Aravind R. 2011. "The Right to Food and Buyer Power." *German Law Journal* 11(11): 1190–244.

Ganz, Marshall. 2009. "Resources and Resourcefulness: Strategic Capacity in the Unionization of California Agriculture, 1959–1966." *American Journal of Sociology* 105(4): 1003–62.

Garay, Candelaria. 2007. "Social Policy and Collective Action: Unemployed Workers, Community Associations, and Protest in Argentina." *Politics and Society* 35(2): 301–28.

Garza, Cecila. 2012. "Meet the Crawfish-Peeling Guestworkers Who Inspired Walmart Walkouts." *Yes! Magazine*, October 12.

Gely, Rafael and Timothy Chandler. 2011. "Organizing Principles; The Significance of Card-Check Laws." *St. Louis University School of Law Public Law Review* 30: 475–516.

Gereffi, Gary and Peter Evans. 1981. "Transnational Corporations, Dependent Development, and State Policy in the Semiperiphery: A Comparison of Brazil and Mexico." *Latin American Research Review* 16(3): 31–64.

Gereffi, Gary and Michael Korzeniewicz, eds. 1994. *Commodity Chains and Global Capitalism*. Westport, CT: Praeger.

Gernigon, Bernard, Alberto Odero and Horatio Guido. 1998. *ILO Principles Concerning the Right to Strike*. Geneva: International Labour Organization.

Ghosh, Joyati. 2009. "Migration and Gender Empowerment: Recent Trends and Emerging Issues." Human Development Research Paper 2009/4. United Nations Development Programme.

Gibbon, Peter. 2003. "The African Growth and Opportunity Act and the

Global Commodity Chain for Clothing." *World Development* 31(11): 1809–27.

Givan, Rebecca Kolins and Lena Hipp. 2012. Public Perceptions of Union Efficacy: A Twenty-Four Country Study." *Labor Studies Journal* 37(1): 7–32.

Glass, Amy. 2008. "India Sets Minimum Wage for UAE Domestic Workers." *Arabian Business*, February 21. http://www.arabianbusiness.com/511923-indian-govt-sets-minimum-wage-for-uae-domestic-workers

Gleave, Jonathan. 2011. "Spain's Indignant Movement Gears for New Struggle." Reuters, November 18. http://www.reuters.com/article/2011/11/18/spain-elec tion-indignant-idUSL5E7MH2F020111118 (accessed February 18, 2013).

Gonzalez, David. 2003. "Latin Sweatshops Pressed by U.S. Campus Power." *The New York Times*, April 4. http://www.nytimes.com/2003/04/04/international/ americas/04LABO.html?pagewanted=1 (accessed November 5, 2012).

Gordon, Jennifer. 2009. "Towards Transnational Labor Citizenship: Restructuring Labor Migration to Reinforce Workers' Rights. A Preliminary Report on Emerging Experiments." Fordham Law School, New York.

Gordon, Jennifer. 2011. "Free Movement and Equal Rights for Low-Wage Workers? What the United States Can Learn from the New EU Migration to Britain." Chief Justice Earl Warren Institute on Law and Social Policy, Issue Brief, May, Berkeley, CA: University of California Berkeley.

Gottfried, Heidi. 2012. *Gender, Work and Economy: Unpacking the Global Economy*. Cambridge: Polity Press.

Gould IV, William B. 2007. "Independent Adjudication, Political Process, and the State of Labor-Management Relations: The Role of the National Labor Relations Board." *Indiana Law Journal* 82(2): Article 8.

Greenhouse, Steven. 2010. "Factory Defies Sweatshop Label, But Can it Thrive?" *The New York Times*, July 17. http://www.nytimes.com/2010/07/18/business/ global/18shirt.html?pagewanted=all (accessed November 2, 2012).

Greenhouse, Steven. 2012a. "More Lockouts as Companies Battle Unions." *The New York Times*, January 22. http://www.nytimes.com/2012/01/23/business/ lockouts-once-rare-put-workers-on-the-defensive.html?pagewanted=all&_r=0 (accessed October 19, 2012).

Greenhouse, Steven. 2012b. "Walmart Labor Protests Grow, Organizers Say." *The New York Times*, October 9. http://www.nytimes.com/2012/10/10/busi ness/organizers-say-wal-mart-labor-protests-spread.html (accessed February 27, 2013).

Greider, William. 2013. "Why Was Paul Krugman So Wrong?" *The Nation*, April 1.

Grinyer, John, Alex Russell and David Collison. 1998. "Evidence of Managerial Short-Termism in the UK." *British Journal of Management* 9: 13–22.

Hacker, Jacob S. 2006. *The Great Risk Shift: The Assault on American Jobs, Families, Health Care and Retirement – And How You Can Fight Back*. Oxford: Oxford University Press.

References

Hahnel, Robin. 2005. *Economic Justice and Democracy: From Competition to Cooperation.* New York: Routledge.

Hall, Peter A. and David Soskice. 2001. *Varieties of Capitalism: The Institutional Foundations of Comparative Advantage.* Oxford: Oxford University Press.

Hall-Jones, Peter. 2010. "Strike Wave Signals Global Shift." New Unionism Network blog, October 21. http://newunionism.wordpress.com/2010/10/21/strikes/ (accessed October 26, 2012).

Hallward-Driemeier, Mary. 2003. "Do Bilateral Investment Treaties Attract Foreign Direct Investment? Only a Bit . . . And They Could Bite." World Bank Policy Research Working Paper No. 3121.

Hamann, Kersten and John Kelly. 2010. "The Puzzle of Trade Union Strength in Western Europe since 1980." *Indian Journal of Industrial Relations* 45(4): 646–57.

Hananel, Sam. 2012. "Unions Gearing up to Spend Big in 2012 Elections." *Huffington Post*, February 22. http://www.huffingtonpost.com/2012/02/22/labor-unions-obama-elections-2012_n_1293173.html (accessed February 5, 2013).

Harris, David and Diego Azzi. 2006. "Venezuela's answer to 'free trade': the Bolivarian Alternative for the Americas." Focus on the Global South Occasional Paper No. 3.

Hart-Landsberg, Martin. 2009. "The Promise and Perils of Korean Reunification." *Monthly Review* 60(11): 50–59.

Harvey, David. 2005. *A Brief History of Neoliberalism.* Oxford: Oxford University Press.

Hattingh, Shawn. 2009. "Workers Creating Hope: Factory Occupations and Self-Management." *MRZine*, June 15. http://mrzine.monthlyreview.org/2009/hattingh150609.html

Hayter, Susan and Bradley Weinberg. 2011. "Mind the Gap: Collective Bargaining and Wage Inequality." In Susan Hayter, ed. *The Role of Collective Bargaining in the Global Economy: Negotiating for Social Justice.* Geneva: International Labour Organization.

Hayter, Susan, Tayo Fashoyin and Thomas A. Kochan. 2011. "Review Essay: Collective Bargaining for the 21st Century." *Journal of Industrial Relations* 53(2): 225–47.

Hébert, Gérard. 2012. "Labour Organization." *The Canadian Encyclopedia.* Toronto, ON: Historica-Dominion.

Henwood, Doug. 2003. "Beyond Globophobia." *The Nation*, December 1.

Hepple, Bob. 2005. *Labour Laws and Global Trade.* Oxford: Hart Publishing.

Hewison, Kevin and Arne L. Kalleberg. 2013. "Precarious Work and Flexibilization in South and Southeast Asia." *American Behavioral Scientist* 57(4): 395–402.

Hill, Jennifer. 2010. "Binational Unions: New Hope for Guestworkers." *Labor: Studies in Working-Class History of the Americas* 7(4): 9–15.

References

Hirsh, Barry T. and David A. Macpherson. 2013. "Union Membership and Coverage Database from the CPS." http://www.unionstats.com/ (accessed June 21, 2013).

Hochschild, Adam. 2005. *Bury the Chains: Prophets and Rebels in the Fight to Free an Empire's Slaves*. Boston, MA: Houghton Mifflin.

Hochschild, Arlie. R. 2000. "Global Care Chains and Emotional Surplus Value." In Will Hutton and Anthony Giddens, eds. *On The Edge: Living with Global Capitalism*. London: Jonathan Cape.

Hoerr, John. 1997. *We Can't Eat Prestige: The Women Who Organized Harvard*. Philadelphia, PA: Temple University Press.

Hoffman, Christy. 2011. "G4S Global Framework Agreement and the OECD Process." *International Union Rights* 18(2): 5–6.

Holland, Joshua. 2012. "Romney's Bain Capital is Sending Many Jobs to China the Day Before the Election." Alternet, October 17. http://truth-out.org/news/item/12151-romneys-bain-capital-is-sending-many-jobs-to-china-the-day-before-the-election

Holman, David, Rosemary Batt and Ursula Holtgrewe. 2007. "The Global Call Center Report: International Perspectives on Management and Employment." Report of the Global Call Center Network. http://www.ilr.cornell.edu/global callcenter/upload/GCC-Intl-Rept-US-Version.pdf (accessed March 12, 2013).

Hometown Advantage. 2001. "Wal-Mart Settles Predatory Pricing Charge." October 1. www.ilsr.org/walmart-settles-predatory-pricing-charge/.

Hondagneu-Sotelo, Pierrette. 2007. *Domestica: Immigrant Workers Cleaning and Caring in the Shadows of Affluence*. Berkeley, CA: University of California Press.

Hong, Jane C. 2000. "Enforcement of Corporate Codes of Conduct: Finding a Private Right of Action for International Laborers against MNCs for Labor Rights Violations." *Wisconsin International Law Journal* 19: 41–69.

Hugill, Peter J. 2006. "The Geostrategy of Global Business: Wal-Mart and Its Historical Forbears." In Stanley D. Brunn, ed. *Wal-Mart World: The World's Biggest Corporation in the Global Economy*. New York: Routledge.

Human Rights Watch. 2000. "'Deck is Stacked' against U.S. Workers." News Release, August 31. http://www.hrw.org/news/2000/08/30/deck-stacked-against-us-workers

Humphries, Jane. 1977. "Class Struggle and the Persistence of the Working-Class Family." *Cambridge Journal of Economics* 1: 241–58.

Hurd, Richard. 2004. "The Failure of Organizing, the New Unity Partnership and the Future of the Labor Movement. Cornell University ILR School. http://digitalcommons.ilr.cornell.edu/articles/297/

Hussmanns, Ralf. 2004. "Measuring the Informal Economy: From Employment in the Informal Sector to Informal Employment." Working Paper No. 53. Geneva: International Labour Organization.

References

Hyman, Richard. 1971. *Marxism and the Sociology of Trade Unions*. London: Pluto Press.

Ingersoll, Richard. 1997. "Teacher Turnover and Teacher Quality: The Recurring Myth of Teacher Shortages." *Teachers College Record* 99(1): 41–44.

International Labour Organization. 2008. "Declaration on Social Justice for a Fair Globalization." Geneva: ILO.

International Labour Organization. 2011. "Statistical Update on Employment in the Informal Sector." Geneva: ILO.

International Labour Organization. 2013. "Global Wage Report 2012/13: Wages and Equitable Growth." Geneva: ILO.

International Trade Union Confederation. 2012 and various years. "Annual Survey of Violations of Trade Union Rights." Brussels: ITUC.

Jaccarino, Mike. 2009. "Stella D'Oro Protesters Lean on Goldman Sachs." *Daily News*, September 28. http://www.nydailynews.com/new-york/bronx/stella-oro-protesters-lean-goldman-sachs-article-1.383866#ixzz22PhCuaUB (accessed August 2, 2012).

Jakarta Globe. 2012. "More Than 2 Million Workers Strike in Indonesia." October 3. http://www.thejakartaglobe.com/achive/more-than-2-million-workers-strike-in-indonesia/ (accessed March 28, 2013).

Jamieson, Dave. 2012. "Walmart-Contracted Warehouse Workers Strike Ahead of Black Friday." *Huffington Post*, November 14. http://www.huffington-post.com/2012/11/14/walmart-strike-black-friday_n_2130389.html (accessed January 7, 2013).

Jarley, Paul and Cheryl L. Maranto. 1990. "Union Corporate Campaigns: An Assessment." *Industrial and Labor Relations Review* 43(5): 505–24.

Jenkins, Steve. 2002. "Organizing, Advocacy and Member Power: A Critical Reflection." *WorkingUSA* 6(2): 56–89.

Jones, Jeffrey M. 2012. "In U.S., Labor Union Approval Steady at 52%." Gallup Politics, August 31. http://www.gallup.com/poll/157025/labor-union-approval-steady.aspx (accessed September 8, 2012).

Joshi, Yadav Raj. 2012. "S Asia agrees on minimum wage for house-maids." *The Himalayan*, June 26. http://www.thehimalayantimes.com/fullNews.php?headline=S+Asia+agrees+on+minimum+wage+for+housemaids&NewsID=337393 (accessed March 28, 2013).

Juamotte, Florence, Subir Lall, Chris Papageorgiou and Petia Topalova. 2007. "Technology Widening Rich-Poor Gap." *IMF Survey Magazine*, October 10.

Kabeer, Naila. 2000. *The Power to Choose: Bangladeshi Women and Labour Market Decisions in London and Dhaka*. London: Verso.

Kalleberg. Arne L. 2009. "Precarious Work, Insecure Workers: Employment Relations in Transition." *American Sociological Review* 74: 1–22.

Kay, Tamara. 2011. *NAFTA and the Politics of Labor Transnationalism*. Cambridge: Cambridge University Press.

References

Keating, Joshua E. 2012. "America's long history of training future coup leaders." *The Nation*, May 30. http://www.nation.com.pk/pakistan-news-newspaper-daily-english-online/international/30-Mar-2012/america-s-long-history-of-training-future-coup-leaders (accessed September 18, 2012).

Kelly, Robin D. G. 1996. *Race Rebels: Culture, Politics and the Black Working Class*. New York: Free Press.

Kim, A. E. 2004. "The Social Perils of the Asian Financial Crisis." *Journal of Contemporary Asia* 34(1): 221–37.

Klotz, Audie. 2002. "Transnational Activism and Global Transformations: The Anti-Apartheid and Abolitionist Experiences." *European Journal of International Relations* 8(1): 49–76.

Kugler, Adriana D. 2004. "The Effect of Job Security Regulations on Labor Market Flexibility. Evidence from the Colombian Labor Market Reform." In James J. Heckman and Carmen Pagés, eds. *Law and Employment: Lessons from Latin American and the Caribbean*. Chicago, IL: University of Chicago Press.

Kumar, Pradeep and Christopher Robert Schenk. 2006. *Paths to Union Renewal: Canadian Experiences*. Toronto, ON: University of Toronto Press.

Kumhof, Michael, Claire Lebarz, Romain Rancière, Alexander W. Richter and Nathaniel A. Throckmorton. 2012. "Income Inequality and Current Account Imbalances." IMF Working Paper, WP/12/08, January.

La Botz, Dan. 2011. "Strike Wave Sweeps Brazil." *Labor Notes*, October 7.

La Botz, Dan. 2012. "Mexico's Labor Law Changes Undermine Worker Rights." *Labor Notes*, December 25. http://www.labornotes.org/blogs/2012/09/mexico%E2%80%99s-labor-law-changes-undermine-worker-rights (accessed June 21, 2013).

Lafer, Gordon. 2005. "Hospital Speedups and the Fiction of a Nursing Shortage." *Labor Studies Journal* 30(1): 27–46.

Lambert, Susan J. 2008. "Passing the Buck: Labor Flexibility Practices that Transfer Risk onto Hourly Workers." *Human Relations* 61(9): 1203–27.

Laverty, K. J. 1996. "Economic Short-termism: The Debate, the Unresolved Issues, and the Implications for Management Practice and Research." *Academy of Management Review* 21(3): 825–50.

Lazos, Sylvia R. 2007. "The Immigrant Rights Marches (Las Marchas): Did the 'Gigante' (Giant) Wake Up or Does it Still Sleep Tonight?" *Nevada Law Journal* 7: 780–825.

Leary, Elly and Jean Alonso. 1997. "The Women Who Organized Harvard: A Feminist Model of Labor Organization?" *Monthly Review* 49(7): 1–9.

Lederer, Shannon. 2012. Interview with the author. September 13.

Lee, Chang Hee and Mingwei Liu. 2011. "Collective Bargaining in Transition: Measuring the Effects of Collective Voice in China." In Susan Hayter, ed. *The Role of Collective Bargaining in the Global Economy: Negotiating for Social Justice*, Geneva: ILO.

References

Lee, Cheol-Sung. 2007. "Labor Unions and Good Governance: A Cross-National, Comparative Analysis." *American Sociological Review* 72(4): 585–609.

Lee, Jennifer. 2009. "Stella D'Oro Factory to Close in October." *The New York Times*, July 6. http://cityroom.blogs.nytimes.com/2009/07/06/stella-doro-fac tory-to-close-in-october/ (accessed August 2, 2012).

Lee, Minjin. 2012. "Varieties of Community Unionism: A Comparison of Community Unionism in Japan and Korea." In Akira Suzuki, ed. *Cross-National Comparisons of Social Movement Unionism: Diversities of Labour Movement Revitalization in Japan, Korea and the United States*. Vol. 18. Oxford: Peter Lang.

Leiva, Aldo M. 2000. "Cuban Labor Law: Issues and Challenges." *Cuba in Transition. Papers and Proceedings of the Tenth Annual Meeting of the Association for the Study of the Cuban Economy, Miami, Florida*. Silver Spring, MD: Association for the Study of the Cuban Economy.

Levi, Margaret, David Olson, Jon Agnone and Devin Kelly. 2009. "Union Democracy Reexamined." *Politics & Society* 37(2): 203–28.

Levitsky, Steven. 2003. "From Labor Politics to Machine Politics: The Transformation of Party-Union Linkages in Argentine Peronism, 1983–1999." *Latin American Research Review* 38(3): 3–36.

Lin, Justin Yifu. 2012. *New Structural Economics: A Framework for Rethinking Development and Policy*. Washington, DC: The World Bank.

Lindenberg, Gail. 1993. "The Labor Union in the Cuban Workplace." *Latin American Perspectives* 76(20): 28–39.

Lloyd, Gloria. 2012. "Alta Gracia Model Shown as 'Viable'." *The Chronicle* (Duke University), February 8. http://www.dukechronicle.com/article/alta-gracia-model-shown-viable (accessed November 2, 2012).

Lochhead, Carolyn. 2006. "Give and Take Across the Border." *San Francisco Chronicle*, May 21. http://www.sfgate.com/news/article/Give-and-take-across-the-border-1-in-7-Mexican-2496634.php (accessed September 9, 2013).

Logan, John. 2006. "The Union Avoidance Industry in the United States." *British Journal of Industrial Relations* 44(4): 651–75.

Longshore and Shipping News. 2012. "Charleston Longshoremen Join Walmart Protest." December 22. http://www.longshoreshippingnews.com/2012/12/charleston-longshoremen-join-walmart-protest/ (accessed February 27, 2013).

Looise, Jan Kees and Michiel Drucker. 2002. "Employee Participation In Multinational Enterprises: The Effects of Globalisation on Dutch Works Councils." *Employee Relations* 24(1): 29–52.

Luce, Stephanie. 2004. *Fighting for a Living Wage*. Ithaca, NY: Cornell University Press.

Luce, Stephanie. 2005. "The Case for International Labor Standards: A Northern Perspective." IDS Working Paper 250. Brighton: Institute for Development Studies.

References

Luce, Stephanie. 2011. "What Can We Learn from Wisconsin?" *Organizing Upgrade*, April 1. http://www.organizingupgrade.com/index.php/modules-menu/labor/item/114-luce-what-can-we-learn-from-wisconsin (accessed February 27, 2013).

Luce, Stephanie. 2012. "Labour and Community Coalitions: Challenges for Growth." In Akira Suzuki, ed. *Cross-National Comparisons of Social Movement Unionism: Diversities of Labour Movement Revitalization in Japan, Korea and the United States*. Vol. 18. Oxford: Peter Lang.

Luce, Stephanie and Naoki Fujita. 2012. "Discounted Jobs: How Retailers Sell Workers Short." New York: Retail Action Project.

Ludlam, Steve. 2009. "Cuban Labour at 50: What about the Workers?" *Bulletin of Latin American Research* 28(4): 542–57.

Luxemburg, Rosa. 1906. "The Mass Strike, The Political Party and the Trade Unions." http://www.marxists.org/archive/luxemburg/1906/mass-strike/index.htm

Lynch, Caitrin. 2007. *Juki Girls, Good Girls: Gender and Cultural Politics in Sri Lanka's Global Garment Industry*. Ithaca, NY: Cornell University Press.

Lynd, Staughton and Daniel Gross. 2008. *Labor Law for the Rank and Filer*, 2nd edn. Oakland, CA: PM Press.

Lynn, Barry C. 2006. "Breaking the Chain." *Harper's* 313: 29–36.

Maher, Kris. 2005. "Unions' New Foe: Consultants." *Wall Street Journal*, August 15.

Maher, Kris. 2008. "Labor Wants Obama to Take on Big Fight." *Wall Street Journal*, November 8.

Maiti, Dibyendu. 2013. "Precarious Work in India: Trends and Emerging Issues." *American Behavioral Scientist* 57(4): 507–30.

Makanza, Tendai. 2011. "The Quest For Alternatives In Southern Africa: An ANSA Initiative." Die Rosa-Luxemburg-Stiftung auf dem Weltsozialforum, January 26. http://wsf.blog.rosalux.de/2011/01/26/the-quest-for-alternatives-in-southern-africa-an-ansa-initiative/ (accessed June 24, 2013).

Manning, Alan. 2003. *Monopsony in Motion: Imperfect Competition in Labor Markets*. Princeton, NJ: Princeton University Press.

Marr, Chuck and Brian Highsmith 2012. "Six Tests for Corporate Tax Reform. Center on Budget and Policy Priorities." Washington, DC. http://www.cbpp.org/cms/index.cfm?fa=view&id=3411

Mason, Paul. 2012. "Greece: Trying to Understand Syriza." BBC News, May 14. http://www.bbc.co.uk/news/world-europe-18056677

Mattson, Sean. 2007. "Union Rep's Slaying Called Revenge." *San Antonio Express-News*, April 13. http://www.smfws.com/articles2007/april2007/art04132007.htm

May, Martha. 1985. "Bread Before Roses: American Workingmen, Labor Unions and the Family Wage." In Ruth Milkman, ed. *Women, Work and Protest: A Century of U.S. Women's Labor History*. New York: Routledge.

References

McCallum, Jamie K. 2011. "Trade Union Renewal and Labor Transnationalism in South Africa: The Case of SATAWU." *WorkingUSA* 14(2): 161–76.

McIntosh, Don. 2000. "Religious Employers Don't Always Practice What They Preach." *Northwest Labor Press*, August 4.

Megginson, William L. and Jeffrey M. Netter. 2001. "From State to Market: A Survey of Empirical Studies on Privatization." *Journal of Economic Literature* 39(2): 321–89.

Mello, William. n.d. "The Labor Movements ABC: Unions and Working Class Education in Brazil." Indiana University. http://www.sindlab.org/download_up/The%20Labor%20Movements%20ABC.pdf

Merk, Jeroen. 2008. *The Structural Crisis of Labour Flexibility*. Amsterdam: Clean Clothes Campaign.

Michel, Heiner. 2007. "Co-Determination in Germany: The Recent Debate." Johann Wolfgang Goethe-Universität, Frankfurt.

Milkman, Ruth, ed. 1985. *Women, Work and Protest: A Century of U.S. Women's Labor History*. New York: Routledge.

Milkman, Ruth. 2011. "Immigrant Workers, Precarious Work, and the US Labor Movement." *Globalizations* 8(3): 361–72.

Milkman, Ruth and Kim Voss, eds. 2004. *Rebuilding Labor: Organizing and Organizers in the New Union Movement*. Ithaca, NY: Cornell University Press/ILR Press.

Miller, Tom. 2012. *China's Urban Billion: The Story Behind the Biggest Migration in Human History*. London: Zed Books.

Mines, Richard and Jeffrey Avina. 1992. "Immigrants and Labor Standards: The Case of California Janitors." In Jorge A. Bustamante, Clark Reynolds and Raul A. Hinojosa Ojeda, eds. *U.S.-Mexico Relations: Labor Market Interdependence*. Palo Alto, CA: Stanford University Press.

Ministry of Overseas Indian Affairs. 2008. "Minimum Wage Fixed for Indian Guestworkers in Oman." http://twocircles.net/node/78219

Moody, Kim. 1997. *An Injury to All*. London: Verso Books.

Moody, Kim. 2000. "The Rank and File Strategy." Solidarity Working Paper, Detroit, MI.

Moran, Theresa. 2012. "Chicago Teachers Raise the Bar." *Labor Notes*, September 19. http://labornotes.org/2012/09/chicago-teachers-raise-bar (accessed October 31, 2012).

Muncks, Ronaldo. 2002. *Globalization and Labour: The New "Great Transformation"*. London: Zed Books.

Murillo, M. Victoria. 2000. "From Populism to Neoliberalism: Labor Unions and Market Reforms in Latin America." *World Politics* 52(January): 135–74.

Murillo, M. Victoria and Andrew Schrank. 2005. "With a Little Help from My Friends: Partisan Politics, Transnational Alliances, and Labor Rights in Latin America." *Comparative Political Studies* 38(8): 971–99.

Naduris-Weissman, Eli. 2010. "Worker Centers & Traditional Labor Law: How to Stay on The Good Side of the Law!" Worker Center Strategy Guide on Traditional Labor Law.

Needleman, Ruth. 2004. "Going Back to School, What Should Union Education Be About?' *New Labor Forum* 13(2): 101–10.

Neikirk, William R. 1987. *Volcker: Portrait of the Money Man*. New York: Congdon and Reed.

Ness, Immanuel. 2011. *Guest Workers and Resistance to U.S. Corporate Despotism*. Urbana, IL: University of Illinois Press.

Ness, Immanuel and Dario Azzellini. 2011. *Ours to Master and To Own: Worker Control from the Commune to the Present*. Chicago, IL: Haymarket Books.

Nova, Scott and Ben Hensler. 2011. Memo to WRC Affiliate Universities and Colleges. Re: Business Review Process for the Designated Suppliers Program, December 11. http://www.workersrights.org/university/memo/121611.html (accessed November 2, 2012).

Novelli, Mario. 2004. "Globalisations, Social Movement Unionism and New Internationalisms: The Role of Strategic Learning in the Transformation of the Municipal Workers Union of EMCALI." *Globalisation, Societies and Education* 2(2): 161–30.

OECD. 2013. *OECD Factbook 2013: Economic, Environmental and Social Statistics*. Paris: Organization for Economic Co-operation and Development.

Ortiz, Paul. 2013. "Charging through the Archway of History: Immigrants and African-Americans Unite to Transform the Face of Labor and the Power of Community." *Truthout*, February 16. http://www.truth-out.org/opinion/item/ 14540-charging-through-the-archway-of-history-immigrants-and-african-ame ricans-unite-to-transform-the-face-of-labor-and-the-power-of-community (acc essed February 18, 2013).

Palmquist, Rod. 2010. "Student Campaign Takes on Nike Like Never Before." *Huffington Post*, July 12.

Palpacuer, Florence, Peter Gibbon and Lotte Thomsen. 2004. "New Challenges for Developing Country Suppliers in Global Clothing Chains: A Comparative European Perspective." *World Development* 33(3): 409–30.

Panitch, Leo and Sam Gindin. 2012. *The Making of Global Capitalism*. London: Verso.

Parker, Mike and Martha Gruelle. 1999. *Democracy is Power: Rebuilding Unions from the Bottom Up*. Detroit, MI: Labor Education and Research Project.

Parker, Mike and Jane Slaughter. 1995. *Working Smart: A Union Guide to Participation Program and Reengineering*. Detroit, MI: Labor Notes.

Parreñas, Rhacel Salazar. 2001. *Servants of Globalization: Women, Migration, and Domestic Work*. Stanford, CA: Stanford University Press.

Patrick-Knox, Natalie. 2012. "In an Unprecedented Victory, Federal Government Issues U-Visas to Striking Guestworkers." Jobs with Justice. http://www.jwj.

org/blog/unprecedented-victory-federal-government-issues-u-visas-striking-guestworkers (accessed March 30, 2013).

Penninx, Rinus and Judith Roosblad, eds. 2000. *Trade Unions, Immigration, and Immigrants in Europe, 1960–1993: A Comparative Study of the Actions of Trade Unions in Seven West European Countries*. Oxford: Berghahn Books.

Perez, Sofia A. 2004. "Constraint or Motor? Monetary Integration and the Construction of a Social Model in Spain." In Andrew Martin and George Ross, eds. *Euros and Europeans: Monetary Integration and the European Model of Society*. Cambridge: Cambridge University Press.

Phelan, Craig. ed. 2006. *The Future of Organized Labor: Global Perspectives*. Bern, Switzerland: Peter Lang.

Piazza, James A. 2005. "Globalizing Quiescence: Globalization, Union Density and Strikes in 15 Industrialized Countries." *Economic and Industrial Democracy* 26(2): 289–314.

Piketty, Thomas and Emmanuel Saez. 2006. "The Evolution of Top Incomes: A Historical and International Perspective." *American Economic Review: Papers and Proceedings* 96(2): 200–5.

Plant, Roger. 2008. "Forced Labor: Critical Issues For US Business Leaders." Background paper prepared for conference on "Engaging Business: Addressing Forced Labor," Atlanta, Georgia. Geneva: ILO.

Pollin, Robert. 2012. *Back to Full Employment*. Cambridge, MA: MIT Press.

Prashad, Vijay. 2007. *The Darker Nations: A People's History of the Third World*. New York: The New Press.

Public Citizen. 2003. "Water Privatization Fiascos: Broken Promises and Social Turmoil." A special report by Public Citizen's Water for All Program. Washington, DC: Public Citizen.

Pun, Ngai. 2005. *Made in China: Women Factory Workers in a Global Workplace*. Durham, NC: Duke University Press.

Rahman, Mohammad Mafizur, Rasheda Khanam, and Nur Uddin Absar. 1999. "Child Labor in Bangladesh: A Critical Appraisal of Harkin's Bill and the MOU-Type Schooling Program." *Journal of Economic Issues* 33(4): 985–1003.

Reagan, R. 1980. "Labor Day address at Liberty State Park," September 1. Available at http://www.americanrhetoric.com/speeches/ronaldreaganlibertypark.htm (accessed September 14, 2013).

Remmer, Karen L. 1980. "Political Demobilization in Chile, 1973–1978." *Comparative Politics* 12(3): 275–301.

Reuters. 2012. "Tunisia's Largest Union Cancels General Strike." December 12. http://www.reuters.com/article/2012/12/12/us-tunisia-strike-idUSBRE8BB1G720121212 (accessed February 14, 2013).

Reyes, Teófilo. 2004. "8000 'Guest Workers' Join Farm Union in North Carolina." *Labor Notes*, September 30.

References

Rhomberg, Chris. 2012. *The Broken Table: The Detroit Newspaper Strike and the State of American Labor*. New York: Russell Sage Foundation.

Riddell, Chris. 2004. "Union Certification Success under Voting versus Card-Check Procedures: Evidence from British Columbia, 1978–1998." *Industrial and Labor Relations Review* 57(4): 493–517.

Roach, Stephen S. 2007. "The Davos Disconnect." *Newsweek International*, January 30.

Rockwell, Mark. 2011. "Human Trafficking Decision Will Allow Class Action Suits for Guest Workers, Says Civil Rights Groups." *Government Security News*, December 21. http://www.gsnmagazine.com/node/25291?c=access_control_identification (accessed December 17, 2012).

Rodriguez, Robyn Magalit. 2010. *Migrants for Export: How the Philippine State Brokers Labor to the World*. Minneapolis, MN: University of Minnesota Press.

Rodrik, Dani. 2002. "After Neoliberalism, What?" Paper Presented to the Alternatives to Neoliberalism Conference Sponsored by the New Rules for Global Finance Coalition, May 23–24.

Rose, Joseph B., Gary N. Chaison and Enrique de la Garza. 2000. "A Comparative Analysis of Public Sector Restructuring in the U.S., Canada, Mexico and the Caribbean." *Journal of Labor Research* 21: 601–25.

Ross, Andrew. 2006. *Fast Boat to China: Corporate Flight and the Consequences of Free Trade*. New York: Pantheon.

Ross, Andrew. 2009. *Nice Work if You Can Get it: Life and Labor in Precarious Times*. New York: New York University Press.

Ross, Robert J. S. 2004. *Slaves to Fashion: Poverty and Abuse in the New Sweatshops*. Ann Arbor, MI: University of Michigan Press.

Sbragia, Alberta M. 2004. "Shaping a Polity in an Economic and Monetary Union: The EU in Comparative Perspective." In Andrew Martin and George Ross, eds. *Euros and Europeans: Monetary Integration and the European Model of Society*. Cambridge: Cambridge University Press.

Schiavone, Michael. 2007. "Rank-and-File Militancy and Power: Revisiting the Teamster Struggle with the United Parcel Service Ten Years Later." *WorkingUSA* 10(June): 175–91.

Schmitter Heisler, Barbara. 2000. "Trapped in the Consociational Cage: Trade Unions and Immigration in Switzerland." In Rinus Rinus and Judith Roosblad, eds. *Trade Unions, Immigration, and Immigrants in Europe, 1960–1993: A Comparative Study of the Actions of Trade Unions in Seven West European Countries*. Oxford: Berghahn Books.

Schneider, Geoffrey. 2003. "Neoliberalism and Economic Justice in South Africa: Revisiting the Debate on Economic Apartheid." *Journal Review of Social Economy* 61(1): 23–50.

Schurman, Susan J. and Adrienne E. Eaton. 2012. "Trade Union Organizing in the Informal Economy: A Review of the Literature on Organizing in Africa,

References

Asia, Latin America, North America and Western, Central and Eastern Europe." Report to the Solidarity Center, Rutgers University.

Schwartzman, Kathleen. 2008. "Lettuce, Segmented Labor Markets, and the Immigration Discourse." *Journal of Black Studies* 39(1): 129–56.

Scipes, Kim. 2011. *AFL-CIO's Secret War against Developing Country Workers: Solidarity or Sabotage?* Lanham, MD: Lexington Books.

Segelod, Esbjörn. 2000. "A Comparison of Managers' Perceptions of Short-Termism in Sweden and the U.S." *International Journal of Production Economics* 63(3): 243–54.

Seidman, Gay. 1994. *Manufacturing Militance: Workers' Movements in Brazil and South Africa, 1970–1985.* Berkeley, CA: University of California Press.

Seidman, Gay. 2007. *Beyond the Boycott: Labor Rights, Human Rights, and Transnational Activism.* New York: Russell Sage Foundation.

Selwyn, Ben. 2007. "Labour Process and Workers' Bargaining Power in Export Grape Production, North East Brazil." *Journal of Agrarian Change* 7(4): 526–53.

Shaw, Randy. 2010. "Labor's Missed Opportunity." *BeyondChron*, November 30.

Silver, Beverly. 2003. *Forces of Labor: Workers' Movements and Globalization since 1870.* Cambridge: Cambridge University Press.

Simms, Melanie, Jane Holgate and Edmund Heery. 2013. *Union Voices: Tactics and Tensions in UK Organizing.* Ithaca, NY: Cornell University Press.

Skarlicki, Daniel P. and Gary P. Latham. 1997. "Leadership Training in Organizational Justice to Increase Citizenship Behavior within a Labor Union: A Replication." *Personnel Psychology* 50(3): 617–33.

Slaughter, Jane. 2010. "Anger over Health Care Bill Creates Uncertain Future." *Labor Notes*, January 20.

Smith, Adam. 1776. *An Inquiry into the Nature and Causes of the Wealth of Nations.* London: W. Strahan

Song, Sophie. 2013. "China Now Has More Than 260 Million Migrant Workers Whose Average Monthly Salary Is 2,290 Yuan ($374.09)." *International Business Times*, June 5. http://www.ibtimes.com/china-now-has-more-260-million-migrant-workers-whose-average-monthly-salary-2290-yuan-37409-1281559 (accessed June 25, 2013).

Standing, Guy. 2011. *The Precariat: The New Dangerous Class.* New York: Bloomsbury USA.

Stepan-Norris, Judith and Maurice Zeitlin. 2002. *Left Out: Reds and America's Industrial Unions.* Cambridge: Cambridge University Press.

Stevis, Dimitris and Terry Boswell. 2007. "International Framework Agreements: Opportunities and Challenges for Global Unionism." In Kate Bronfenbrenner, ed. *Global Unions: Challenging Transnational Capital through Cross-Border Campaigns.* Ithaca, NY: Cornell University Press.

References

Stiglitz, Joseph E. 2006. *Making Globalization Work*. New York: W.W. Norton.

Suggett, James. 2010. "Venezuelan Unions March to Control Companies, Throw Out 'Reformist' State Management." *Venezuela Analysis*, October 28. http://venezuelanalysis.com/analysis/5744 (accessed August 7, 2012).

Sukthankar, Ashwini and Kevin Kolben. 2006. "Indian Labor Legislation and Cross-Border Solidarity in Historical Context." In Kate Bronfenbrenner, ed. *Global Unions: Challenging Transnational Capital Through Cross-Border Campaigns*. Ithaca, NY: Cornell University Press.

Sundar, K. R. Shyam. 2000. "Second National Commission on Labour: Not up to the Task." In Shekhar Krishnan and Mihir Desai, eds. *Workers Rights' and Labour Laws: A Backgrounder for the Workshop on Labour to be held from 29–31 December 2000 at the National Conference on Human Rights, Social Movements, Globalisation and the Law at Panchgani, Maharashtra*. Mumbai: India Centre for Human Rights & Law.

Suzuki, Akira, ed. 2012. *Cross-National Comparisons of Social Movement Unionism: Diversities of Labour Movement Revitalization in Japan, Korea and the United States*. Vol. 18. Oxford: Peter Lang.

Takasu, Hirohiko. 2012. "The Formation of a Region-Based Amalgamated Union Movement and Its Possibilities." In Akira Suzuki, ed. *Cross-National Comparisons of Social Movement Unionism: Diversities of Labour Movement Revitalization in Japan, Korea and the United States*. Vol. 18. Oxford: Peter Lang.

Tanguy, Jeremy. 2013. "Collective and Individual Conflicts in the Workplace: Evidence from France." *Industrial Relations* 52(1): 102–33.

Tattersall, Amanda. 2010. *Power in Coalition: Strategies for Strong Unions and Social Change*. Ithaca, NY: Cornell University Press.

Tattersall, Amanda and David Reynolds. 2007. "The Shifting Power of Labor-Community Coalitions: Identifying Common Elements of Powerful Coalitions in Australia and the U.S." *WorkingUSA* 10(1): 77–102.

Taylor, Jeffrey. 2001. *Union Learning: Canadian Labour Education in the Twentieth Century*. Toronto, ON: Thompson Educational Publishing.

Taylor, Jeffrey. 2007. "From Union Education to Worker Education." In Lesley Farrell and Tara Fenwick, eds. *World Yearbook of Education 2007: Educating the Global Workforce*. New York: Routledge.

Teubal, Miguel. 2004. "Rise and Collapse of Neoliberal in Argentina: The Role of Economic Groups." *Journal of Developing Societies* 20(3–4): 173–88.

The Economist. 2012. "One Billion Workers." *The Economist*, January 23. http://www.economist.com/blogs/freeexchange/2012/01/chinas-labour-force

The Hindu. 2012. "All Trade Unions to Strike Work on Tuesday." *The Hindu*, February 25. http://www.thehindu.com/news/national/article2932593.ece (accessed October 24, 2012).

Thomson, Robert. 2007. "Time to Comply: National Responses to Six EU

References

Labour Market Directives Revisited." *West European Politics* 30(5): 987–1008.

Trubek, David M. 2006. "Review Essay: The Emergence of Transnational Labor Law." *The American Journal of International Law* 100(3): 725–33.

Tufts, Stephen. 1998. "Government and Opposition." *Antipode* 30(3): 227–50.

Turner, Lowell. 2004. "Why Revitalize? Labour's Urgent Mission in a Contested Global Economy." In Carola Frege and John Kelly, eds. *Varieties of Unionism: Strategies for Labor Renewal in Comparative Perspective*. Oxford: Oxford University Press.

Turner, Lowell. 2009. "Institutions and Activism: Crisis and Opportunity for a German Labor Movement in Decline." *Industrial and Labor Relations Review* 62(3): 294–312.

Uetricht, Micah and Jasson Perez. 2012. "Democratic to the CORE." *In These Times*, November 30. http://inthesetimes.com/article/14207/democratic_to_the_core

UNCTAD. 2007. "The Universe of the Largest Transnational Corporations." New York and Geneva: United Nations.

UNCTAD. 2012. *Global Investment Report*. New York and Geneva: United Nations.

United Nations. 2012. "The Millennium Development Goals Report: Gender Chart 2012." http://www.unwomen.org/en/digital-library/publications/2012/12/the-millennium-development-goals-report-gender-chart-2012

United Nations Centre on Transnational Corporations. 1991. *World Investment Report: The Triad in Foreign Direct Investment*. New York: United Nations.

Vahapassi, Antero E. E. 2004. "Social Protection and the Informal Sector: Challenges, Obstacles and Possibilities." Jakarta: ASEAN Security Meeting.

van Vliet, Olaf and Henk Nijboer. 2012. "Flexicurity in the European Union: Flexibility for Outsiders, Security for Insiders." Department of Economics Research Memorandum 2012.2. Leiden, The Netherlands: Leiden University.

Vandaele, Kurt. 2011. "Sustaining or Abandoning 'Social Peace'? Strike Developments and Trends in Europe Since the 1990s." Working Paper 2011.05, European Trade Union Institute.

Vander Stichele, Myriam and Bob Young. 2009. "The Abuse of Supermarket Buyer Power in the EU Food Retail Sector: Preliminary Survey of Evidence, Agribusiness Accountability Initiative." Amsterdam: SOMO.

Vanderborght, Yannick. 2006. "Why Trade Unions Oppose Basic Income." *Basic Income Studies* 1(1).

Visser, Jelle. 2006. "Union Membership Statistics in 24 Countries." *Monthly Labor Review* 129(1): 38–49.

Vivas, Esther. 2009. "Food Crisis: Causes, Consequences and Alternatives." *International Viewpoint*, December 14.

Vogel, David. 2006. *The Market for Virtue: The Potential and Limits of Corporate Social Responsibility*. Washington, DC: Brookings Institution Press.

References

Vosko, Leah F. 2000. *Temporary Work: The Gendered Rise of a Precarious Employment Relationship*. Toronto, ON: Toronto University Press.

Vosko, Leah F. 2010. *Managing the Margins: Gender, Citizenship and the International Regulation of Precarious Employment*. New York: Oxford University Press.

Voss, Kim and Rachel Sherman. 2000. "Breaking the Iron Law of Oligarchy: Union Revitalization in the American Labor Movement." *American Journal of Sociology* 106(2): 303–49.

Vuotto, Mirta. 2012. "Organizational Dynamics of Worker Cooperatives in Argentina." *Service Business* 6(1): 85–97.

Wainwright, Hilary. 2012. "Transformative Power: Political Organization in Transition." *Socialist Register* 49.

Ward, Alex. 2012. "Mass Anti-Austerity Protests Engulf Europe." *The New Statesman*, November 14. http://www.newstatesman.com/economics/econom ics/2012/11/mass-anti-austerity-protests-engulf-europe

Warner, Malcom. 2010. "Labour Markets in China: Coming to Terms with Globalization." Working Paper Series 1. Cambridge Judge Business School.

Warren, Dorian T. 2010. "The American Labor Movement in the Age of Obama: The Challenges and Opportunities of a Racialized Political Economy." *Perspectives on Politics* 8(3): 847–60.

Washington Post. 2012. "Shopkeepers Flood India Streets with Strike, Protests against Walmart." *Washington Post*, September 21. http://www. bostonglobe.com/news/world/2012/09/20/shopkeepers-india-protest-plans-for-foreign-retailers/PIaYWTejnAdqoECYq1CdnN/story.html (accessed March 28, 2013).

Webb, Sydney and Beatrice Webb. 1987. "The Origins of Trade Unionism." In Simeon Larsen and Bruce Nissen, eds. *Theories of the Labor Movement*. Detroit, MI: Wayne State University Press.

Weil, David. 1991. "Enforcing OSHA: The Role of Labor Unions." *Industrial Relations: A Journal of Economy and Society* 30(1): 20–36.

Weinbaum, Eve S. 2004. *To Move a Mountain: Fighting the Global Economy in Appalachia*. New York: The New Press.

Wells, Don. 2007. "Too Weak for the Job: Corporate Codes of Conduct, Non-Governmental Organizations and the Regulation of International Labour Standards." *Global Social Policy* 7: 51–74.

Wente, Margaret. 2013. "Teachers Unions are Obsolete." *The Globe and Mail* (Toronto), January.

Western, Bruce. 1993. "Postwar Unionization in Eighteen Advanced Capitalist Countries." *American Sociological Review* 58(2): 266–82.

Western, Bruce and Jake Rosenfeld. 2011. "Unions, Norms, and the Rise in U.S. Wage Inequality." *American Sociological Review* 76(4): 513–37.

Weststar, Johanna. 2006. "Union Education, Union Leadership and Union Renewal: The Role of PEL." In Pradeep Kumar and Christopher Robert

Schenk, eds. *Paths to Union Renewal: Canadian Experiences.* Toronto, ON: University of Toronto Press.

Wibowo, Ignatius. 2009. "China's Soft Power and Neoliberal Agenda in Southeast Asia." In Mingjiang Li, ed. *Soft Power: China's Emerging Strategy in International Politics.* Lanham, MD: Lexington Books.

Williams, Charles. 2012. "Americanism and Anti-Communism: The UAW and Repressive Liberalism before the Red Scare." *Labor History* 53(4): 495–515.

Williams, Colin C. 2009. "Formal and Informal Employment in Europe: Beyond Dualistic Representations." *European Urban and Regional Studies* 16(2): 147–59.

Williams, Peter. 2010. "The World's Worst Immigration Laws." *Foreign Policy*, April 29.

Witherell, Rob. 2009. "Steelworkers Form Collaboration with MONDRAGON, the World's Largest Worker-Owned Cooperative." United Steelworkers Press Release, October 27. http://www.usw.org/media_center/releases_advisories?id=0234 (accessed August 7, 2012).

Witwer, David. 2011. "The Chapter Left Untold: Labor Historians and the Problem of Union Corruption." *Labor: Studies in Working-Class History of the Americas* 8(2): 37–57.

Wolf, Martin. 2009. "Seeds of its Own Destruction." *Financial Times*, March 8.

Woodside, Arch G. and Drew Martin. 2008. *Tourism Management: Analysis, Behaviour, and Strategy.* Wallingford, Oxon: CABI.

Worker Rights Consortium. 2008. "Worker Rights Consortium Assessment re: Mexmode, S.A. De C.V. (Mexico), Findings and Recommendations. July 3, 2008." Washington, DC: Worker Rights Consortium.

World Bank. 2011. *Migration and Remittances Fact Book*, 2nd edn. Washington, DC: The World Bank.

Wrench, John. 1986. "Unequal Comrades: Trade Unions, Equal Opportunity and Racism." Policy Papers in Ethnic Relations No. 5. Coventry: University of Warwick.

Wright, Erik Olin. 2000. "Working-Class Power, Capitalist-Class Interests, and Class Compromise." *American Journal of Sociology* 105(4): 957–1002.

Xinhua. 2012. "20% of Chinese Join Trade Unions." January 7. http://www.chinadaily.com.cn/china/2012-01/07/content_14400312.htm

Yates, Michael D. 2003. *Naming the System: Inequality and Work in the Global Economy.* New York: Monthly Review Press.

Yates, Michael D. 2008. *Why Unions Matter*, 2nd edn. New York: Monthly Review Press.

Zenglein, Max J. 2008. "Marketization of the Chinese Labor Market and the Role of Unions." Global Labour University Working Papers, Paper Number 4, Berlin.

References

Zhong, Ang and Xioahui Zhang. 2011. "Strike at PepsiCo Bottling Plants in China." *The Economic Observer*, November 14. http://www.eeo.com.cn/ens/2011/1114/215661.shtml (accessed February 14, 2013).

Index

237

Index

Index

Index

Index

Index